JACK HOULIHAN

Beginner's Guide to **Processing and Printing**

Clyde Reynolds

Newnes Technical Books

Newnes Technical Books
is an imprint of the Butterworth Group
which has principal offices in
London, Sydney, Toronto, Wellington, Durban and Boston

First published 1981

British Library Cataloguing in Publication Data

Reynolds, Clyde
Beginner's guide to processing and printing.
1. Photography – Processing
I. Title
770.28 TR330

ISBN 0 408 00550 5

Photoset by Butterworths Litho Preparation Department
Printed in England by Fakenham Press Ltd, Fakenham, Norfolk

Contents

1

Why process?

For most photographers, operating the camera is the creative part of photography. Once the image is on the film, they can rely on others to carry out its mechanical transformation from an (as yet) invisible image into a finished picture, colour or monochrome.

Basically, there are two categories of photographic processor: totally professional (or custom) laboratories employing skilled craftsmen to turn out the best possible results; and automated photofinishers relying heavily on machines to perform accurately repeatable process and print operations.

The staff of professional laboratories expect to be able to interpret pictures just as the photographer wants. They rely on precision machinery to process negatives or transparencies as well as possible, matching the process as closely as possible to the photographer's requirements and altering the times to suit special instructions on film speed. They can also make individual enlargements with the composition the photographer asks, even adjusting the exposure on different parts of the print if needed.

Obviously, such services are costly, they cannot be justified for most ordinary pictures, and they depend heavily on the photographer's ability to visualise the result as he takes each shot, and to be able to communicate his vision to the printer. For most films, automatic photofinishing is the best choice of commercial processing and printing services. That is why most professional labs also offer high quality automatic printing services.

Photofinishers

Today, most photofinishers concentrate on developing and printing colour negative films. The 'D & P' operations vie with one another to offer the lowest cost and quickest turn-round. Given a well exposed film and normal subjects, most photofinishers can provide a set of excellent 'enprints' 9 cm (approx. 3½ in) wide at very low cost. The exact size depends on the format. Square pictures produce prints 9 cm square; size 110 9×11.5 cm (3½×4½ in), and 35 mm 9 ×13 cm (3½×5 in).

Photofinishers can also offer a small range of enlargements, usually printing to widths of 13, 18, 20.5, 25.5 or 28 cm (5, 7, 8, 10 or 11 in). Unfortunately, few offer more than the most rudimentary selective enlargement service. The picture must be composed exactly in the camera; just as it is with transparency film.

Printing your own pictures allows you to crop and tilt them however best it suits the subject, even creating a straight Tower of Pisa (Clyde Reynolds)

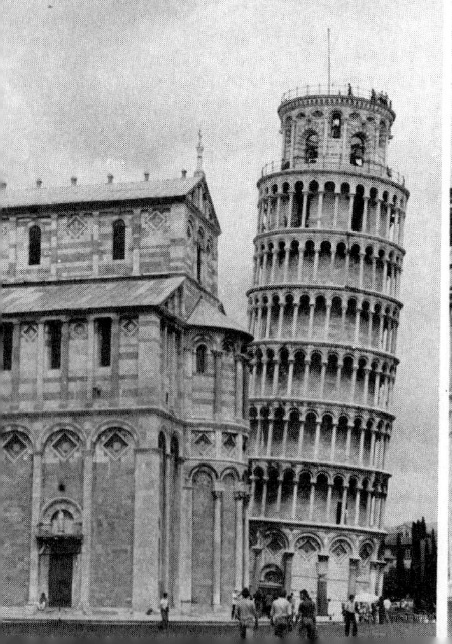

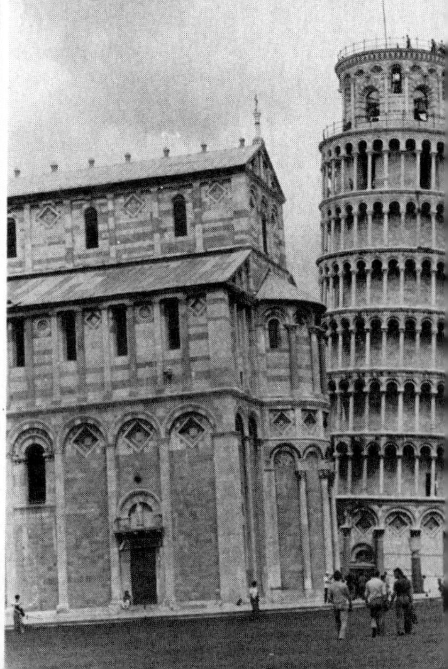

To be well printed on automatic machinery, pictures must be well composed and well exposed. Neither is difficult; but the third requirement is highly restrictive: the pictures must be of normal subjects. That is because the printer is calibrated on one essential assumption: that the whole of each scene integrates (averages) to a mid-grey. The calculations of exposure and colour balance are all based on this. The automatic printer adjusts the overall colour and tone to 'compensate' for any deviation from the normal. Imagine a small child in a white dress standing in the shade in front of a brightly sunlit grassy bank. The picture is composed to show the girl small against a brilliant green surround. By measuring mainly from the brilliant green, the electronics in the printer will almost ignore the child. The brilliant green grass will be adjusted to a dull almost grey colour. Worse, though, will be the effect on the child. Not only will she be much too dark – she will also be wearing a pink dress!

Naturally, a gross example like this should be rejected and reprinted before the pictures are returned to the photographer. In fact, many photofinishers have experienced machine operators who can spot unusual negatives in advance and print them more normally. But even then, a difficult scene may not be satisfactory. The problem is exacerbated when the picture has no independent reference – no people and no grass – so that even the human operator has no idea of what the overall colour or brightness should be.

All in all, once you start to take out-of-the-ordinary pictures, the photofinisher is unsuitable. Prints have to be made by hand; either at considerable cost or by yourself. Making your own prints gives you the control you need to get the colour and density exactly how you, the photographer, want them. It is the final stage in translating your vision into a pictorial reality.

The transparency user is much better served. His films are simply processed, and come back with all the special and spectacular colours of each scene. However, when it comes to having prints made, there is not much advantage in sending transparencies to a photofinisher. Even on the latest materials, the prints tend to lose the brilliance of the original. The paper has a lower brightness range than the transparency film, and it needs skill and patience to make the print best suited to the subject. In fact, printing from transparencies is now almost as easy as printing from negatives, so home processing is an especially good prospect if your colour work in mainly on slides. That way, you can make occasional prints from suitable shots.

It is becoming harder and harder to get black-and-white prints made. Good hand made prints need as much time and trouble as do hand made colour prints; so the costs are becoming comparable. Anything less than individual attention loses the joy of monochrome work, which involves translating a multicoloured scene into an exactly appropriate pattern of tones.

Prints and control

Let us first look at the possibilities offered by black-and-white printing. You can choose exactly which part of the image you want in the picture, leaving out unwanted areas. You can enlarge the picture to virtually any size you choose. Varying the print exposure time controls the density, which allows the choice of light or dark prints to suit the subject and the mood. This also offers the means to compensate, at least partly, for exposure errors in the camera, thus saving otherwise wasted pictures.

Monochrome prints are a translation of the world into a range of tones. Some scenes call for harsh blacks and whites, with little grey to relieve the impact. Others need a much more subtle range of intermediate tones to tell their story. This *contrast* is controlled by two factors – the film development and the choice of paper. For most purposes, it is well to follow normal film development. That leaves one control – the paper. Printing paper comes in a range of grades (or, more conveniently, can be altered by selection of the colour of the printing light), which means that you can select the contrast that you want to suit any particular image.

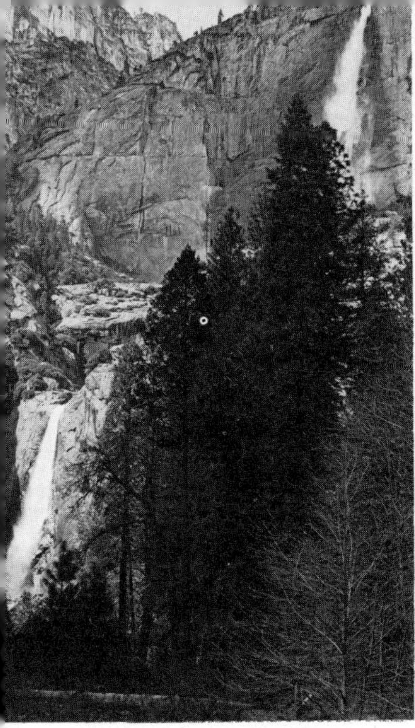
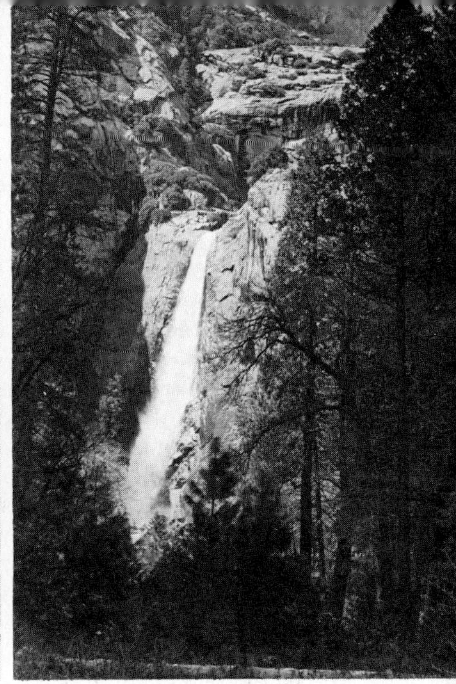

Selecting part of a negative allows one picture to be taken from a single shot (Clyde Reynolds)

While many negatives produce fine prints with suitable choice of paper grade (or variable contrast filter), others are quite unsuitable for 'straight' printing. Perhaps the foreground is too light, or when the rest is right, the shadows lack detail. The answer usually is to expose different parts of the image for different lengths of time. This is quite simply done by interposing a suitable mask in the enlarger light beam for part of the exposure time. With variable contrast paper, it is even possible to print different parts of the picture through filters to give them suitable contrasts.

Another advantage of making your own prints is that the image can be modified to suit the picture. Expose the paper through any one of a thousand different materials to give it a special look. Gauze, cloth or smeared glass, midway between the lens and baseboard, can soften or diffuse the image;

while materials in contact with the negative or paper are sharply imaged – offering an infinite choice of textures. Some of the more popular are meshes and lattices, grain effect and stipples.

Some photographers find that the most satisfying way to create the images they want is to derive them in the dark room. The basis of most of this work is high contrast film – usually that intended for preparing material for photomechanical printing, to produce books, magazines and so forth. Such films can produce an image (from a normal negative) in pure black and white. From a pure black-and-white negative, it is possible to produce a whole range of striking images by following a few fairly simple processes.

All this creative control is lost when the film is handled by a normal develop-and-print service. Furthermore, the processing may take several days, while by working at home one can produce prints within an hour of taking the pictures.

Colour printing

Printing from colour, while a little more tricky than monochrome work, offers most of the same creative control. Naturally, you can choose which part of the image you want to print – and the size you want it. Exposure again controls the density, allowing delicate pastel prints or gloomy darkness. Further, altering the colour of the printing light changes the overall colour of the print; you can create a warm rosy glow, or a cold greenish barren waste. When the subject requires, you can hold back part to change the tonal balance or alter the colour of just one section.

When it comes to contrast control, though, colour is much more limited. Most brands of paper come in only one contrast grade, and it may be surprising to the monochrome worker that most negatives print well on the single grade of paper. With a problem colour negative there are two solutions: different brands of paper offer slightly different contrasts, and with some processing chemicals the process times can be varied to alter the print contrast.

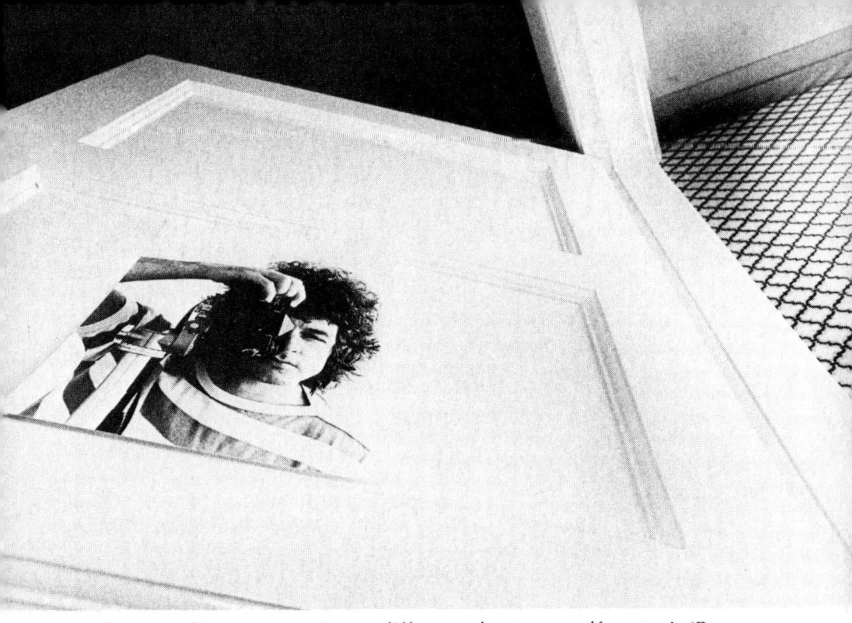

Rephotographing a print gives a different slant on a self-portrait (Roy Pryer)

All the means of modifying the image by using screens work equally as well in colour as in black-and-white, but there are no extra-contrast colour materials to match the monochrome printers' films. However, it is quite possible to make brilliant colour prints from one or more high-contrast monochrome negatives if you wish.

Slides, too

It is now possible to print from transparencies almost as easily as from negatives. In fact, making the exposure is much easier, it is just that the processing is a little more complicated. The latest transparency printing materials are so good that the prints can virtually match those made from colour negatives.

There is much to be said for starting colour printing by working from transparencies. In fact, this is a good way to start printing of any kind. The basic reason for this is that you know when a transparency is good – you can see the image projected on to a screen or on to an enlarger baseboard, which avoids the wasted time of trying out negatives. Also, because transparencies are inherently much more contrasty than prints, the print materials must be much less so. That, in turn, means that they are much less sensitive to variations in exposure or in the colour of the enlarger light.

Monochrome film processing

If you want the control over your images that is offered by printing, you need the best possible negatives. Film processing is easy; it takes virtually no special skill, just a little care. Follow some very simple routines and make sure that the film stays for the right length of time in the right developer at the right temperature, assuming correct exposure in the first place, you will produce excellent negatives. Even if you stray far from the ideal time and temperature, the results are still printable – albeit on an unusual grade of paper, with little margin for creative choice of tones and contrast.

It is this very ease and flexibility that is the problem with commercial processing. There is no need for strict control, or special care, to produce negatives that look fine on enprints from an automatic printer. So you are lucky if you can find a custom black-and-white processor who really takes good care of your films. It is far easier to ensure good negatives by processing the material yourself. Obviously, to get prints quickly after a shooting session this is essential.

Processing variations

Following the manufacturer's time and temperature information with a normal developer produces high quality negatives, but they may not exactly suit particular requirements.

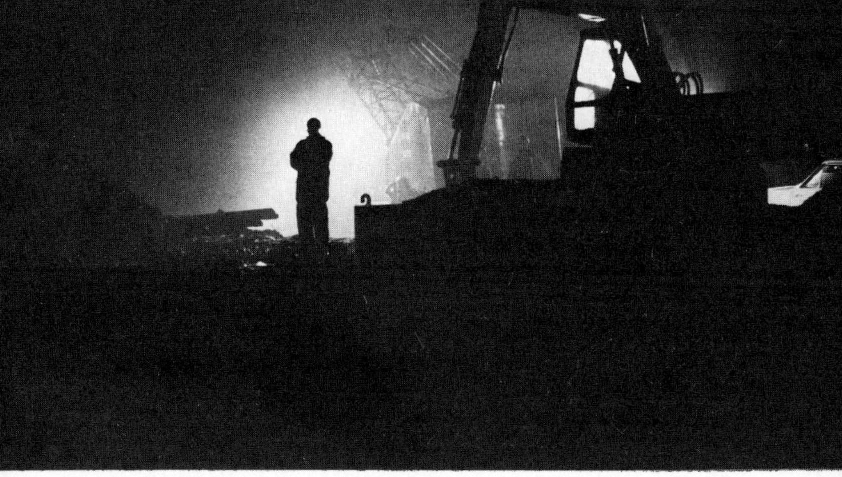

Uprating a 400 ASA film to 1600 ASA allows pictures to be taken at night (Ed Buziak)

The ideal negative contrast varies with the printing equipment, and with the photographer's vision. It is simple, with a few tests, to alter the process times to suit any purpose, which makes printing a lot easier.

In addition to varying the contrast, changes in development can change the grain structure and the effective film speed. Choose a fine-grain developer to produce negatives capable of the greatest enlargement. This may entail giving extra exposure in the camera, but that is usually no problem.

When the situations calls, you may want to give less exposure than the film normally needs, to that you are able to use a smaller lens aperture or a faster shutter speed. Within reason, speed-increasing developers can produce good negatives from underexposed films. Naturally, the whole film is affected and usually the result is much grainier than normal. However, uprating (pushing) the film offers much greater flexibility for picture-taking when the lights are low.

Chromogenic materials, such as Ilford XP-1 and Agfa Vario XL, use colour film technology to produce monochrome negatives. They can accept a wider range of exposure variation before needing abnormal processing.

Colour film processing

If you can process a black-and-white film, then you can process a colour negative one. Of course, the chemicals are different, but the principles are the same: bathe the film in developer for a fixed time at the correct temperature, fix it and wash it. The two major reasons for processing your own colour films are speed of access and quality of processing. There is also some latitude for altering the contrast and film speed.

Transparency films are more complicated to process, but no more difficult. They are, though, in a way much more daunting. The image on each frame is the final picture, and if the processing goes wrong, all is lost. The film may be too light, too dark, or the wrong colour. The shots cannot be 'redeemed' by careful printing, as can many negative 'failures'. Of course, the same applies to commercially processed material, and some awful results are possible – poor contrast, false colours, splotches and scratches are unfortunately widespread. While transparency processing needs care and application, it is not beyond the simplest home equipment. Furthermore, the chemicals now available are vastly simpler and much quicker to use than those of even a few years ago.

Costs

Chapter 2 details the equipment for processing and printing – the essential, the desirable, and the luxury. As with any other pastime, it is possible to spend a small fortune on equipping a darkroom. However, it is also possible to produce excellent results with quite a small outlay.

For black and white work, a reasonable outfit costs around the price of a moderate 35 mm SLR. Converting that to basic colour printing needs adds the cost of a reasonable quality wide-angle lens. Buying the best and most convenient equipment is naturally more expensive: a good home colour darkroom costs around the price of a top quality 35 mm system camera and two or three accessory lenses.

Clearly, the capital outlay is never going to be recouped by printing a few holiday films each year. On a purely cost basis, you can buy a large number of hand made enlargements for the same money.

Once you are equipped, black-and-white printing is still relatively inexpensive. 100 sheets of variable contrast paper 20 × 25 cm (8 × 10 in) cost about as much as 10–15 rolls of black-and-white film. The chemicals add little to the cost – for film or paper.

Colour papers are around twice the price of monochrome – and the chemicals much more expensive, so you need to be quite efficient to make a large saving over machine made prints, and wasting materials here and there soon brings the cost up. With care, though, you can produce prints at around two-thirds of the machine reprint cost. If you are making good prints, that is great value, because professional hand made prints are about three times the price of automatic ones.

The most expensive materials and chemicals are Cibachrome, which produce superb prints from transparencies with a remarkably low failure rate. Each 20 × 25 cm (8 × 10 in) print costs around one-third the price of a 20-exposure cassette of Kodachrome (including processing). However, most workers achieve good prints on at least three-quarters of the sheets that they use, which makes the material more economic than its price suggests.

Getting started

So, what's needed to get going? The basic outfit for black-and-white work is: a developing tank, developing dishes, enlarger and lens, thermometer, measuring beakers and suitable storage bottles. The chemicals are: film developer, print developer and fixer. For colour films, no extra equipment is needed, but for colour prints you need filters: either three primary colours, or a set of secondary (white light) printing filters, an enlarger with a colour drawer and a colour print processing drum. Colour negative chemicals usually work for films or paper and most now consist of developer and bleach fix. Colour transparency chemicals are more complicated, but come in easy-to-follow kits.

The whole range of creative control is available with the most basic equipment and suitable chemicals. As long as the equipment is good, even the simplest outfit is capable of matching the print quality given by the most sophisticated; so it is best to start with simple basic equipment. Slow it might be, but the best way to learn. Once you become enthusiastic, then is the time to look for greater sophistication – mainly as an aid to quicker and more convenient working.

While colour work has a special attraction, most photographers start with black-and-white. Working in bright safelighting hardly differs from the familiar; and the excitement of seeing the picture 'appear from nowhere' in the developing dish is almost universal.

This book gives all the basic information you need to get started. The equipment, the chemistry, the routines, and lots of hints. Of course, with improved materials, times, temperatures and routines are constantly being changed. Even so, the basic procedures will still apply for many years after you have bought the book. For exact dilutions, times and temperatures, follow the instructions packed with each set of chemicals. That really means *each* set. Don't just file one set of instructions and keep using it. Things change, and last year's practice may well have been superseded, even though the material still bears the same name.

2

Selecting and using equipment

It is quite possible to process films and paper in cooking utensils, and even to make enlargements using a slide projector. However, the basic photographic equipment makes life a lot easier. Furthermore, there is a wide range of gadgets for the darkroom. Some are a great help, others mere decoration.

Darkness and safelight

Photographic materials react to light. That is how they produce pictures. Stray light reaching unprocessed paper or

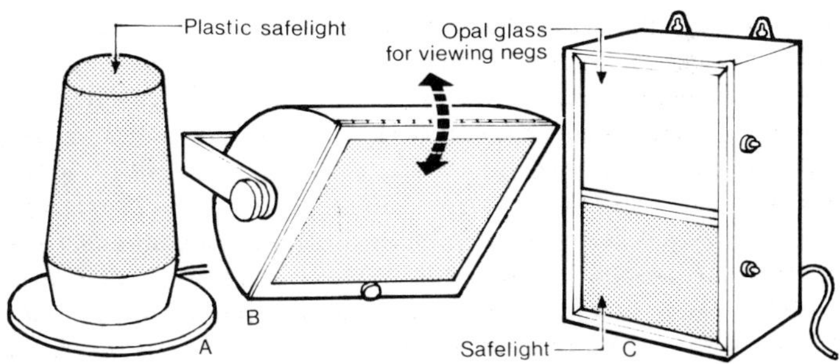

Safelights come in various shapes and sizes. Their important feature is the colour of the light. A. Free-standing moulded unit. B. Wall-mounted unit with interchangeable filters. C. Wall or bench unit opal glass viewing light as well

film exposes it, producing fogging, so materials must be protected from light until the image is fixed. Some materials, including most films, are sensitive to light of all colours, so they must be handled in total darkness. Other materials, though, react only to light of particular colour. For example, most monochrome papers and a number of darkroom films (for copying negatives and so on) are sensitive only to blue light. Yet other films, and a few papers, are sensitive to blue and green light, but not to red.

These materials – called blue-sensitive and orthochromatic respectively – are normally handled in light of the appropriate colour. Safelights for blue-sensitive materials are usually yellow-orange or yellow-green. Orthochromatic materials can be processed in ruby red light.

Space and shape

The first requirement for processing and printing is a room that can be light proofed and illuminated with light of a suitable colour if appropriate. For most people working at home, this means the kitchen or the bathroom – neither is ideal.

Some photographic chemicals are highly toxic, and ideally should never be handled in the kitchen. However, if you can use no other room, take very careful precautions. Put away all food and cooking utensils before you start. Cover the working surface with polythene sheeting, and make quite sure that no spillage can possibly seep into any drawer or cupboard. Always restrict work with chemicals to the sink (or draining board) and keep the outsides of all the containers washed with clean water. Keep the enlarger and other electrical equipment away from wet areas.

The problem with bathrooms is that the close proximity of electricity to plumbing can be dangerous. That is why building regulations call for string-pull switches and ban socket outlets. Note that shaver sockets work through a small

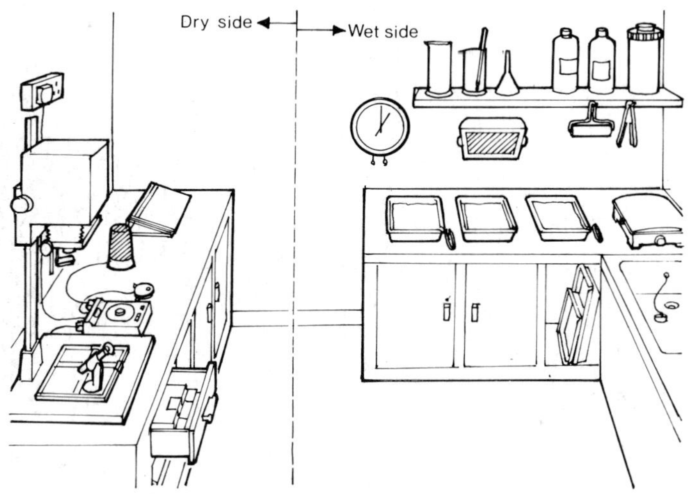

If possible separate the exposure equipment from the processing equipment to prevent contamination or electrical problems

isolating transformer, to avoid any chance of electric shock. They are not suitable for running enlargers, safelights or other photographic equipment. With no power sockets, you have to work from an extension lead, which is less than ideal. Also, few bathrooms are large enough to make a comfortable darkroom. Most workers build a suitable cover for the bath, and stand their processing dishes on that. This can work well, but you must have another good firm support for the enlarger.

Ideally, the darkroom should be separate from the normal domestic living areas. Many photographers use a large cupboard, a shed, or the loft. A room of about 2.5 × 2 m (8 × 6 ft) is ideal. It needs two clearly defined areas: wet and dry. The wet area should have space for four processing trays. For example, if you use 30.5 × 25.5 cm (12 × 10 in) paper, the trays are about 36 × 30 cm (14 × 11 in) outside. So you need a space at least 38 × 122 cm (15 × 48 in) to accommodate them comfortably. The best processing table is a shallow sink with duckboards to keep the dishes above any water. However, most people just use a bench.

The enlarger should stand well away from the wet area so that no splashes can reach it, or the dry paper. Such an arrangement also avoids the dangers of keeping electrical equipment close to water.

The most convenient height for an enlarger bench is about 90 cm (35 in). It should be sturdy enough to avoid vibration, and large enough to provide temporary storage space for paper and negatives. A good size is 1 m × 65 cm (3 × 2 ft). In a permanent darkroom, it is often convenient to mount an enlarger column on the bench (or on the wall behind it). This allows greater freedom than does composing on the enlarger baseboard. However, it can restrict the maximum enlargement possible.

A simple solution to this is to make a section of the bench top removable, and to arrange one more lower positions to hold the enlarging easel. Note that the shelves need to be considerably larger than the removable section of the bench.

Blacking out

There are three basic ways to black out a window: with curtains, with a roller blind, or with a removable cover. If the room is used for other purposes, light-proof curtains may be an attractive proposition. They can be of normal curtain material lined with light-proofing material, and if necessary lined again with something more attractive. If the curtains fit tightly within the window reveal, or overlap the opening by 30 cm (12 in) or more, they should darken the room enough for black-and-white processing except, perhaps, on brilliant sunny days.

After a few minutes in the dark, though, you will be able to see that light creeps round the edges. For loading films into tanks, or for colour printing, this is too much stray light. So the answer is to use more tightly fitting blackout material. An alternative is to use a properly constructed roller blind which runs in channels either side of the window and into a slot in

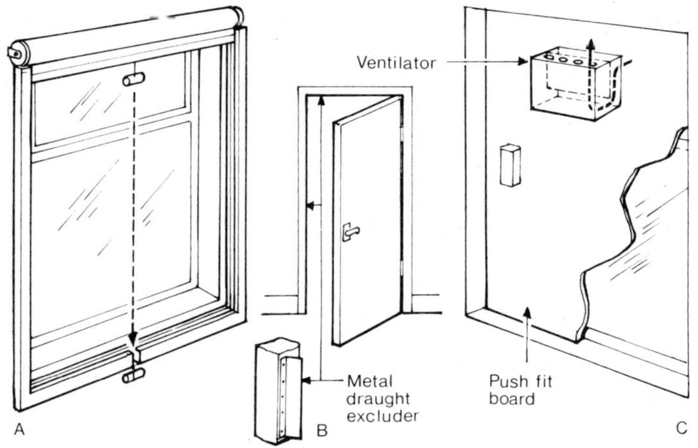

A darkroom needs black-out. A. A roller blind is a good permanent fixture. B. Metal draught excluder can seal doors effectively. C. Boards to fit windows are simple to make and use; but include a ventilator in small rooms

the sill. The joinery, though, tends to look rather obtrusive on windows of any distinction.

The most economical and often the most satisfactory method is to make up a tight-fitting opaque cover for the window. A sheet of hardboard edged with rubber trim is ideal. The cover should be a good push fit into the window reveal. Put a small handle on the inside to allow easy fitting and removing. For longer term work a ventilator is needed. Cut a hole in the board and cover it with another piece about twice the size of the hole about 2.5 cm (1 in) away stuck on suitable blocks. With the inside of the ventilator painted matt black, no light should get in.

The door, too, may need attention. Light can usually get round the edges. The best way to stop this is to fit copper draught excluder right round it.

To test the blackout, sit in the room for 20 minutes. If, after your eyes have accommodated to the darkness, you can only just see the edges of the window and door, the room is dark enough for film loading and colour printing. If, however, you can detect the light reaching other walls, then films may get fogged and the room needs more attention.

Ventilation

A small closed room can quite quickly become stuffy especially if heated with a gas or oil heater which competes for oxygen. Damp conditions, produced through lack of ventilation, can soon lead to condensation problems in a permanent darkroom. Also, a number of photographic chemicals are acrid, some are poisonous. It is no pleasure to work in a close atmosphere, especially if it is fume-laden, and it can be dangerous.

So darkroom ventilation is very important. Careful exclusion of all external light can exclude virtually all fresh air as well. A small cupboard may be fine for loading a developing tank, but do not consider processing paper in such confined conditions without proper ventilation. Tank or drum processing, as used for films and colour materials, is less of a problem than is dish processing. It is normal to emerge from the darkened room every few minutes to process the exposed colour papers, so any but the smallest darkroom is probably acceptable – as long as the processing area is well ventilated.

For longer-term occupancy (more than 20 minutes at a stretch) some provision for air circulation is essential. A simple ventilator in the blackout board, as described above, is fine for casual use, if the window is open. With a more permanent construction it is well worth fitting a light-trapped extractor fan. Such fans are readily available from photographic laboratory suppliers, and are best wired directly to the safelight circuit in a black-and-white darkroom. For open-tray or roller-transport colour work, the fan should have a separate switch.

Portable darkrooms

It is possible to buy a complete folding darkroom, or to construct one. The basic principle is to start with a large wardrobe-type cupboard, which houses the enlarger on a bench, and provides storage for paper, chemicals and equipment. The doors open out to form a wood and light-proof polythene room, with space for processing dishes.

Safelights

The main aim of safelighting is to provide as much illumination as possible without affecting the film or paper in use.

SAFELIGHTS

Material	Filter colour
Contact printing papers Blue sensitive copy films	Yellow-green or pale amber
Projection (enlarging) papers (bromide or chlorobromide)	Amber or olive green
Variable-contrast papers	Amber
Orthochromatic materials (lith films etc.)	Ruby red
Panchromatic papers Very slow panchromatic films	Dark green
Medium speed panchromatic films	Very dark green or dark bluish-green
Colour print materials	Very dark amber or dark brown
Fast panchromatic films Colour films	Total darkness

Safelights come in three basic forms: an opaque (usually metal) housing which holds a bulb and coloured filter; complete moulded safelights, which just take a bulb; and units with special light sources – most commonly sodium lamps – which need little extra filtration. All types are equally effective when used to the manufacturer's directions. The most important of these are to use a bulb of low enough power, and to keep the safelight a little away from the paper or film – usually at least 1 m (3 ft).

Safelight filters come in a range of colours to suit various purposes. However, most people need only one, or at most two. The most widely needed is an amber or yellow light for black-and-white printing. A good safelight lets you see easily, especially if the darkroom has light-coloured walls. *Orthochromatic* materials (sensitive to blue and green) are used for making high-contrast (line) copies and other derivations. These need a red safelight.

There are also particular safelights recommended for colour printing and film loading, which give very little light. The brightest are pulsating, because human eyes can see more in such lighting than they can with an equivalent level of constant light. However, none of them are particularly useful for ordinary work. You have to wait 20 or 30 minutes before you can see more than the faintest glow, and most photographers want to go into the light at much shorter intervals than this. So it is much simpler just to work in total darkness.

When setting up a new darkroom, it is best to test the safelighting. Put a sheet of photographic paper on the enlarger baseboard, and place a coin on top of it. Leave the safelight on for five minutes. Then take away the coin, give the paper an overall exposure that should produce a mid grey print (without a negative in the enlarger). With most enlargers, about 1 second at *f*/16 is right for 25 × 20 cm (10 × 8 in) paper. Process the paper in the usual way. When it is fixed, it should be an even tone all over. If you can see a pale area where the coin was, then the lighting is not safe and you need to check the blackout, use a smaller safelight bulb, or move the safelight further away.

Developing films

Films can be processed in an open dish or box. However, it is now virtually universal in small dark rooms to process them in a light-tight tank.

Normally, the film is wound onto a spiral, which goes into the tank. There are two basic types: plastics and stainless steel. The plastics ones have a spiral groove in each end

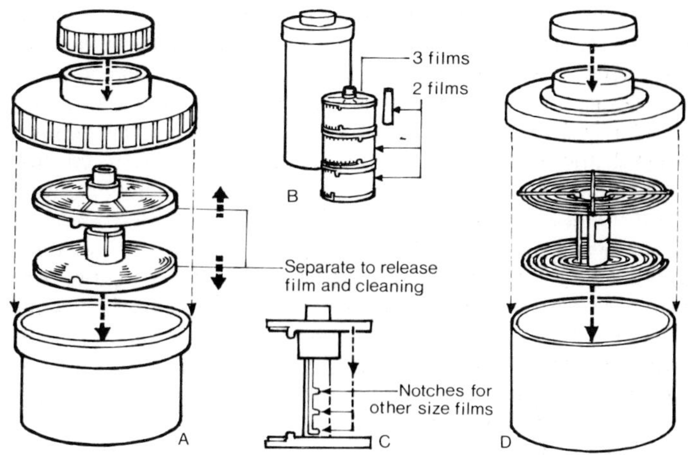

Small tanks are ideal for film processing. A. Plastics tanks and spirals are ideal for occasional use. B. Tanks are available to take a number of films at once. C. Stainless steel tanks with centre-load spirals are durable and quicker to use *after* practice. Some have plastics lids

plate. Most of them load from the edge inwards. The end of the film is pushed into the start of the grooves, where it is gripped by a ball bearing held in a slot in each side. The two ends of the spiral are then held one in each hand and contra-rotated back and forth about 30°. The film is pulled in by the two ball bearings. This works well with new completely dry spirals. However, once they are worn, or even slightly damp, they can jam up. If you need to develop several films in quick succession, before the spiral can be dried properly, it is possible to load the spiral under water, but extra care is needed so as not to damage the emulsion. It is extremely sensitive to damage when wet.

Stainless steel spirals are simply a pair of spirals of thick wire welded to a central core. The film is attached to the core (by one of a number of different methods) curved slightly, and wound round the spiral. It springs out to lie between adjacent coils of the wire.

The plastics spirals are less expensive, and fit into considerably less expensive plastics tanks. Many of them can be adjusted to take different film formats. There are certainly easier to learn to use, and probably the best choice for occasional use. The metal ones are used with stainless steel tanks, and can also be used in professional 15-litre processing lines. They are not as easy to load at first, but with a little practice are much faster than the plastics ones. There is considerable variation in quality of stainless steel spirals. The least expensive are flimsy, and have rather awkward central spring catches. They need to be treated with utmost care if they are not to be bent or disjointed. Good quality spirals costs about 30% more. They are made more robust, and the 35 mm size have a much easier film holder – two prongs which engage with the last pair of perforation. This type is a joy to load.

As an alternative to spirals, a few tanks use crinkly edged plastics 'aprons' which are rolled up together with the film. The apron touches the film at its edges only, and allows the chemicals to reach the exposed emulsion.

Daylight loading

Films need complete darkness, so all the manipulations must go on in the dark. In the absence of a suitably darkened room

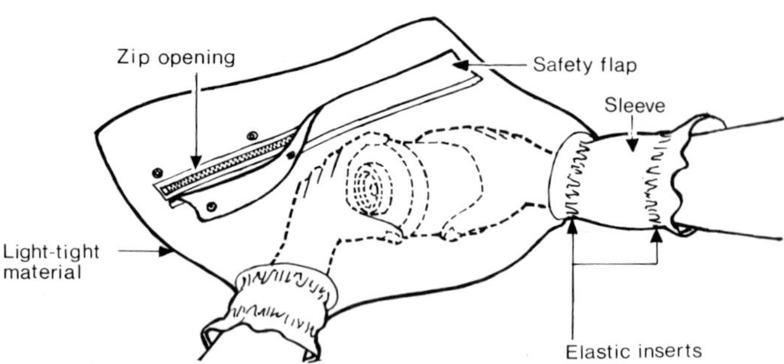

For film loading, a changing bag is a good substitute for a darkroom

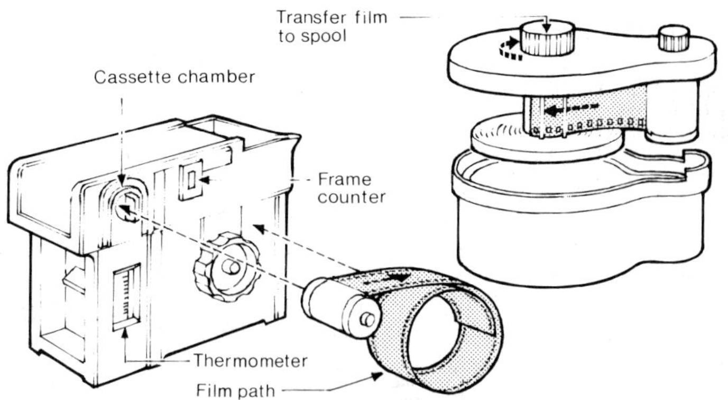

Without a darkroom, films can be developed in daylight-loading tanks. The film is pulled out of the cassette and slightly engaged on the reel. Then the tank is closed and the film wound into the processing chamber

there are two possibilities: a changing bag, or a daylight-loading tank. Changing bags are light-tight bags with two sleeves which usually have elastic cuffs to hold them on the arms and to ensure a complete seal. The bag has a zipped opening. The tank, spirals, film cassette, scissors for trimming and so on, all go in the bag, which is then zipped up. After the arms are inserted into the sleeves the tank can be loaded with confidence in broad daylight. It is a good idea to shake out the changing bag after each use to keep it clear of dust or film debris.

Daylight loading tanks are exactly what their name implies. The film cassette is placed in the tank, the leader connected to the mechanism, and the tank closed. Then the film can be wound out into the processing chamber and processed in full daylight.

Beakers and measures

To process a film, the right quantity of chemicals at the right dilution need be left in the tank for the right length of time.

This requires measuring vessels of large enough capacity to take a tankful of developer. The best material for photographic vessels is glass, but perfectly suitable plastics measures are available. Get them from photographic suppliers though; many culinary measures are made from unsuitable materials.

For most work, a set of calibrated beakers – 50 ml, 250 ml, and 1 litre – are fine. They are accurate enough for diluting liquid or powdered processing chemicals. For more precise work, mixing up solutions from raw chemicals, for example, a measuring cylinder is essential. When working from powdered chemicals, the solutions should be filtered. This needs a funnel and filter papers. A funnel is, in any case, a great help in filling storage bottles and processing tanks.

Mixing chemicals

Few photographic chemicals come in working strength solutions. They are concentrated or dehydrated for convenient storage. Before use they must be made up to the correct volume with water. Tap water is perfectly adequate virtually anywhere. If it leads to constant contamination problems, boiled and cooled water is usually satisfactory. Failing that, use distilled or de-ionised water. Battery top-up fluid is *not* suitable, it is seldom pure distilled water. A number of

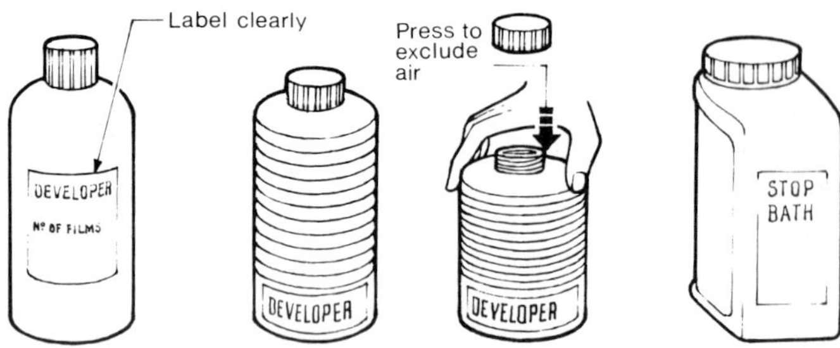

Storage bottles are essential for any darkroom. Flexible ones allow airless storage which prolongs the life of developers

purifying filters are available, producing photographically acceptable water direct from the tap.

Virtually all chemicals come with instructions which are worth following. Often mixing the constituents in the wrong order makes them difficult to dissolve, and may even reduce their activity. Some formulae allow you to mix up part packs as you need them; others do not permit division. Follow the temperature recommendations, too. That can speed things up a lot.

When mixing up powdered chemicals, mix them all – in the instructed order – with about two thirds of the total volume of water at about 50°C (unless the instructions are different). When all is mixed in, make the solution up to the full indicated quantity, and filter it into a bottle. Do not try to divide powdered chemicals unless so advised in the instructions. Working from liquid concentrates is easier. Most can be diluted as and when required to produce working strength solution, thus calling for less storage space.

Sometimes the same containers or measuring vessels are needed to mix up several different solutions in turn. Always mix them up in the order that they will be used (developer, bleach, fix, stabiliser, for example). Some solution is always carried forward during processing; so a little transferred in mixing has no noticeable effect. Back-contamination (fix in developer, for example) is usually disastrous, and may happen even with careful washing between steps.

Naturally, you need a container to mix up the total volume of solution. Once mixed, though, it is often better to store the solutions in small bottles. Full, dark, airtight containers increase the storage life of some chemicals dramatically. So select the best series of containers for the process you are using. Dark glass bottles are the best universal containers. Black and white developers keep for many months in them. Colour chemicals for several weeks.

Flexible bottles allow the air to be squeezed out when they are part full. They work well until about half empty. With less than that in them, most tend to suck air slowly through their cap seals. The concertina type have a further problem – they are virtually impossible to clean once a solution has dried.

Thermometers

The temperature of processing solutions must be right as well, so a good thermometer is essential. Most are glass, with a bulb of liquid which expands with temperature to form a column. Top quality ones use mercury, though most have a column of coloured spirit. Those with red liquid are quite useless in the darkroom, as they cannot be read in safelighting. Photographic thermometers use blue fluid.

Dial thermometers were once very popular; insted of a column of liquid, they have a pointer which rotates against a scale. Their main use is in plastics developing tanks. The main body of the thermometer goes down the central hole (used to fill the tank and for spiral agitation) leaving the dial to be seen from outside. The modern equivalent is a digital electronic thermometer with a probe on the end of a lead.

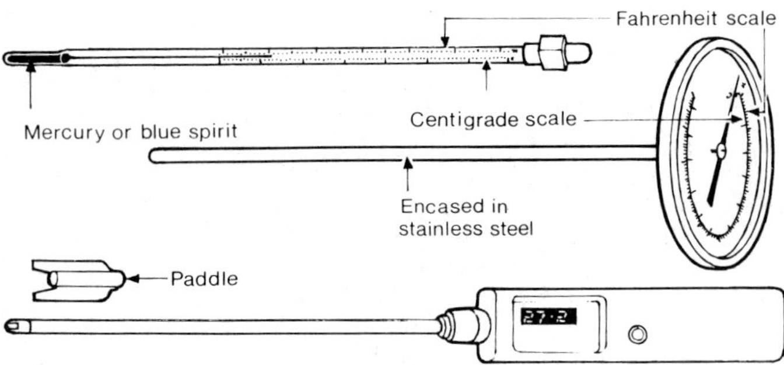

A good photographic thermometer is essential for accurate processing, especially in colour

With any type of thermometer, its consistency is more important than its accuracy. Once you have evolved a satisfactory processing time for any temperature indicated on your thermometer, you can stick to that. Be careful, though, if you change thermometers. Check the new one against the old (if it is unbroken) to ensure that you keep to the same temperature.

Black-and-white processing takes place at around 20°C (68°F) so a thermometer reading up to 25°C is quite sufficient. Colour processes, though, need much high temperatures, mostly around 38°C (100°F). Many colour printing routines call for a pre-wash at a considerably higher temperature than this. So a thermometer that reads 45°C is essential, and one that reads to 60°C is useful.

Film dryers

The ideal way to dry a film is in a heated cabinet. The film hangs in a gentle stream of filtered air rising by convection.

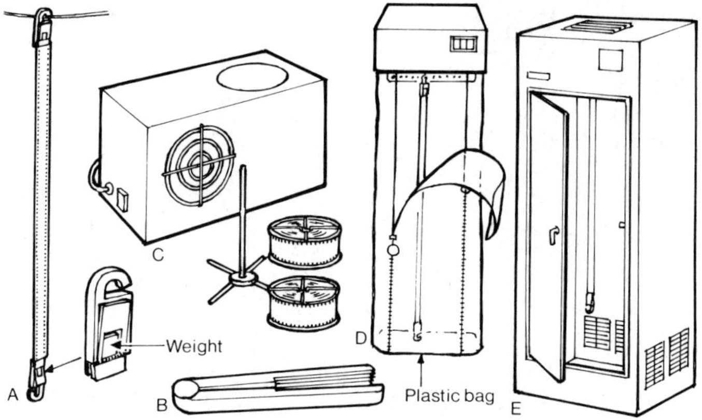

Drying films without letting them get dusty is important. A. The simplest way is to hang them in a dust-free place. B. A squeegee to remove excess water helps prevent drying marks. C. Some bench dryers take films on their spirals. D. For occasional use, a hanging foldable drying cabinet is excellent. E. In a permanent darkroom, a fixed drying cabinet is ideal

However, this is by no means essential. Films can be hung up to dry in any dust-free room, warmed or not as required. There are small folding film dryers which hang on the wall. Providing a stream of filtered air, they ensure dust-free drying.

Rubber squeegee tongs can be used to clear off most of the water, which is a good idea in hard water areas, where films often end up with white drying marks. The problem with the tongs is that they can pick up grit and so scratch the film. They are best avoided unless drying marks are a problem.

Enlargers

To make a print, the image of the negative is focused on to the paper for a measured time. This is done with an enlarger,

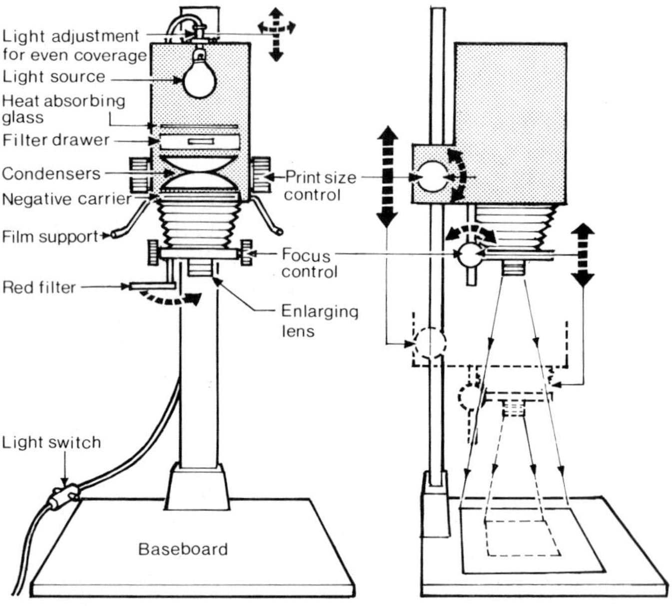

The features of a typical enlarger

which is much like a slide projector. It has a light source, a film holder and a lens. It differs, though, in some important aspects. Most enlargers operate vertically. The projection unit (or held) travels up and down a column to adjust the magnification. Some use a hinged parallelogram movement instead of, or as well as, the sliding one. The film needs to be held more accurately flat than in a projector, and the whole outfit must be virtually light-tight.

Basically, an enlarger is quite simple. It must provide an even light over the whole negative area; and hold the negative flat, parallel with the lens mount and the baseboard. The head must move up and down with reasonable ease, and must be well away from the column at large magnifications so that the paper can be positioned exactly as needed. The focus mechanism must be capable of retaining the focus. Beyond that, all else is just added convenience. The most useful basic addition is a series of calibrations on the enlarger column from which you can calculate magnifications. This makes it much easier to work out the correct exposure when changing picture size.

There are two basic types of illumination system: condenser and diffuser. Condenser systems focus the light from the lamp through the film into to lens. Virtually all enlargers use opal bulbs, so the light is still quite diffuse. The advantages of the focused light beam are high light output and increased contrast in black-and-white. The main disadvantage is that it shows up blemishes and dirt on the negative surfaces. However, it is much to be recommended for monochrome printing. To be most effective, the condensers must be matched in focal length to the enlarging lens, and so should be changed for different film sizes.

Diffuser systems are normally used for colour, because colour print contrast is the same whatever system is used. Also, colour heads must diffuse the light at some stage to mix it thoroughly. Because they are being widely chosen for colour work, diffuser enlargers are becoming much more widely accepted for black-and-white. Many workers find that they offer better control of highlight details. The latest chromogenic monochrome films, introduced with Ilford XP-1 400 and Agfa Vario XL, like colour films, offer the same contrast with diffuser or condenser systems.

Enlargers are normally supplied without lenses. Most have a 39 mm screw mount to take virtually any lens. Adaptors or alternative flanges allow them to be converted to take lenses with different mounts.

Two different focus mechanisms are used. Either the lens mount rotates in a helical movement, or the whole mount is tracked up and down with a rack and pinion. There is little to choose between the systems. Whether they use bellows or sliding metal tubes, focusing systems are all effectively light-tight.

Negative carriers

The most basic way of holding film in an enlarger is to press it between two sheets of metal with holes which are the size of one negative. Naturally, the two pieces must be keyed together, usually by pins and holes, and must slot into the enlarger at the right place. More sophisticated versions are hinged, and may carry the film in a groove. Any of these carriers can work well enough used with care. The problem comes when changing from one negative to the next. All

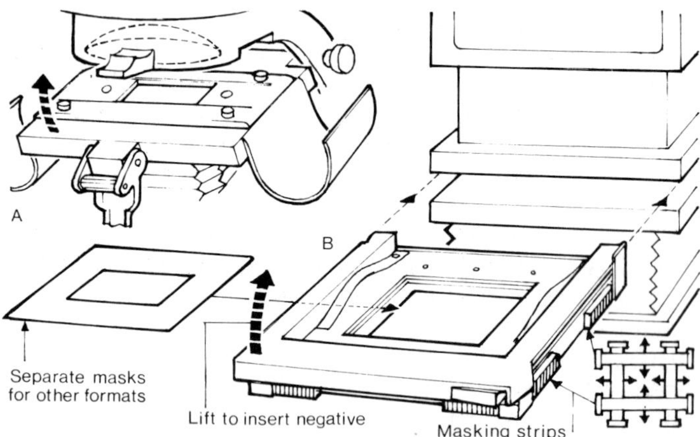

Most enlargers allow several sizes of negatives. A. A 35mm glassless carrier, with the negative held down by the condenser lens. B. Adjustable carriers may have interchangeable masks or movable masking strips

enlargers have a system of releasing the pressure from the carrier to allow the film to be pulled through. However, some still have the danger of scratching.

There is nothing in a glassless carrier like this to hold the negative flat. Films wider than 35 mm tend to bow considerably, making a sharp print impossible. So they must be held with glass at least above, and preferably on both sides. Some enlargers use the condenser lens to hold the film down flat, others use sheets of glass. Once again the carrier needs to be designed with care to avoid scratching the film. In practice, with a wide aperture lens, even prints from 35 mm film are noticeably sharper using a glass carrier.

The problem with glass is keeping it clean. Every speck of dust shows on the print, and some can cause the strange interference pattern called Newton's rings. The best way to keep the glasses clean is to polish them with an artificial fibre non-woven cleaning cloth – the disposable sort used in the kitchen. These generate very little static electricity when polishing glass. Do not use them on lenses, or other pieces of optical glass, though, they may well damage the surface. The glasses in an enlarger carrier are relatively inexpensive to replace if they get damaged.

One important consideration is the ability to hold mounted transparencies (slides). Printing from transparencies is becoming easier and easier, and is a good way to begin colour printing. When choosing an enlarger, make sure that it has a carrier which can hold slides as well as negatives.

For colour printing, it is important that the carrier does not leak too much light. Most modern designs are well sealed, and fit closely into the enlarger. All, though, let some light out, so do not expect complete light-tightness.

Rangefinders and autofocus

Some enlargers incorporate a rangefinder. This usually operates by projecting a line image onto the baseboard – exactly linear when the focus is correct, broken when out of focus. This is of little practical use. It is easy to focus the image visually to well within the accuracy of the rangefinder. Its main use is in providing an accurately focused light beam for making some types of contact print.

A number of enlargers have autofocus mechanisms. These couple the focusing movement to the head travel, so that the image remains in focus as its size is altered. In some models

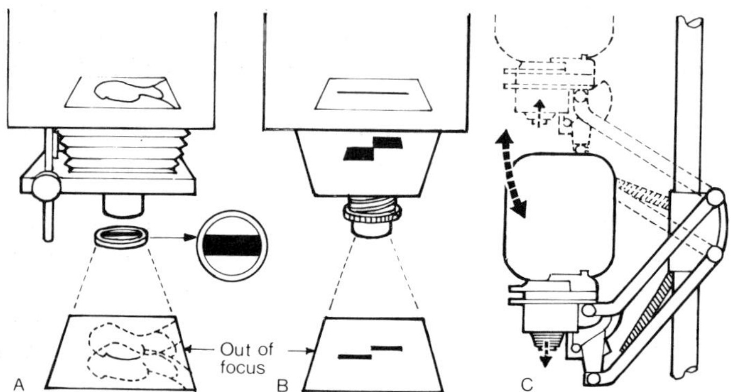

Several enlargers have rangefinding devices fitted. A. Coincident image attachment works with the negative in place. B. More common split-line versions allow the range finder to replace the negative carrier. C. In autofocus enlargers, the lens moves with the head travel to keep the picture sharp at all magnifications

this movement is preset, so that the image is always focused exactly in one plane. These enlargers need easels of exactly the right height. More sophisticated models retain focus once the image has been focused on the baseboard or easel. Either way, autofocus is a great boon.

Colour printing

To make colour prints the colour of the enlarger light has to be accurately controlled. This can be done by making three separate exposures through primary red, green and blue filters, but most photographers prefer to make a single 'white light' exposure. Most recent enlargers have a colour drawer.

This holds one or more coloured acetate filters to give the correct colour light.

Colour printing filters (CP filters) are made in a series of densities of cyan, magenta and yellow. For most films and papers, only magenta and yellow are used. In fact some combinations need so much yellow and magenta filtration that strong red filters are also available. The densities are calibrated in units of absorption, usually varying from the palest 05 to 50. Each filter carries a density and colour designation: C for cyan, M for magenta, Y for yellow and R for red. A typical set contains: 05, 10, 20, 30, 40, 50 of each cyan, magenta and yellow, a CP50R and a UV absorbing filter, which is used for all colour printing.

Most colour drawer enlargers incorporate a heat absorbing glass. This, too, is needed for colour printing, as otherwise too much infra-red radiation reaches the film.

While it is possible to make excellent prints with filters in a colour drawer, altering the colour balance is rather tedious. To overcome this, most manufacturers offer enlargers with colour heads. These have built-in filter wedges which can be moved into the light path at the turn of a knob. The systems vary – one at least controls the brilliance of three separately coloured light sources – the effect is the same. You simply dial in the correction needed, and the enlarger light changes colour. Colour heads can also be used to change the contrast of variable-contrast black-and-white papers.

Paterson's Colour 35 enlarger, shown first at Photokina 1980, introduced a simple and elegant low-cost solution. Between the light source and condensers is a housing with a series of sliding controls. Each moves one acetate filter into (or out of) the light path. Thus, basic filter pack changes are made by the push of a knob. Of course, the range of filters has to be restricted, but they cover all normal colour-printing needs, and a range of suitable colours for variable-contrast papers.

Because the exact colour is so important it is well worth using a stabilised power supply for any colour enlarger, otherwise voltage changes can alter the colour. Many enlargers now use 12-volt bulbs, and can be supplied with a stabilised transformer to overcome the problem. For a mains voltage enlarger, the best source of a stabilised supply is an electrical shop.

Lenses

Enlarging lenses are chosen to match the film format. They are nearly all of normal optical construction, and so should be the same focal length as the standard for the camera: 25 mm for size 110, 50 mm for 35 mm film, 80 mm for 6 × 6 and 105 mm for 6 × 9. Wide-angle lenses allow larger prints to be made at the same column height, but good ones are expensive. Zoom lenses, too, are a luxury needed only when column travel is restricted.

The quality of any print is restricted by the quality of the enlarging lens. There is no point in using a top quality camera and then a second-rate enlarging lens. However, this is not an area in which image quality is always closely related to price.

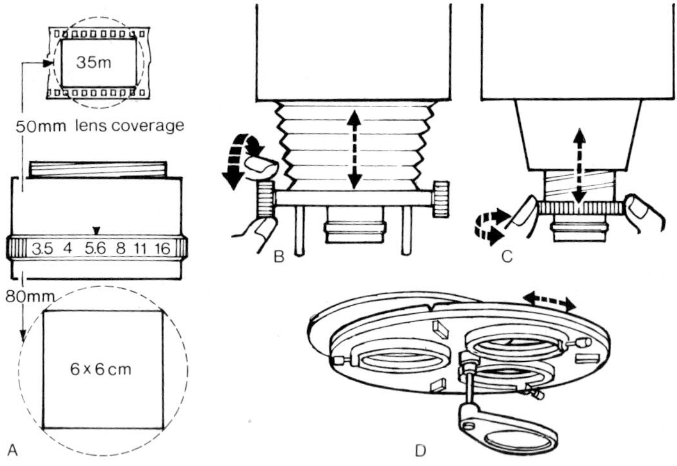

A. Enlarger lenses must be chosen to cover the whole negative area. B. Commonly, focus is by rack and pinion. C. Some models have a helical focusing control. D. For tricolour printing, or special effects, a filter turret below the lenes is useful

The top quality (and price) German lenses are extremely good and virtually essential for the most critical work. However, with moderate enlargements from ordinary quality negatives, the results are not noticeably better than those produced by a good reasonably priced lens. Prints from good lenses in the next price bracket down are usually indistinguishable from those made through a reasonably priced lens. The major difference among mid-range lenses in practice is that the more expensive models have a wider aperture (usually *f*/2.8 instead of around *f*/4). This is of little advantage in printing. It is much more cost effective to use a higher powered enlarger bulb than to pay three times the price for a lens one stop wider in aperture.

A top quality lens costs as much as a good compact 35 mm camera; and is clearly the best choice of the perfectionist. For those who choose to aim just a little lower, the optimum choice of lens is the best one you can get with a moderate maximum aperture (*f*/3.5 to *f*/4.5 for a 50 mm lens). Expect to pay around the price of five or six process-paid colour transparency films. Avoid cheap unknown brands; they really can degrade the whole system irretrievably. The difference between a good moderately priced *f*/4 lens and the poor examples available at around half the price can be staggering. However most of the lenses supplied *with* enlargers offer reasonable performance.

One of the least reliable features of a cheap enlarging lens is its diaphragm. It is often not possible to rely on its calibrated apertures. As it is normal practice to print at one aperture, altering exposures by changing the time, this is not an insuperable problem, but it does mean that new exposure tests are needed if the aperture is altered.

Easels and printers

Once you have composed and focused the picture, you must place a sheet of paper flat below the enlarger. Modern resin coated papers lie virtually flat, and it is quite possible just to put a piece of paper on the enlarger baseboard. This is quite simple for black-and-white work if the board is ruled with a suitable grid. It can also be lined up using the red safelight filter built into most enlargers.

However, in colour printing the paper must be positioned accurately in total darkness. The best way to do this is in a printing easel. The easiest type to use is a flat box with a dark slide. First the picture is composed and focused on the inside surface of the box. Then (in the dark) the box is loaded, and the paper covered with the dark slide. The box can then be

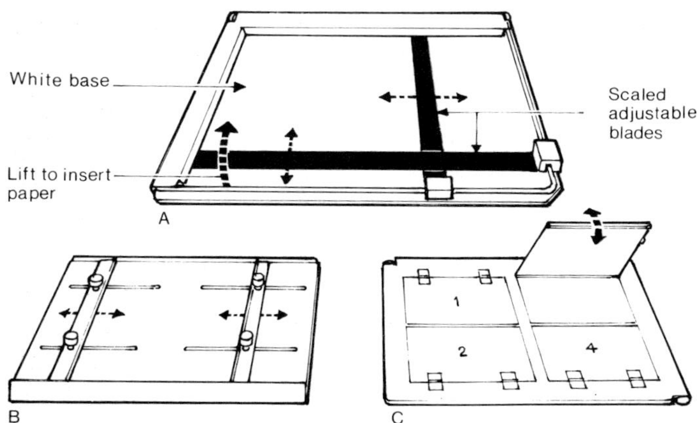

Enlarging easels make placing and holding the paper simpler. A. The traditional masking frame has adjustable blades to hold the paper and produces unexposed borders. B. A borderless easel holds the paper by side pressure. C. A number of systems allow multiple printing on a single sheet

positioned in the enlarger light beam. (Of course, the image will not be quite sharp on the slide, but do not refocus.) Then the enlarger is turned off, the dark slide removed, and the paper exposed. Some versions used hinged covers instead of a removable dark slide.

Most printing boxes have a series of blocks or flaps which allow small sections of the paper to be exposed in turn. This is very useful for making test prints – especially in colour.

The classic 'masking frame' is much simpler. It has a pair of adjustable blades mounted on a hinged frame. The blades are set to the paper size and when the picture has been composed the frame is raised, the paper set against stops, and the frame lowered. Quite a simple operation even in the dark. These easels produce prints with white borders.

Focus finders

For small prints, it is easy to see the exact point of best focus. At greater enlargements, this becomes more difficult, especially in deliberately soft-focus pictures. The best way to be

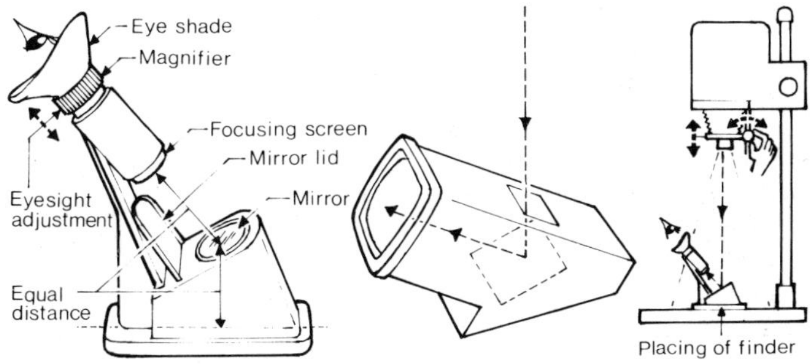

Focus finders allow the negative grain to be sharply focused for the crispest prints

sure is to use a focus finder. A focus finder magnifies a small section of the picture so that you can see the grain structure. When that is focused sharply, you can be sure that you have the best possible sharpness all over the print.

Measuring exposure

The classic way of determining print exposures is to make a test strip at a series of different exposure times (see page 115). This can be a time-consuming and costly process especially in colour. It is much quicker to measure the light level, and calculate the exposure time from that.

Most enlarging exposure meters work on the whole negative. A diffuser held under the lens (set for the printing aperture) produces an even tone for the meter to measure. Adjusting the control until the meter's light goes on (or off) sets the scale to read out the exposure time. Some versions have a digital exposure time read out. It is that simple. There is, of course one complication: paper speeds are nowhere near as accurately controlled as film speeds, and individual processing techniques and preferences can also influence the exposure needed.

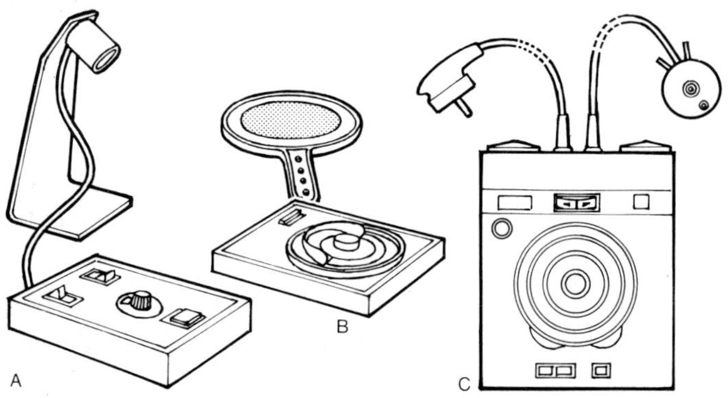

Printing exposure meters: Automatic exposure control adjusts exposure time according to light reflected from print. B. A straightforward enlarging meter is adjusted to a null point for a diffused reading. C. For greater sophistication, some meters have a spot-reading probe

The normal practice is to calibrate the meter for each type of paper used. Simply make the best print possible using the test strip method. Then measure the enlarger light (with the negative in place) at the same magnification and lens aperture, and adjust the meter so that it gives its correct exposure indication at the correct time setting. Read off the paper index (often a letter) and mark it on the paper box. The index should work every time. Every time, that is, that the negative has a normal density range.

With unusual subjects – very light or very dark backgrounds for example – the meter will prove wrong just as a normal through-the-lens camera meter fails in the same conditions. Such problem subjects are few enough to be printed using a test strip. However, with some meters they, too, can be measured. The meter may allow you to measure the exposure from a small section of the image. Then, if you have have previously calibrated the meter, from say flesh tone or green grass, you can set the exposure from a similar section of the problem negative.

Enlarging meters can be influenced by safelighting, so it is normal to switch off the safelights when metering. Some meters can be wired into the safelight circuit to extinguish them automatically when the meter is switched on.

Measuring colour

With colour printing, the colour needs to be right as well. The most economical way to calculate the colour needed is with a filter mosaic. There are several different types, all basically doing the same thing – providing a range of tiny patches of filter to be placed in contact with the paper. They work on a scrambled image, and provide a series of coloured patches on the processed paper, one of which is neutral grey. Following the instructions allows the printing light to be altered to give the correct colour balance (see page 164).

Colour analysers are more sophisticated. They measure in turn the red, green and blue light (usually from a scrambled image, but they can be used selectively) and display filter changes in cyan, magenta and yellow needed to return the colour to match the original reference negative. Used carefully, such aids can reduce wasted time and materials very considerably.

Timing the exposure

Once everything else is settled, the paper (monochrome or colour) has to be exposed for exactly the right time. It can be done by looking at a clock or watch or by counting. In fact, there is available a device which just flashes once a second to aid accurate timing.

However, undoubtedly the simplest and most repeatable way to work is with an enlarger timer. This is simply a timed

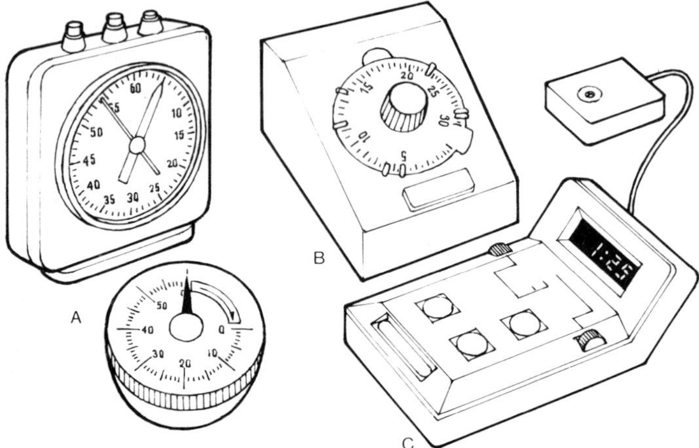

Accurate timing is an essential part of photography. Most timers count back to zero. For process control, a multistage timer is ideal

switch wired into the enlarger lead. One control allows the light to remain on for composing and focusing. The other switches the enlarger on and off again after a preset time interval. Timers use clockwork, electromagnetic or electronic mechanisms. There is little to choose between them. Once again, repeatability is far more important than is absolute accuracy.

A number of manufacturers offer timers coupled to enlarging exposure meters, thus avoiding the need to transfer settings – an extra convenience. Some also offer totally automatic exposure control. The meter reads light reflected from the printing paper, and switches off the enlarger after a suitable amount of light has reached the print. These are fine – so long as they can display the time that the print needs. Otherwise it is impossible to calculate the times needed for 'dodging' or burning in (see page 124). One small accessory gives extra freedom – a foot switch. This can be used to operate the enlarger with or without a timer and so leaves both hands free for manipulating the negative image as it falls on the printing paper.

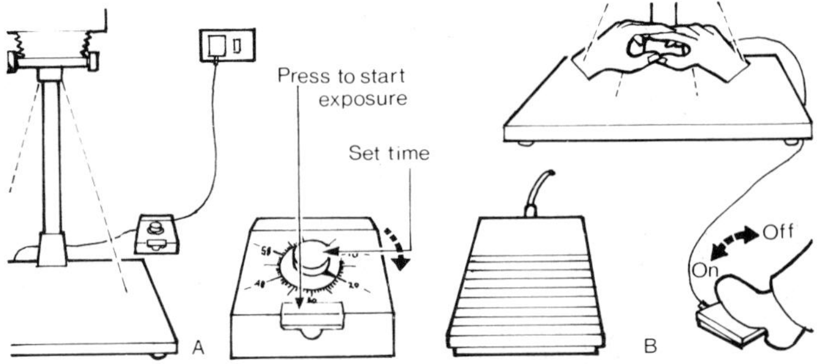

Enlarger light controls. A. For repeatable results, a repeat timer can be wired into the enlarger lead. B. A foot switch leaves both hands free for manipulating the printing light

Processing dishes

Black-and-white paper is processed in a series of dishes or trays, one each for developer, stop bath and fixer. It is then washed, either in another tray, or in a sink. For greatest economy, it is best to use trays intended for the particular size of paper. Dishes are often about 2.5 cm (1 in) longer each way than the paper. However, a set of trays intended for 30.5 × 25.5 cm (12 × 10 in) paper are good for most common sizes, without taking too much solution. For larger prints, a set of 60 × 50 cm (24 × 20 in) dishes are useful.

The most readily available washing dish is a rectangular washing-up bowl. This can accommodate a large number of prints. However, all prints should finally be washed in running water, and resin-coated ones should not be left for more than five minutes or so in the 'holding' bowl before being washed.

Monochrome processing takes place at around room temperature. So as long as the solutions start at the right temperature, there is little need for temperature control equipment. In very cold conditions, or when using higher temperature processes, the dishes can be stood on a thermostatically controlled dishwarmer.

Tongs

Processing solutions – even those for black-and-white – can produce skin disorders, so it is best to work without dabbling in the chemicals. The simplest way is to move the print from tray to tray with tongs. Two pairs are needed – one for the developer and one for the other solutions – those with soft rubber tips are best, as hard tips can damage the soft emulsion of resin-coated papers. Select two differently shaped tongs, so that they can be distinguished in the dark. The developer tongs should never go into the other solutions and the other tongs never go in the developer, otherwise they will cause contamination of the developer, reducing its efficiency or even spoiling prints.

Print washers

Most casual photographers wash prints in a sink or bath, although this is messy and not always effective. There are a

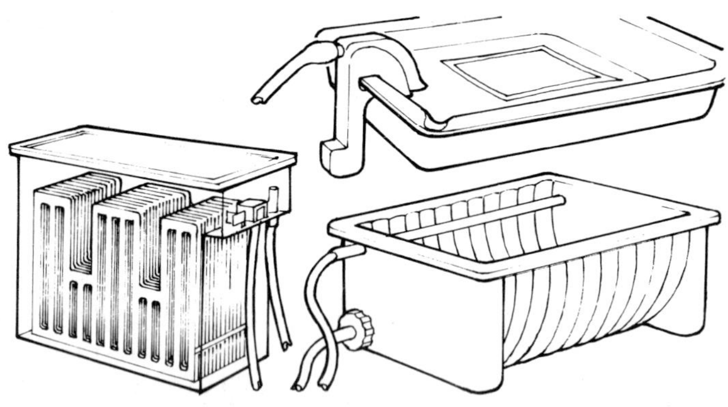

For permanent prints, especially on non-resin-coated paper, a print washer is a great asset

number of print washers on the market which hold the prints apart in a flow of running water, washing them effectively, and avoiding splashes.

It is quite simple to make an effective print washer, starting with a plastics bowl. Fit rods or wires to hold the print upright and apart. Drill a row of holes about 2.5 cm (1 in) from the top towards one end, and lead a tube from the tap to the bottom of the other end. Adjust the flow so that the water swirls round the prints without splashing and flows out of the overflow holes.

Colour print drums

It is quite possible to process colour prints in trays which are standing on a dishwarmer. However, since you are working

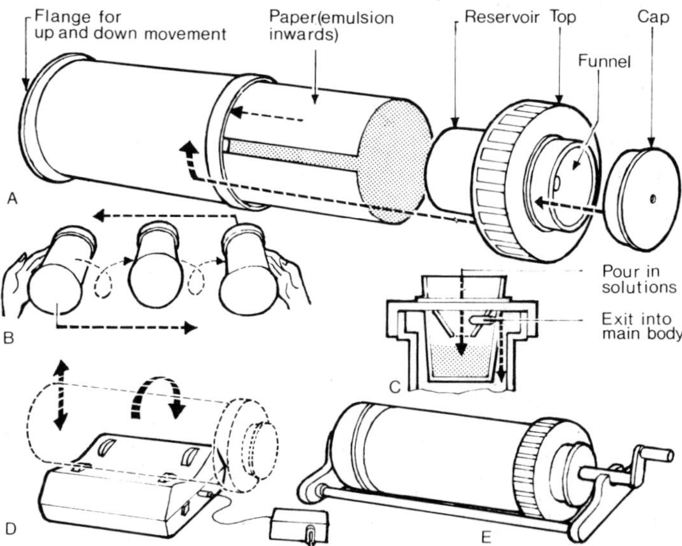

Processing colour prints: A. A typical light-tight print drum. B. Chemicals are agitated by rolling the drum. C. Reservoir holds the solutions until rolling begins for accurate timing. D. A motor base makes agitation easy. E. Some drums have a simple crank handle instead of rolling

virtually in the dark with toxic chemicals this is not to be recommended. The answer is to use a print drum. These light-tight drums are rather like large film tanks. The prints (one or more depending on the size) wrap round the inside, picture inwards.

Once the drum is loaded (in the dark) processing can proceed in full lighting. The drum is first warmed with water of a suitable temperature, then the solutions in turn are poured in at the correct intervals. The drum is rolled up and down the bench to swish the small volume of solution across the print.

This is quite a slow process, and can be made less tedious by using a motor to rotate the drum, instead of rolling it along a bench. The motors reverse motion about every ten seconds to ensure even processing.

Several units now combine motorised rotation with a thermostatically controlled water bath to provide constantly repeatable processing – which is essential for colour work. Some systems take film processing tanks as well – a great convenience. All drums can also be used for black-and-white printing, which is especially convenient with panchromatic papers.

Colour print processors

The motorised, thermostatically controlled print processing drums provide very consistent processing. However, they still take several minutes to process each print (or batch of prints), so a second drum is a great asset. You can be exposing the next batch of prints while one batch is processing itself. However, that calls for some dexterity. The solutions have to be changed every two or three minutes.

There are now sophisticated bench top colour processors. The exposed paper goes in one end, and a dry print comes out of the other. These machines are expensive, and only of interest to the most dedicated enthusiast. However, they open up the prospect of small-scale printing and processing for the freelance photographer or part-time professional.

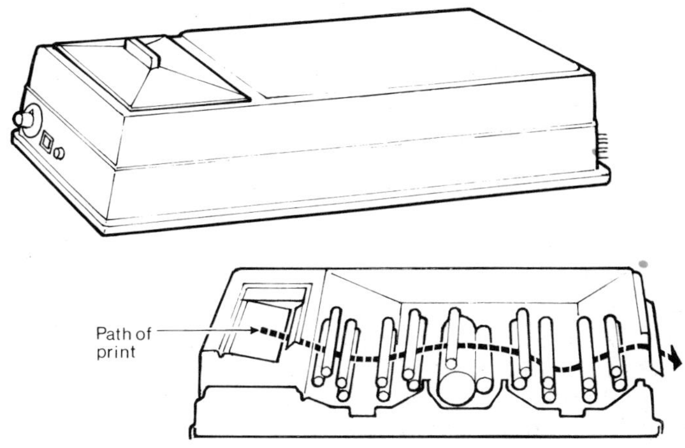

A roller transport process, such as the Durst RCP 20, can be used for automatic colour and black-and-white processing

Simpler and not quite so expensive models, introduced with the Durst RCP 20, makes this type of processing available to a wider range of enthusiasts. They are a great convenience. These processors work well with resin-coated black-and-white paper as well. They cannot, though transport normal (fiber-based) papers. Filled with water, the processors offer a temperature regulated water bath for small tank processing. Note, however, that the compartments *must* be filled with water whenever such a processor is switched on.

Drying and glazing

After washing for the recommended time, the prints must be dried. Resin-coated papers (including colour materials) dry flat and to their designed surface with no special attention. They can be laid either on absorbent paper or in a rack and just left alone. Alternatively, they can be dried in warm air. A hair dryer is the most handy source of warm air. Print driers for resin-coated papers consist of a series of grids to support

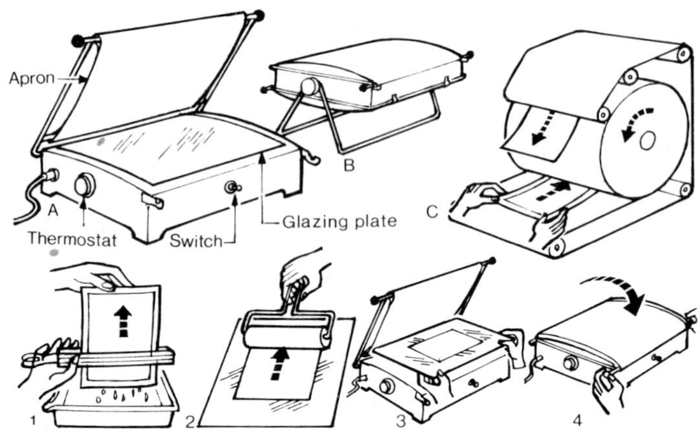

To achieve a high gloss, non-resin-coated papers must be glazed. A. Single sided glazer. B. Double-sided glazer. C. Rotary glazing machine. 1–4 steps in hot glazing a print

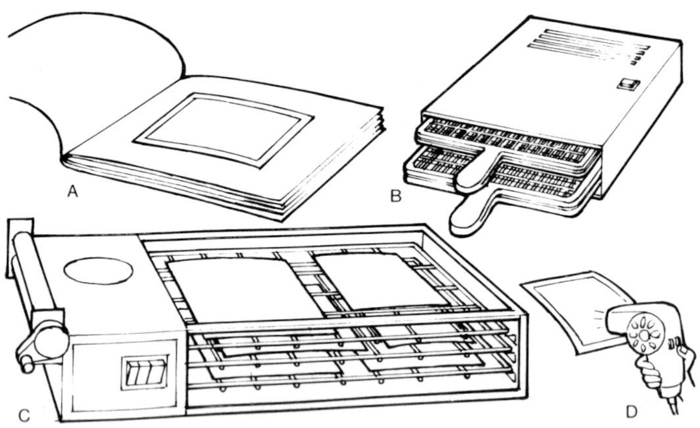

Drying prints. A. A book of blotting paper is good for paper prints. B. Electric print dryer. C. Resin-coated-paper dryer. D. Resin-coated prints can be quickly dried with a hair dryer

prints in a gentle flow of warm air. They ensure the best gloss on glossy prints, and avoid the potential damage and dirt from less organized drying methods.

Older style (fibre-based) papers tend to curl if air dried, and glossy ones dry matt. To produce glossy prints the paper must be glazed. This involves drying the prints in contact with a hard shiny surface – glass or chromium plate are usual materials.

There are two basic types of print glazer and both can be used for non-glazed prints. Flat-bed glazers have a slightly curved heated glazing sheet. The prints are held in tight contact with a piece of spring-tensioned cloth. Rotary glazers have a heated drum, and a belt of cloth. The cloth holds the prints in contact with the drum as it rotates slowly. Both types have heat controls. If they can be set reliably to a temperature of less than 95°C (200°F) they can be used to dry resin-coated materials.

Processing tapes

Some processes are quite long and involved, and need accurate timing for good results. One simple way to pace yourself is to record a tape of instructions. Simple 'pour in fixer now' commands at the right times are best. Combined with some favourite short musical interludes, tapes like this can make processing much simpler and more enjoyable. Tapes to time one or two processes have been commercially available.

Cutting paper and film

While it is usually best to choose paper the size of the final print, this is not always practical. There are often bargains available in large sizes, or even rolls of paper. Also, you may need to trim some prints to unusual shapes to match their images.

Trimming paper accurately with scissors is difficult. The best improvised method is to use a sharp knife and a steel straightedge – on a suitably unimportant flat surface. Much better, though, is to use a guillotine. The classic hinged-blade variety is quite satisfactory for most dividing and

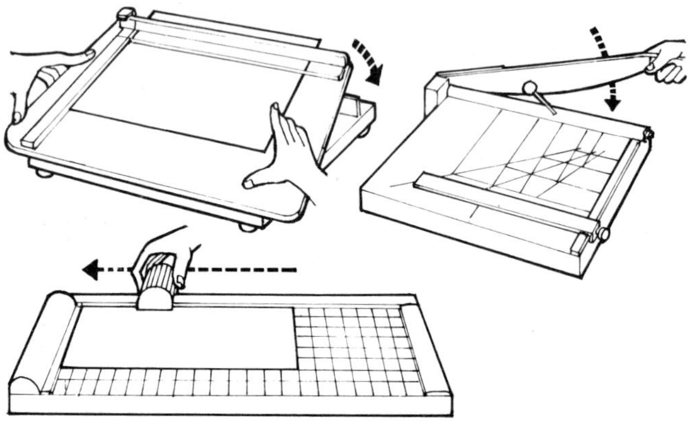

Print trimmers are the best way of cutting paper to size before or after printing

trimming. Choose one with a blade of 30 or 40 cm (12 or 15 in) to allow reasonable versatility. The best trimmers are those with a rotary blade mounted on a slider, which also have the advantage of being much safer if there are children about.

Film, too, can be cut with a trimmer which is useful when working with sheet film. Cutting up negatives, though, is best done with a pair of sharp scissors.

Storing prints and negatives

Start printing, and you soon have too many prints to display them all at once. However, they are easy to store. They can be kept in empty printing-paper boxes, while the black plastic envelopes are excellent for carrying or sending batches of prints.

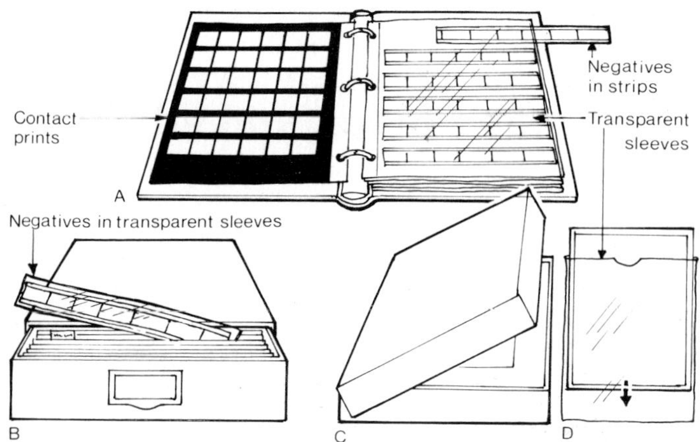

Negatives are delicate and need careful storage. A. Negative file. B. Storage dryer. C. Box file. D. Large negatives go in individual bags

Negatives need more careful storage. Once damaged, they are useless. Keep them in negative files, cut up into suitable lengths, in a loose-leaf binder. It is a good idea also to bind in contact sheets of each batch of negatives so that individual shots can be found virtually instantly.

3

Processing black and white films

Exposing a film correctly in the camera produces an invisible 'latent' image. Developing the film correctly turns the latent image into a visible negative. Everywhere the subject reflected a lot of light the film goes dark. Correspondingly, in the darker parts of the image, the negative is lighter in tone. The film is then 'fixed' to make the image permanent; then film washed and dried, ready for printing.

Processing without equipment

Developing and fixing are usually separate operations. However, they can be accomplished simultaneously in a *monobath*. This is simply a mixture of a fast-acting developer and a slow-acting fixer. The developer acts before the fixer, but in the end, the fixer stops all action, leaving the film ready to be washed.

One of the great advantages of a monobath is that it operates to completion. As long as the film is processed for long enough, the results are the same, irrespective of temperature. Within reason it is not possible to overprocess in a monobath. The main disadvantage is that negative quality is only fair, because the developer needs to act too fast to give really fine grain results.

It is quite possible to process a 20-exposure 35 mm film in its cassette. All that is needed is a beaker or mug, a small rubber band, and a piece of flat stick – such as an iced-lolly (popsicle) stick. When rewinding the film in the camera, make sure that the leader remains outside the cassette. Fix the leader securely outside the cassette by wrapping the rubber band round it.

Pour the monobath solution into the beaker to the depth of the cassette. It works best at about 20°C (68°F). Put in the cassette, and then turn its core back and forth using the flat stick. Agitate this way continuously for 4–5 minutes. The solution is drawn in through the cassette lips, and finds its way to the central core between the coils of film. Although the central part remains dry for a while, the fact that monobaths develop to finality means that the whole film is reasonably evenly developed.

When it is developed, open the cassette, taking care not to scratch the now-delicate emulsion, and wash the film in running water for around 20 minutes (see page 65) and hang it up to dry.

Note that this procedure does not work with normal 36 exposure films because they are packed too tightly in the cassette. Loading 36 or 40 exposures of thinner polyester based film (as used in 72 exposure cassettes) allows longer films to be processed in this manner.

Small-tank processing

The normal small-scale processing method is to load the film wound on spirals into a small cylindrical tank. Tanks take anything from one to ten spirals; some versions allow two short films per spiral. Most tanks need absolute darkness for loading, but a few can be loaded in normal room light. Once closed, the tanks are light-tight and processing is done in normal lighting.

The solutions must at the correct temperature for successful processing. Temperature is especially critical for the developer. Its time, temperature and dilution determine the negative density and contrast. Also, swift temperature changes between one process and the next can reticulate the film. Reticulation at its worst is a pattern of cracks in the emulsion which print as a network of white lines. Often, though, the result is simply a considerable increase in granularity, caused by physical clumping of silver grains as the emulsion moves; a result of differential movement as the soft, water-swollen, emulsion expands or contracts suddenly. The effect is exacerbated because the alkaline developer is replaced by an acid fixer which produces a different degree of swell.

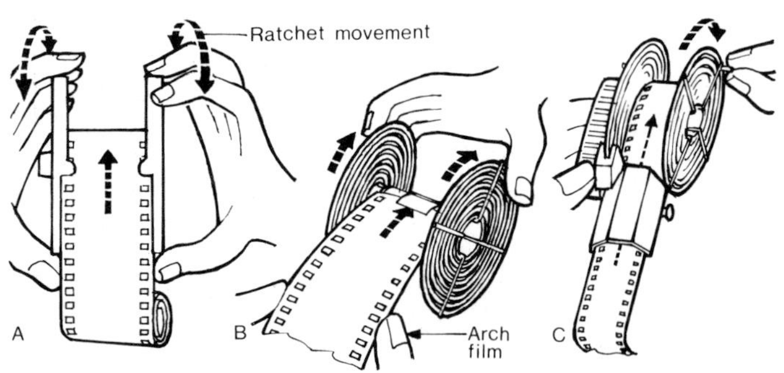

Loading film spirals. A. Plastics spiral. B. Stainless steel spiral. C. Centre-loading spiral with loader

One of the advantages of processing film on spirals is that washing is easy. Some tanks offer a washing unit which takes aerated water to the bottom. The air helps the wash water to rise evenly and carry away the processing by-products. However, a rubber tube led to the bottom of a normal tank is nearly as efficient. Alternatively, the spirals can be placed in a sink in running water, or in a cascade print washer.

The choice of spiral is a personal one; use whichever is easiest and most economical. It is, though, well worth practising many times before embarking on the first important film. In the absence of any old developed film, buy a cassette or roll of outdated material, and practise loading it. If the film goes on to a plastics spiral, it is properly loaded. The

Loading tanks

Most developing tanks are loaded in total darkness. This can be done in a changing bag, or in any small blacked-out space. You need the tank (with its lid), spirals, and cores if they use them, scissors and, for 35 mm crimped cassettes, a cassette opener.

Lay out the spirals (set to the correct film width if adjustable), tank, scissors and films to hand. In the dark, take the first film and remove it from its packing. Break open 110 and 126 cartridges to reveal the film wound in its paper backing. Break the paper seal on 120 films, or pull the end off a 35 mm cassette to take out the spool. With paper-backed film, unwind the backing paper as it leaves the spool until you come to the end of the film. With 35 mm film trim off the leader straight across (with scissors). The process now is different for edge-loading and centre-loading spirals.

Edge-loading spirals take the film in grooves formed in their plastics end plates. At one point the grooves reach the edge. Locate this, and push the film in, emulsion toward the core. It should slide about 5 cm (2 in) into the spiral, and then resist movement. Rotate the two end-plates against one another, and the film is drawn in by two ball-bearing grips. When it is all wound on, detach it from the backing paper or cassette core and put the spiral into the tank.

Centre-loading spirals are usually stainless steel. There are some plastics ones, which use a clip-on loader. To load a steel spiral, unroll about 10 cm (4 in) of film. Press in the sides to curve it slightly toward the emulsion, and attach the end to the core of the spiral. Keeping the film slightly bowed, wind it round and round. As it winds on, the edges spring out to be held between the wire spirals. Put the full reel into the tank.

When all the films are in the tank, it can be finally closed, and taken into the light for processing.

same cannot be said of a metal one. Inexperienced loading can result in adjacent coils touching, and thus not being processed properly.

The emulsion surface of film is very sensitive to contamination. It is important never to touch it. Fingerprints, even from clean fingers, restrict development, leaving permanent marks on the negatives. Avoid contact with the base side, too, wherever possible.

When loading more than one film into a tank, it is always best to put each in turn into the tank, and put the lid on. This reduces the risk of *all* the films fogging should the blackout accidentally fail (because a light is switched on, for example).

Once the films are safely loaded and the top on the tank, they are processed in full room lighting. The sequence is the same as that for paper processing: develop, rinse (or stop), fix and wash. All tanks have a light-trapped lid which allows solutions to enter and leave while keeping light out. Leave the main lid in place until the film is soaked in fixer.

Developers

The slower a film is processed, within limits, the finer will be the grain size. Thus, film developers are a compromise between convenience and fine grain (see page 54). In practice, the almost universal standard is the metol (or phenidone) hydroquinone-borax type typified by Kodak D76 or Ilford ID11. These and a number of newer equivalents, such as Kodak HC 110, provide an almost ideal compromise between fine grain, sharpness and effective film speed.

Working at their normal strength, at 20°C (68°F) ID11 or HC 110 develop a film fully to its rated speed in about 6–9 minutes depending on film type. They can develop about ten 36-exposure films or 120 films or fifteen 20-exposure films per litre. Each subsequent two films calls for an increase of 8% in developing time. The smallest quantity normally available makes 600 ml – enough to use in a two-film tank, which will process six films, with an increase of 10% in time for the second pair and another 10% for the third pair. The developer should be filtered each time it is returned to its container after use. This ensures that no dust or emulsion particles spoil the next film.

Clearly, using developer again and again produces problems in calculating and recording. So many workers prefer to use a one-shot technique. Diluting the same developer with three times its volume of water (one part developer plus three parts water) and using each tankful once only increases the capacity slightly. It also produces slightly finer grain and apparently sharper negatives. However, it also calls for a much longer developing time – usually 15–22 minutes.

Many liquid concentrate developers can be used at greater-than-normal concentration to reduce processing times. This is essential occasionally, as in news photography, but times much shorter than 5 minutes should be treated with care – they may lead to uneven development.

Other developers are formulated for other aims. Most paper and sheet-film formulae are unsuited to film processing – they are far too vigorous and produce very grainy results. Even so-called 'universal' developers at their 'miniature film' dilutions are less than satisfactory. Curiously, though, one high-speed paper developer is finding favour as a film developer when diluted with 60 parts of water (1 + 60). So there is still room to experiment.

Special developers mainly fall into three classes: extra-fine-grain developers, acutance developers, and speed-increasing developers. Let us look at each in turn.

Extra-fine-grain developers, by definition, give a finer grain structure than ID11/D76 types. At the same time, most call for slight overexposure; that is, a reduction in film speed. These are typified by Kodak Microdol X and Ilford Perceptol. Used with care, these formulae produce smoother negatives, which make prints from small formats look more like the results of large-format cameras. As these include some of the lowest priced developers available, they are well worth considering for 35 mm work.

Acutance developers are designed to make the pictures look sharper by enhancing the edges where light and dark areas meet (called the acutance). This happens because they are relatively low concentrations and slow-acting. The denser negative areas soon exhaust the developer in contact with them, and slow down their development. Their edges, though, continue to be developed by chemicals from adjacent lightly exposed areas. On the light side of the border, the converse occurs; near the dark area the developer becomes more exhausted, and thus works slower. So the result is a heightening of edge contrast, and thus an appearance of greater definition.

Some developers are specially formulated to achieve this effect, and work well with fine-grain films. They are not recommended for fast films, because they do not produce particularly fine grain, and they emphasise the grain by increasing the acutance. In fact, using high-dilution one-shot techniques with ID11/D76 type developers introduces a considerable acutance effect, which is one reason why many enthusiasts use this type of development.

Speed-increasing developers produce normal density negatives from underexposed images. They allow the film to be used in less well-lit places than normal. In practice, most do little more than that. Modern films in fact record an enormous range of tones – far more than usually needed. So processing to increase the overall density gives the impression of increasing the speed of the film. The same results could be achieved by printing from the thin negative produced by normal development.

The most substantial speed increase attainable is around 80%, that is, just under one stop. In most cases, extending the time in a standard developer has an equal effect on film speed. However the apparent increase is achieved, it is accompanied by an increase in grain. Thus, it is well to think carefully before setting out to uprate a film.

High-speed developers are used in press work, and in other situations where negatives are needed as soon as possible. Using highly active developer produces negatives with high contrast and considerable grain. That is perfectly acceptable for printing in newspapers, or for large-format materials, such as X-ray films. It is not, though, the best recipe for making high quality prints from 35 mm or smaller negatives.

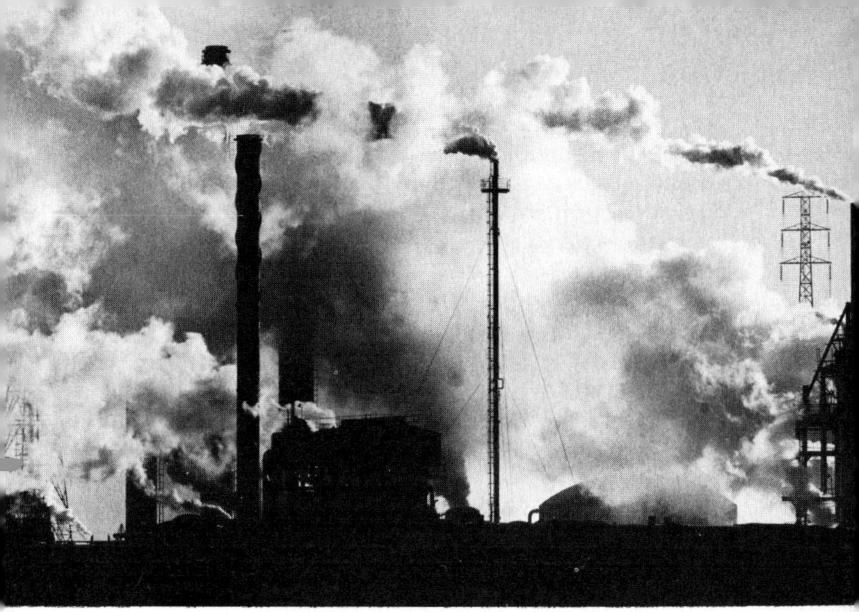

An 'acutance' developer gives a very sharp image on a medium-speed film, and allows it to be uprated slightly (M. C. Dobson)

The same type of developer can provide very stark effects with 400 ASA film, while retaining good tonal balance (Ben Storm)

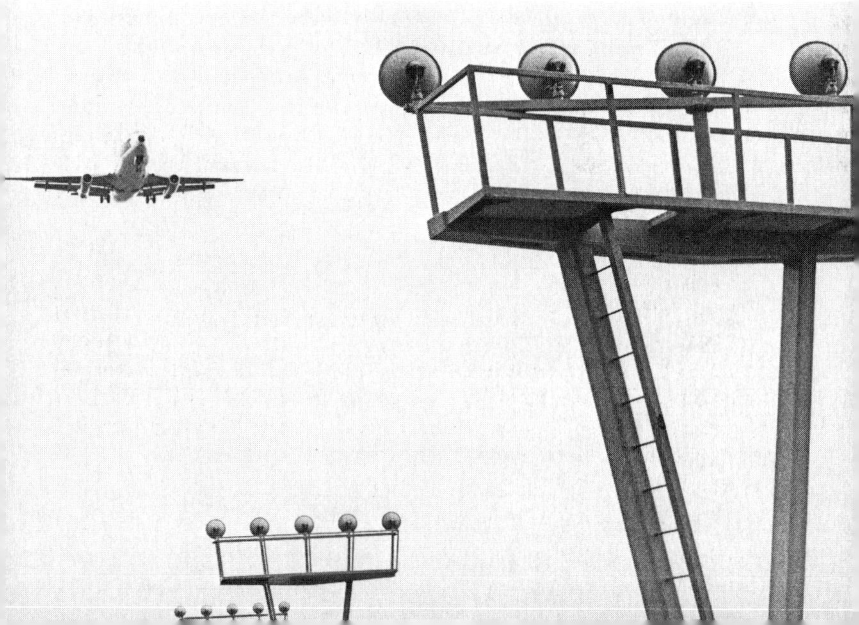

Monobaths are useful in processing tanks as well as for in-cassette developing. They are ideal for use in the field, when temperature and time control can be difficult. The main restriction on their use is that each formula works well with but a small range of films and produces a fixed contrast level. Unless ideally suited, monobaths can severely reduce effective film speed, and most introduce extra grain.

Agitation

The developer in intimate contact with the film becomes exhausted quite quickly. This can lead to reduced image contrast and uneven development. The answer is to stir the solution at regular intervals. At one time, tanks allowed access to the core (on which the spirals are mounted) with a rod. The developer was agitated in this type of tank by rotating the reels. A more modern method is to have a 'waterproof' lid covering the light trap in the main lid. Tanks of this design are agitated by inverting them periodically. Either method works, but inversion agitation is currently thought to give more even development.

The more agitation, the quicker the film develops, so it is essential to establish a regular routine. The recommended practice is to agitate vigorously for the first 30 seconds. This

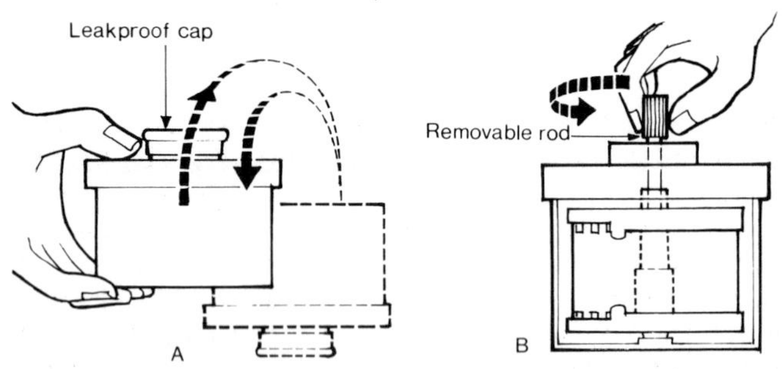

Agitation of film solutions. A. By inversion. B. By rotation

ensures that no air remains trapped against the film – in fact some photographers bang their tank on the bench to dislodge any air. After that, four or five inversions (or twirls) every minute is about right. The exact régime is not so important so long as it is maintained from film to film.

Time and temperature

The film is inside a light-tight box and there is no way to check the progress of development, so it must follow a strict plan. The normal processing temperature is 20°C (68°F). At this temperature a medium-speed film needs around 6½ minutes in normal undiluted developer. Each film/developer combination has its own optimum figure, so check the instructions.

There is, though, nothing sacred about the recommended process. If the negatives turn out to be too dense or too contrasty, it can be changed. Basically, increasing the developing time increases the contrast and density, while increasing the exposure time (reducing the film speed) only increases the density. To achieve the desired results, you have to experiment with film speed settings and processing times. Once you have settled on a régime, though, stick to it rigidly unless you have a good reason to change.

Contrast, speed and grain

Increasing the developing time increases the contrast. The recommended (normal contrast) times are intended to produce negatives that print on normal grade paper (2 or 3) in a condenser type enlarger. Using a diffuser type enlarger (including most enlargers fitted with colour heads) reduces black-and-white print contrast from normal (silver) negatives. Thus, for negatives to print on normal grade paper, they must have higher contrast, produced by a longer developing time. As this also increases the density, it is usually advisable to underexpose the negatives slightly – i.e. set a higher speed on the meter. The increase in developing time is usually around 40%, and the associated increase in effective film speed about 2/3 stop.

As suggested in the section on developers, increased developing time at least appears to increase film speed. In the absence of specific figures increase the time 50% for each stop speed increase needed; for example: normal 10 min, +1 stop 15 min; +2 stops 22½ min. At the same time as increasing the contrast, prolonged development increases

Basic black-and-white film processing

In a small tank, with intermittent agitation, most procedures are similar: pour in the full amount of developer, agitate the tank for 30 seconds continuously, then for 5 seconds every minute until the time is up. Pour out the developer, pour in stop bath, pour out stop bath, pour in fixer, agitate every minute, pour out fixer and wash film.

Typical development times at 20°C (68°F) for normal contrast are:

	Undiluted			1+1			1+3		
Film speed	32–50	125	400	32–50	125	400	32–50	125	400
Time (minutes)	6	6½	7½	8½	9	12	12½	15	21

For high-contrast negatives, the developer time needs to be increased:

	Undiluted			1+1			1+3		
Film speed	32–50	125	400	32–50	125	400	32–50	125	400
Time (minutes)	8½	10	10	12	14	18	18	22	28

After that, the process is: stop bath 30 seconds; fix 5 minutes; then wash 30 minutes in running water. Add a few drops of wetting agent to final rinse. Hang to dry in a dust-free atmosphere.

Too little developer in a small tank leads to uneven development (Clyde Reynolds)

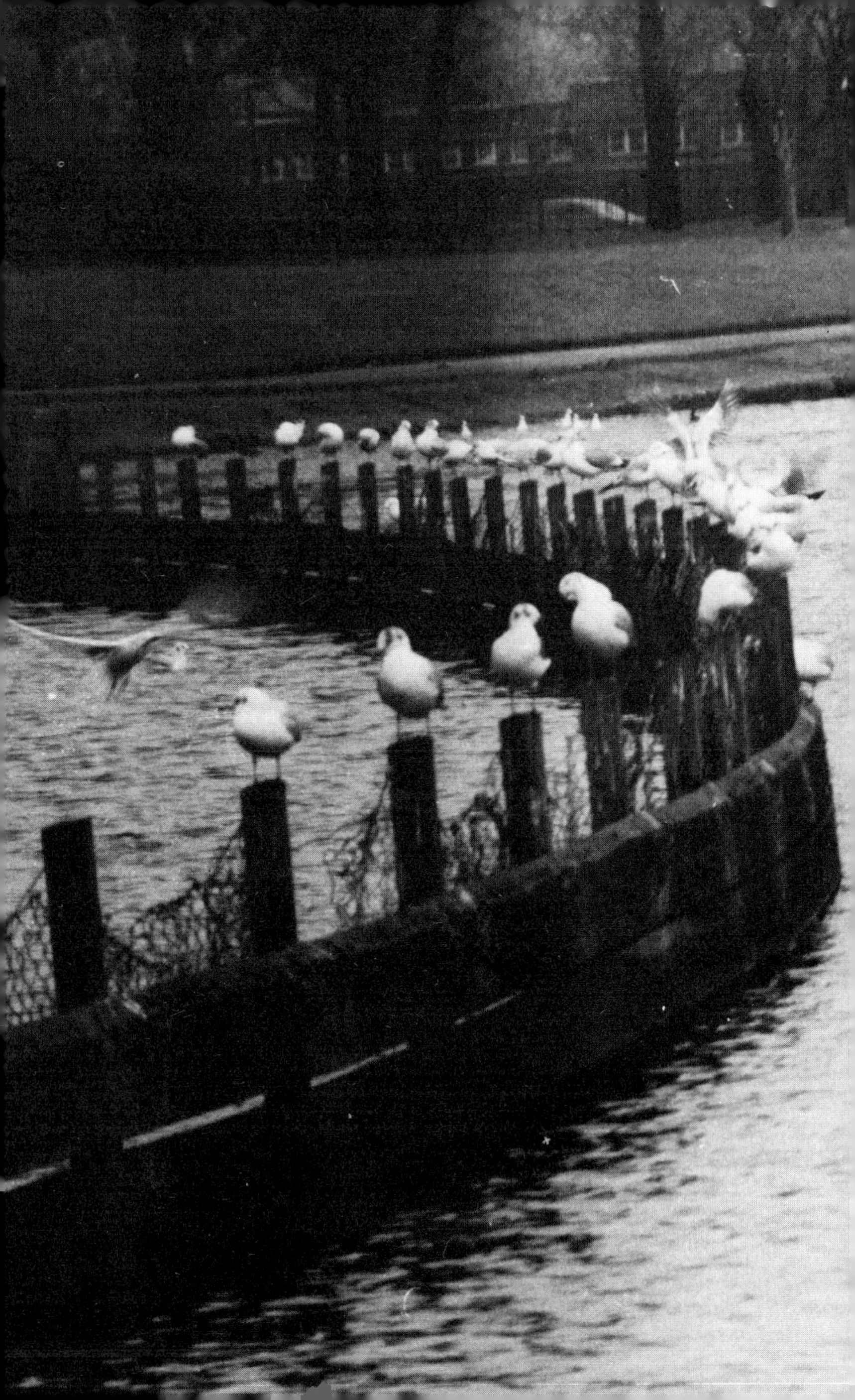

the graininess of the images. This is compensated when using a diffuser enlarger, because it tends to underemphasise grain. However, when the aim is only to increase speed, grain becomes a feature of pictures.

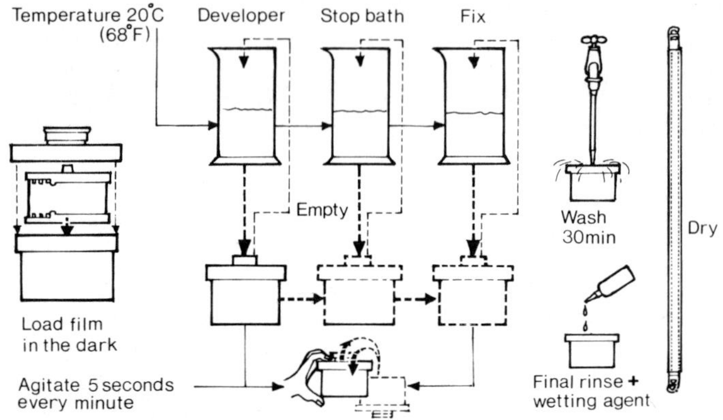

Basic black-and-white film processing

Stop baths

Development must be accurately timed – especially with concentrated fast-acting developers where the times may be as short as 2 minutes. Clearly, an extra half minute can make quite a difference to the contrast and density. There are two parts to ensuring that development stops at exactly the right time: start pouring the developer out before the time is up, and introduce a stop bath to the tank exactly at the moment that the time is up.

Most smallish tanks take around 15 seconds to empty; larger ones can take up to a minute. It is well worth measuring the time when the tank is loaded with filled spirals. Try it while washing processed films. Remember that pouring out the developer does not stop development, since the emulsion is still soaked with developer. An acid solution does stop it.

The most widely used stop bath is dilute acetic acid. Photographic versions usually include an indicator. The yellow solution turns blue when it has lost its acidity and can no longer stop development. Until then it can be used again and again. With long developing times, it is unnecessary to use a stop bath; a water rinse is quite adequate to stop development within a reasonable time. However, an acid bath can help to reduce reticulation if the fixer solution is not at quite the right temperature, because it introduces acidity progressively, rather than in one jump.

Fixing

The function of the fixer is twofold. The thiosulphate forms complex compounds with the unused silver halides in the film, rendering them soluble. The soluble compounds are then dissolved by the water of the fixer. Most fixers take 4 or 5 minutes to fix a film completely, while rapid fixers accomplish it in around 2 minutes.

Some fixers incorporate an emulsion hardener. This toughens up the gelatin, making it much less susceptible to mechanical damage. Hardeners are useful if you wash the film roughly, or want extra strong negatives. With normal care, however, non-hardening fixers are perfectly adequate.

Once the film is thoroughly immersed in fixer, it is totally insensitive to light, so you can look at it. When first in the fixer, the emulsion has its characteristic unexposed creamy look – indicating that it is full of silver halides. As these dissolve in the fixer, so the emulsion becomes progressively clearer. After 1 or 2 minutes it is completely clear. Allow about 4 minutes to be sure that all the halides are totally soluble, and most of the soluble complexes are leached out into the solution, then pour off the fixer. Fixer kept clean by filtering can be used again and again, but always fix the film for double the clearing time. When the clearing time reaches double that of fresh fixer, it is time to throw that batch away and start afresh.

Washing

To achieve any sort of stability, the film needs to be well washed. Thirty minutes in running water is the normal recommendation. This produces negatives which will outlast most photographers. To be sure that they will last virtually for ever, increase the time to one hour.

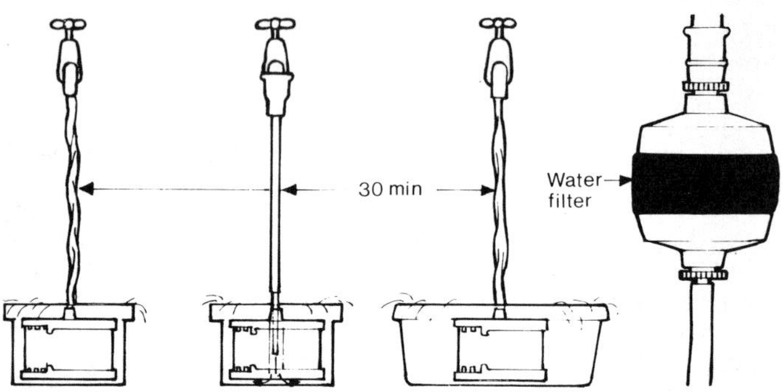

Films need careful washing in running water to remove all process chemicals. In some areas a filter is needed to keep the wash water clean

The simplest way to wash a film is to pour water from a tap straight into the tank (with its top removed). If the stream goes straight down the spiral core, this is very effective. A simple modification is to run a rubber tube down the core to ensure that the water reaches the bottom. As an alternative, the spirals can be taken out and washed in running water either in a sink or in a print washer.

There are a number of proprietary fixer-eliminators which can speed up washing. However, these are not necessary unless wash water is in very scarce supply. They tend to start dissolving the image, so their use is restricted normally to high speed processing routines. The best solution to water

Damaged negative shows torn emulsion turned over and drying marks on sky from hard water (Clyde Reynolds)

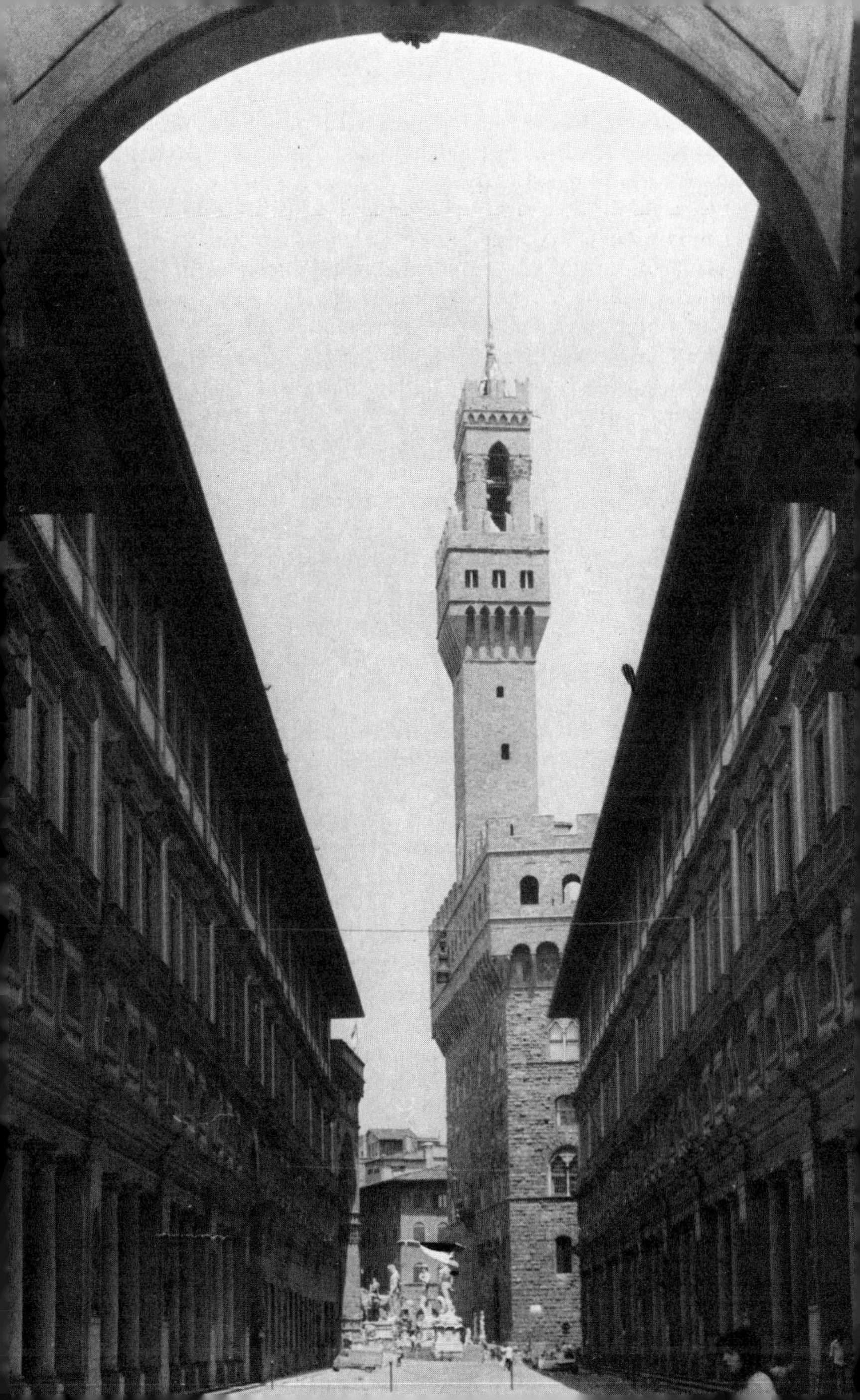

shortage is to fix the film in a non-hardening fixer; then three changes of fresh water, agitated for 5, 10 and 20 inversions, washes the film perfectly well.

This also gets round the problem that can arise with tap water washing – *reticulation* – the crinkling of the emulsion caused by sudden temperature change. Often water supplies are well below 20°C and running really cold water straight on to the film can damage the emulsion. Always reduce the temperature of a running water wash progressively.

One problem encountered in hard water areas is that drops of water dry on the film leaving white marks. To reduce these, give the film a final rinse in water containing a few drops of wetting agent – washing-up detergent is effective. If drying marks are still a problem, try rinsing the film in dilute acetic acid. Stop bath diluted to half the normal strength with a few drops of wetting agent added is about right.

Chromogenic development

Late in 1980, Ilford and Agfa introduced monochrome films based on colour film technology. Like a colour negative, the image is formed of dyes, not silver as in a normal black-and-white material. To produce an acceptable colour, the image is formed from a mixture of coloured dyes, which produces a dark brown negative. This prints perfectly normally on all types of black-and-white paper.

These materials can be processed in normal C41 type colour negative chemistry. Follow the normal routine (see page 80). This is the recommended process for Agfa Vario XL, for all exposure levels from ASA 125 to ASA 1600. Ilford XP1 400 gives its best performance rated at 400 ASA and processed in XP1 developer and bleach-fix which are diluted for one-shot processing. Push processing is not usually needed

Overheating, or changing temperature, too quickly can produce reiculated negatives, with the image cracked or blobbed (Alison Trapmore)

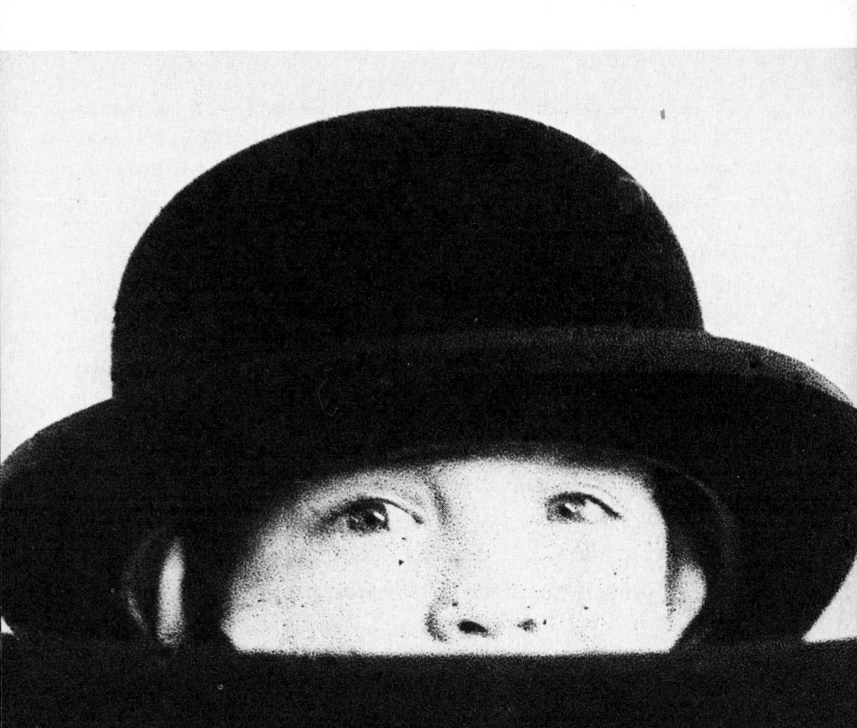

for speeds up to 1600 ASA, but in poor lighting or with low contrast subjects, it is recommended for higher ASA settings. Lower settings are accepted at the normal process times.

XP1 processing

XP1 solutions are supplied as liquids to be mixed to form the concentrates. To prepare the developer stock, mix the contents of bottles A and B in a suitable vessel, add the contents of bottle C and stir thoroughly. The stock solution can then be stored in the component bottles. Rinse them out first, and stick on the stock solution labels. The bleach-fix stock solution is prepared by mixing the two parts A and B. It, too, can be stored in rinsed, labelled component bottles.

XP1 Chromogenic monochrome processing

To make working strength solutions, dilute the developer concentrate 1+3 with water, and the bleach-fix solution 1+4. Note that Ilford XP1 films can be processed in C41 colour negative chemicals, but the results are slightly less sharp than those in XP1 chemistry.

Work with a water-bath at or slightly above process temperature. Keep the containers of solution in the water. Preheat the tank with water 2° above process temperature, then follow the steps outlined.

	Temp °C	*Time*	*Temp °C*	*Time*	*Temp °C*	*Time*
Preheat	40	1	37	1	32	1
Develop	38±0.25	5	35±0.25	6¼	30±0.25	9
Bleach-fix	38±0.25	5	35±0.25	6¼	30±0.25	9
Wash	35–40	3	33–38	4	27–32	5
Wetting agent	35–40	¼	33–38	¼	27–32	¼

Dry the negatives in the usual way.

To increase the ASA rating to 1600, increase the development time to 9 minutes at 40°.

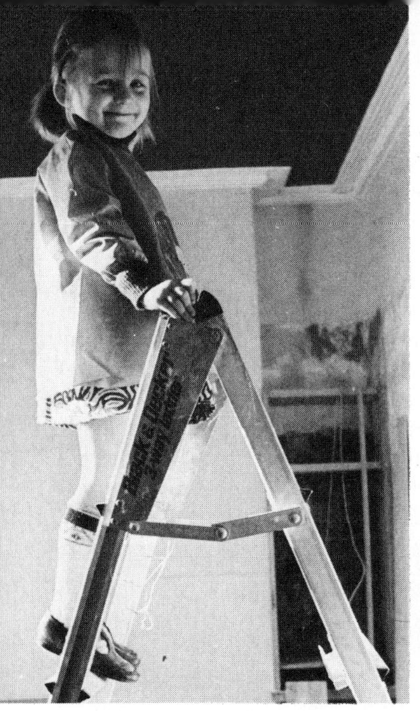

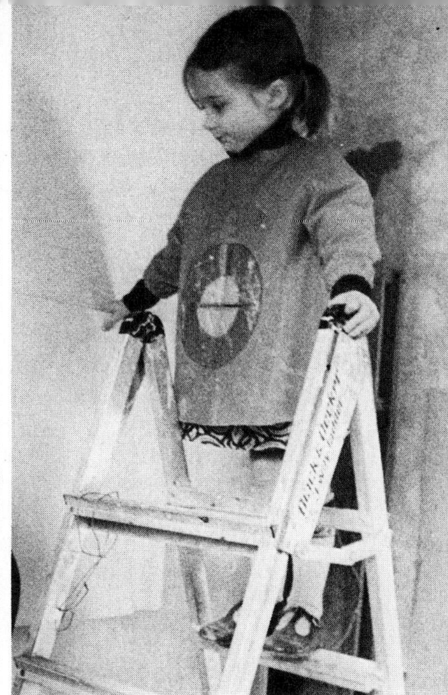

Chromogenic development needs a higher temperature, but yields much finer grain negatives. A.XP-1 rate at 400 ASA. B. HP5 rated at **400 ASA. Each picture shows about ⅛ of 35 mm negative area (Clyde Reynolds)**

Process films in the normal way in small tanks, agitating for the first 10 seconds, then 5 inversions every minute. Washing at about the process temperature is best; but the film can be washed at lower temperatures, as long as it is cooled slowly to avoid reticulation. Wash time at 20°C is 10 minutes.

Drying films

The best way to dry a film is to hang it up in a current of dust-free air. A drying cabinet, often heated, provides this. In the absence of such a facility, hang the film in a dust-free room. Do not use the bathroom – it is likely to be heavily contaminated with talcum powder.

Clip or pin the film to any suitable point. Unroll the spiral carefully, and clip a small weight to the lower end; a spring clothes peg is ideal. Remove excess water by carefully running the film between two fingers. If, with suitable drying aids in the final wash, drying marks still persist, try using a film squeegee. This is like a pair of tongs with rubber blades which are clamped gently either side of the film and slid down to remove most of the water. It really is the last resort, because a squeegee can trap a speck of dirt and scratch the film however carefully it is washed before use.

To speed up drying, for special quickness, use a hair dryer. Play the stream of warm air gently onto the film from a distance of 50–100 cm (2–3 ft). The film can be dry ready to print in about 15 minutes. The danger is that the dryer will embed dust in the emulsion, so restrict its use to occasions when high-speed drying is essential.

Are they right?

Once processed and dried, the negatives are a permanent record of your vision. Naturally, they should be as perfectly processed as possible. The old test used to be that it should be just possible to read clear print through the darkest areas. This is impractical with small-format negatives, and the real test is in their ease of printing. Good negatives should print to 25 × 20 cm (10 × 8 in) at around 10 seconds at *f*/8, giving the best prints on normal grade (2 or 3) paper. If they need too long an exposure, then they were overexposed or overdeveloped. If they need much softer paper, then they were overdeveloped. Conversely negatives which need grade 4 or 5 are underdeveloped.

If the grain is obtrusive on a normal-sized enlargement, then something has gone wrong. Enlarged grain is produced by overexposure, overdevelopment or both. From 35 mm negatives, you can expect grain to be just noticeable in

Film fogged by light entering the cassette (Clyde Reynolds)

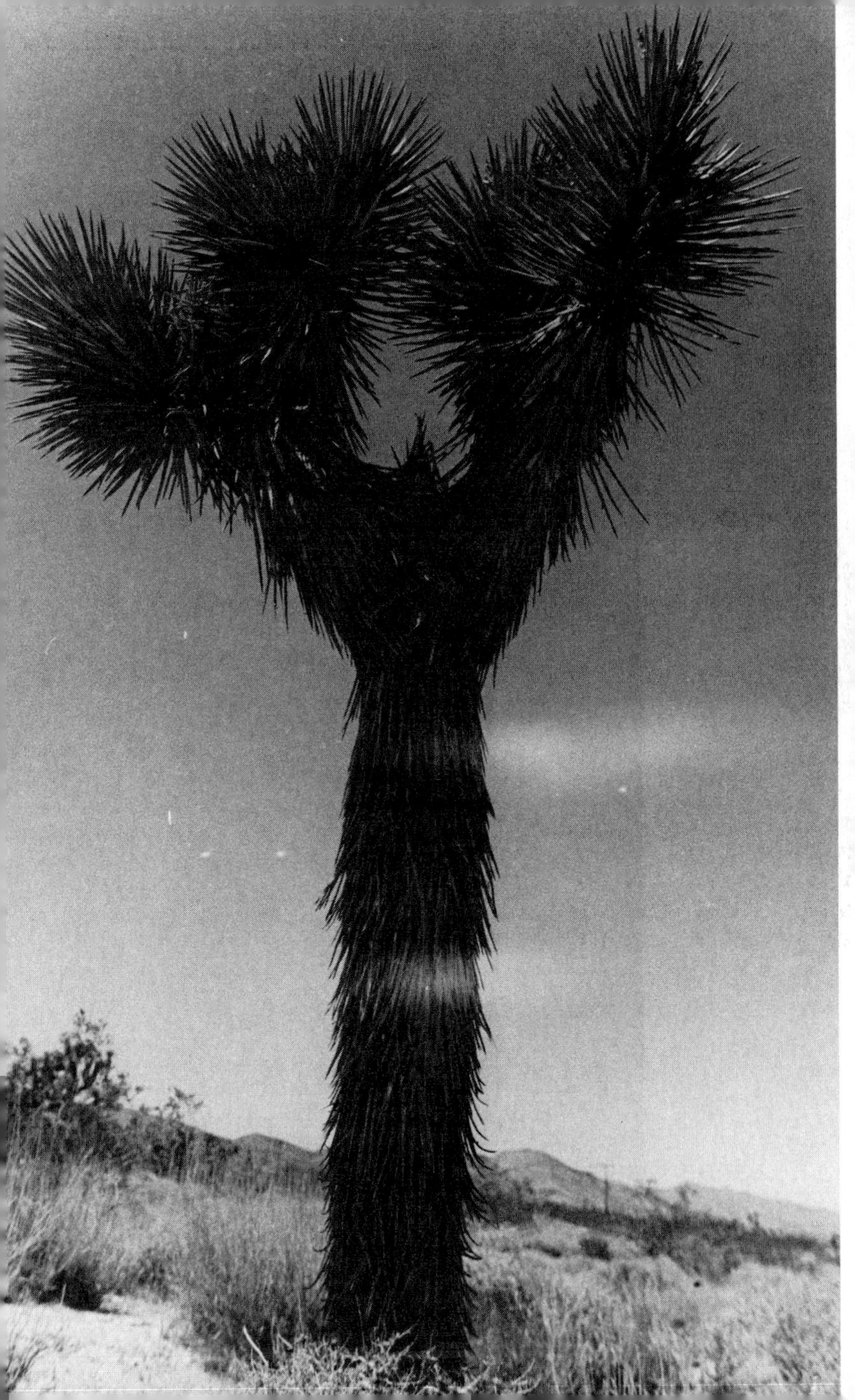

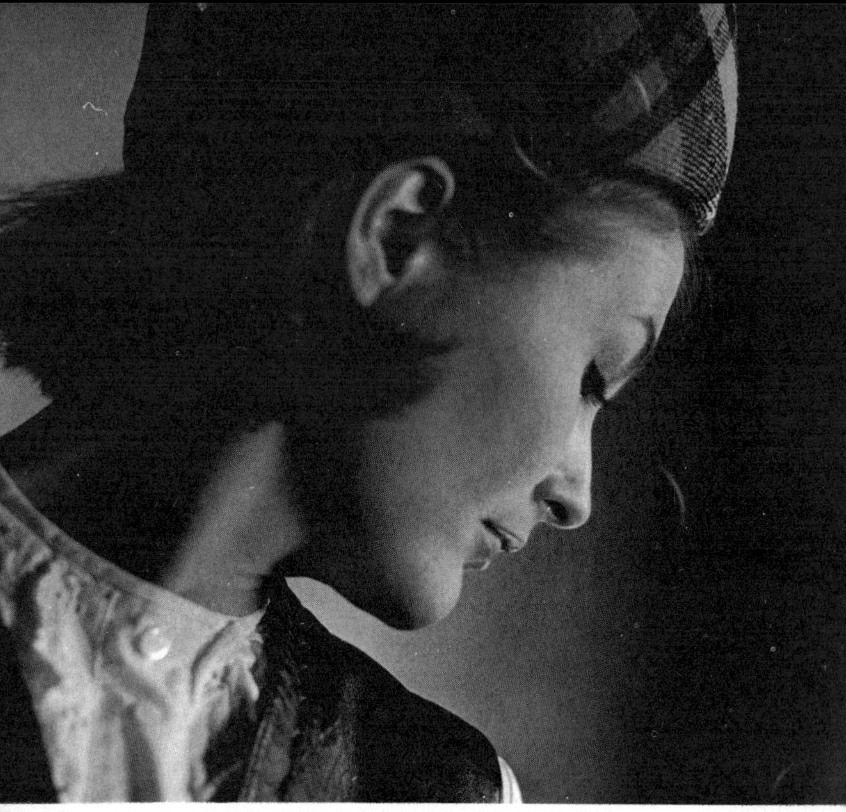

Kink marks on pale area of 6×6 negative (Alison Trapmore)

50 × 40 cm (20 × 16 in) prints from slow film, 30 × 25 cm (12 × 10 in) prints from medium speed films, and 25 × 20 cm (10 × 8 in) prints from fast films.

If there are major faults with many of the negatives, it is essential to find the cause. One great help is the edge numbering. These figures are correctly exposed by the manufacturer. If they have developed to a normal density, then the film processing was reasonably good. In that case a set of unprintable negatives is due to exposure problems in the camera. Note, too, that faulty processing cannot introduce blur or influence the composition.

Flare fogging on single frame (in hair) (Clyde Reynolds)

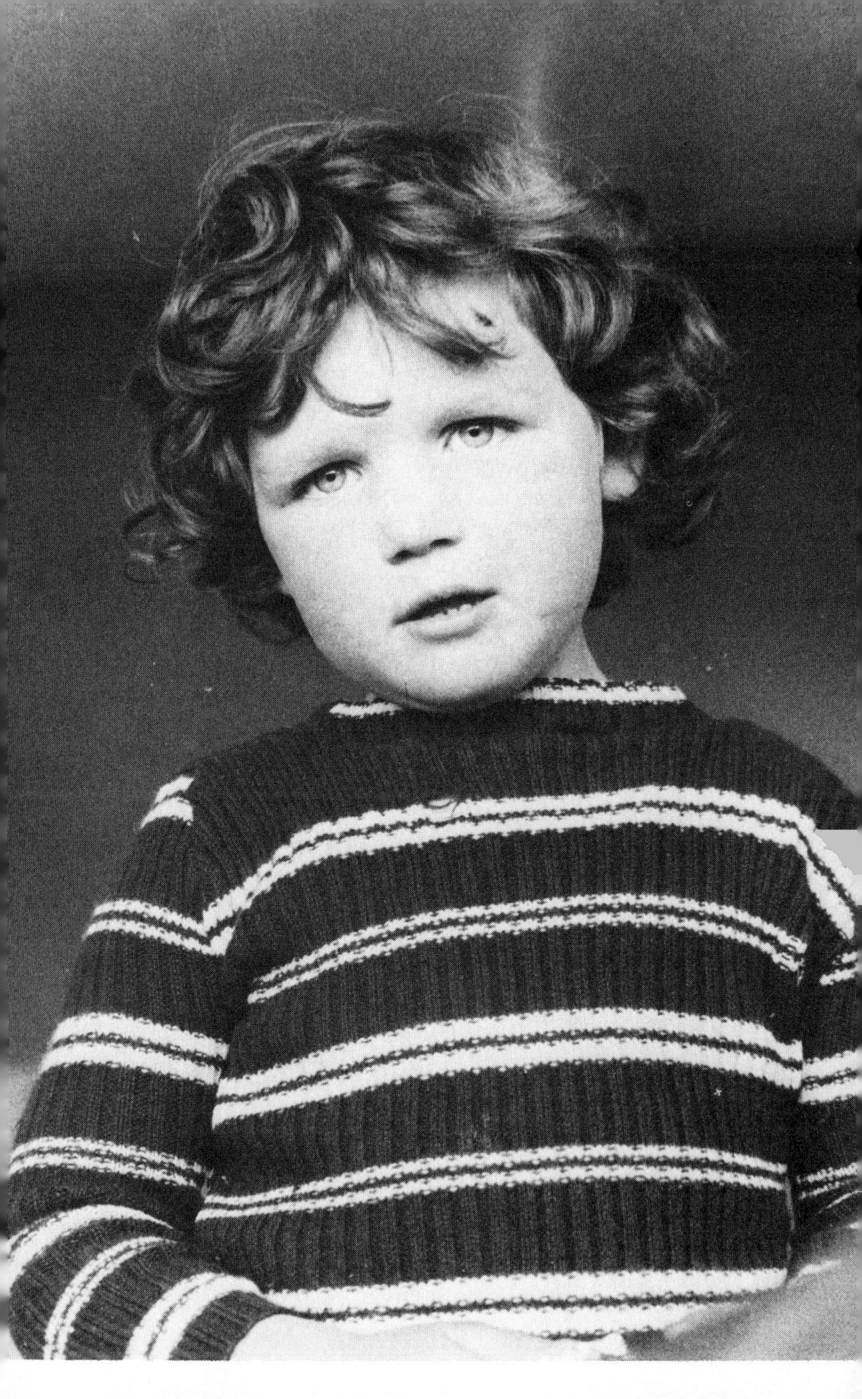

Faults in negatives

Fault		Cause
No image at all on film	*	Undeveloped, or fixed before developing
No images, normal edge markings	*	Unexposed film
Film black all over	*	Film completely fogged
All too light, reasonable contrast, normal edge numbers	*	Underexposed
All too light, little contrast, pale edge numbers	*	Underdeveloped
All too dark, normal contrast, normal edge numbers	*	Overexposed
All too dark high contrast and grain, normal or dark edge numbers	*	Overdeveloped
Too much grain, dark negatives	*	Overexposed and over-developed
Irregular patches of grain	*	Film reticulated
Density varies from frame to frame	*	Inconsistent exposure
Density varies from edge to egde of film	*	Not enough developer in tank
Density uneven, with streaking	*	Too little agitation
Crescent-shaped dark areas	*	Film kinked while loading tank
Parallel lines appear on print	*	Film scratch
Irregular white patches on negative	*	Film scraped during processing
White spots on print	*	Dust on film
Dark spots on print, pale circular patches on negative	*	Air trapped on film during development
Irregular light patches on print	*	Drying marks on film
Pale creamy patches on negative	*	Film touching during processing

Irregular network of lines on print	*	Film reticulated
Irregular black patches	*	Partial fogging before developing
Dark finger marks	*	Developer on fingers when loading
Pale finger marks	*	Fixer or grease on fingers when loading

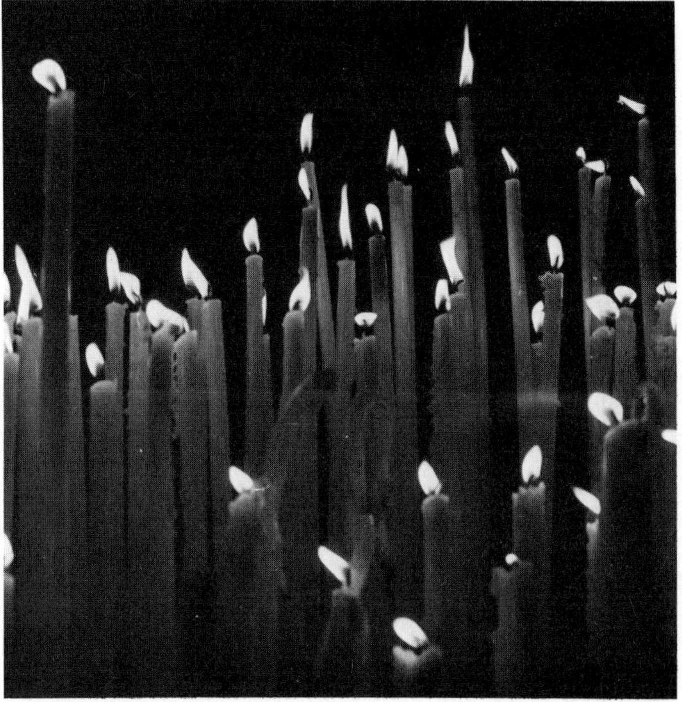

Kink mark centre right almost appears to be flare from candle flame (Beatrice Reynolds)

4

Colour film processing

While most enthusiasts process their own monochrome films, far fewer tackle colour. In practice, colour film processing requires no extra skills: negative films just need a little more care; transparency films a longer and more tedious process.

There are two main reasons for processing at home – speed and quality. There are times when it is much quicker to process colour at home; but the 2–3 hour turn around available from custom laboratories in most large towns is hard to beat. Quality, though is more difficult to find. Most laboratories have their off days, and some are best avoided all the time. With due care, small-tank processing can equal all but the very best laboratory work.

Cost and equipment

Colour processing solutions, once mixed, have quite a short shelf life: few developers are claimed to keep longer than six weeks. While manufacturers are understandably cautious, eight weeks is the longest that most fresh working strength solutions can last, when stored in full airtight bottles. Part-used solution, or those stored in partially full containers last a much shorter time; perhaps 2–3 weeks. Clearly then, the actual cost per film or print is dramatically increased unless the whole volume of solution can be used up before it 'goes off'.

Processing colour negatives is now a great saver. Most of the paper processing kits can also process films. So it is economic to develop a single negative film. Transparency films, on the other hand, need different processing solutions, and transparency kits are usually so complicated that they cannot easily be made up in part quantities. Thus, to be economic, you have to process perhaps six or eight films within a few weeks of opening the kit. So most enthusiasts have to store up transparency films until they have enough to make a kit worth while – thus losing the advantage of immediate access which home processing apparently offers.

Some independent solutions, such as Photocolor's Chrome 6 are all liquid. Thus it is quite simple to make up single film quantities of the solutions. If doing this, it is a good idea to decant the remaining concentrates into smaller bottles to exclude all air and extend their life.

As materials become simpler to process, more dilute-as-needed chemistries are likely to appear. So colour film processing, both negative and reversal, is likely to become the best choice on economic grounds as well as on the ground of convenience and consistency of quality.

The equipment needed to process colour films differs little from that for black-and-white. The only major practical difference is that process temperatures are much higher, so the thermometer must be capable of reading up to 40°C (105°F). The films are loaded into the tank in total darkness in just the same way as are black-and-white films (page 53).

Maintaining temperature

Black-and-white processes are carried out closely enough to room temperature to expect the solutions to retain their heat reasonably well. This is not the case with colour processing. The simplest way to maintain temperatures is to stand the tank in a water bath between agitations. Use a flow of hot and cold water to keep the temperature constant to within half a degree.

For really consistent processing, an automatic temperature controlled tank rotator is recommended. These can be used for both film and paper processing (see page 144). Because the temperatures are high, times are short and they must be maintained with great accuracy. If it takes 15 seconds to

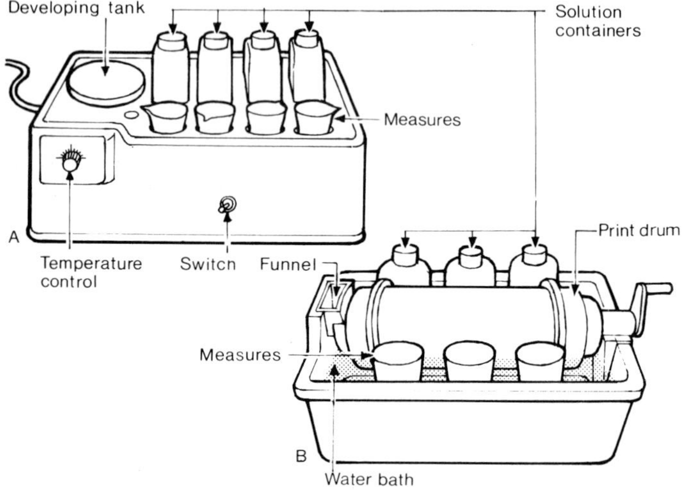

Water baths can maintain colour process temperatures. A. Chemical tempering box for film processing. B. Water bath for drum print processing

empty a tank and 20 seconds to refill it, then start pouring out the developer 35 seconds before the time is up and pour in the next solution at once so that it contacts the film at exactly the right time.

Agitation

There is no point in maintaining accurate times and temperature if agitation is inconsistent. Underagitation leads to underdevelopment and, worse, uneven density. Overagitation produces overdevelopment. Follow the instructions packed with the processing chemicals.

Alternatively, establish a constant régime, and if necessary change your process times slightly to work with it. The simplest is to agitate for 20 seconds immediately after adding the solution, then for 5 seconds every 30 seconds until the time is up.

Colour negative films

Colour negative processing is now as simple as monochrome processing. Using a typical C41 alternative kit takes about 12 or 13 minutes for the five-stage process including preheating

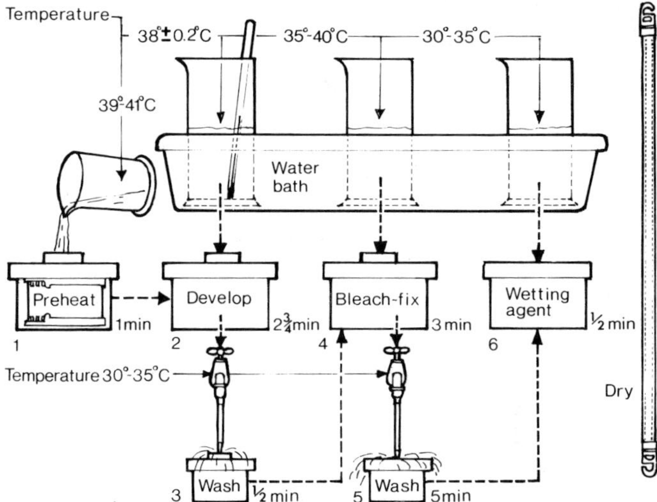

Processing a colour negative film

the tank and washing the film. The two major solutions are made up simply by diluting liquid concentrates with the right volume of water. They can be mixed in exactly the quantities needed. The remaining concentrates keep better than do working strength solutions

The developer includes a colour forming chemical, which reacts with colour couplers already included in the film emulsion. These produce coloured dye images as well as the normal silver image. After a wash, or a normal stop bath, the silver image is bleached out and the film fixed in a bleach-fix

Colour negative processing

Most currently available films use one of two basic processes: Kodak C41 for all type II films of any make, and all 400 ASA colour negative films; and Agfacolor type N for Agfacolor CN, CNS and CNS-2 films. Note that Agfacolor CNS 400 uses C41 type chemistry. Photocolor II is one simple home processing kit for all C41 type negative films.

Work with a water bath at process temperature. Keep the containers of solution in the water. Preheat the tank and film with water (for high temperature processes), then follow the steps outlined below.

	Kodak C41 Flexicolor		Photocolor II (C41)		Agfacolor N	
	Temp °C	*Time (min)*	*Temp °C*	*Time (min)*	*Temp °C*	*Time (min)*
Preheat	39–41	1	39–41	1	–	–
Develop	37.8 ± 0.15	3¼	38 ± 0.2	2¾	20 ± 0.2	8
Intermediate	–	–	–	–	20 ± 0.5	4
Wash (or stop)	–	–	35–40	½	14–20	14
Bleach	24–41	6½	–	–	20 ± 0.5	6
Wash	35–41	3¼	–	–	14–20	6
Fix	24–41	6½	–	–	18–20	6
Bleach-fix	–	–	35–40	3	–	–
Wash	35–41	3¼	30–35	5	14–20	10
Stabilise	24–41	1½	–	–	–	–
Wetting agent	–	–	30–35	½	14–20	1

Dry the negatives in the normal way.

Note that some processes allow a choice of times and temperatures to give standard processing. Make sure to follow the same régime throughout. Note also that some films (400 ASA ones, for example) may need slightly different times in some solutions.

solution. Some processes perform these two operations separately, but the principle is the same.

The film manufacturers' own processes tend to be more complicated both to mix and to use because they are designed for large scale automated processing. So, the home process kits, designed specially for the job, are a much better choice for the small scale user. While there is a summary of the basic processes on the previous page, the instructions packed with each kit can vary from month to month, so always follow the latest booklet.

Like any chemicals, colour developers become exhausted with use. So after the first film each subsequent one developed in the same solution needs a longer time. For example, 300 ml of one colour developer will process three 36-exposure 35 mm films or 120 films. To process the second and third films correctly needs 12% and 30% more time respectively.

It is normal to process colour negatives exactly as instructed, although one or two kits now allow some variation in developer time. As with monochrome developers, increasing the time increases the contrast and the effective film speed. An increase of about 45% varies the effective film speed, in low contrast conditions, the equivalent of about one stop. Do not be tempted to experiment with chemistries which do not suggest modifications. Altering the development time can change the contrasts of each of the three different coloured dye layers differently, producing totally unprintable negatives.

Some processes include a stabiliser, others do not. Most films can benefit from one if the negatives are to be stored for a long while. A solution containing 2% formaldehyde (formalin) and 2% wetting agent can be used after the final wash. Do not wash again – that will remove the stabiliser.

Negative quality

The only way to test colour negatives is to print from them. To be sure that all is well, set up the colour printing facility and make a print from a good commercially processed negative (see page 160). Then try a well-exposed home processed one of a normal subject. Do not expect to use the same filtration, but expect to be able to make an excellent print, with good neutral shadows and clean highlights. The contrast may be a little different, but you can alter that in some chemicals, or compensate by changing to another brand of colour paper – or to a different negative film for future work.

The major problem that can occur is that the contrasts of two (or all) of the three different coloured dye images can be different. The result is that either the shadows or the highlights *must* show a colour cast on the print. For example, the highlights may be pink and the shadows green. To compensate for one simply exaggerates the other.

Colour negative faults

Fault		Cause
Film clear, no edge markings	*	Undeveloped developer/fixer switched
Film black all over	*	Totally fogged
Film clear with edge markings	*	Unexposed
Film black with edge markings	*	Fogged in camera
Image pale – edge marks normal	*	Underexposed
Image dark – edge marks normal	*	Overexposed
Image and edge marks pale	*	Underdeveloped
Image and edge marks dark, contrasty	*	Overdeveloped
Print with shadows and highlights different colours	*	Inappropriate time/temperature

See also black-and-white negative faults for physical problems.

Processing colour slide films

The basis of all normal photography is that silver halides can be converted to metallic silver when they have been excited by light. In colour photography the conversion is accom panied by dye formation, and the silver image is then bleached and fixed out, so the basic result is a negative.

Transparency films are basically similar to colour negative films, and react to processing in the same way. Given negative processing, most of them form strange, but print-able, negatives. To produce normal colour slides requires a multi-stage process.

First the exposed silver halides are converted to metallic silver in a normal type of black-and-white developer. Then the remaining (unexposed) emulsion is totally fogged, either by a strong light or chemically. The halides activated by the second exposure are developed in a colour developer, much like colour negative developer. A colour dye image is formed with the silver image.

The silver formed in the first and second developers is now bleached and fixed out. The film is finally washed, stabilised and dried. Because the image passes through a (black-and-white) negative stage and finally produces a positive image, the process is described as *reversal.*

Two reversal processes are widely used – Kodak E6 and Agfachrome process 41 (not to be confused with C41 nega-tive processing). A third process, the obsolescent Kodak E4, is still used with a number of specialised films. Kits of alternative chemicals are available for all three processes. As with colour negatives, they can prove to be more economic-al, easier, and to give better results in small scale processing than can the film manufacturers, own processing plants.

One group of films, Kodachromes, use a much more complicated process which (after the first development) involves exposing each of the three separate colour dye forming layers sequentially, and processing each in turn in the correct colour-forming developer. This adds the colour to what is otherwise a sophisticated black-and-white emul-sion. As a result, Kodachrome cannot be processed at home and it must be handled in a specialised laboratory. All other colour films include colour formers (colour couplers) in the emulsion, and are thus quite easily home processed. Films with couplers in their emulsion are called *substantive* colour films.

Time and temperature control is even more important for transparencies than for colour negatives. The first development determines the density of the final picture as well as its contrast. Faulty first development can also alter the colour balance.

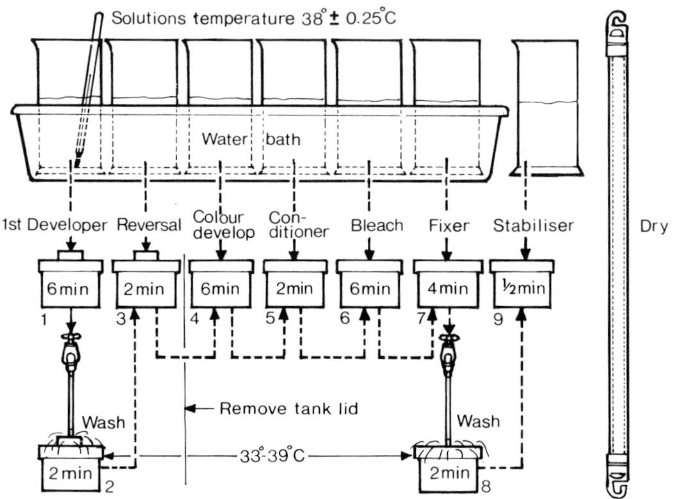

Processing a colour reversal film

As with negative films, it is important to increase first development time as the solution becomes more exhausted. For 120 or 36-exposure 35 mm films, increase the time by 30 seconds for each of the third, fourth and fifth films processed in each 600 ml. For smaller films, increase the time by 15 seconds for each film after the first two processed in 600 ml.

Changing film speeds

Most transparency films have considerably more exposure latitude than is revealed by normal processing. This can be used to alter the effective film speed quite dramatically. Most

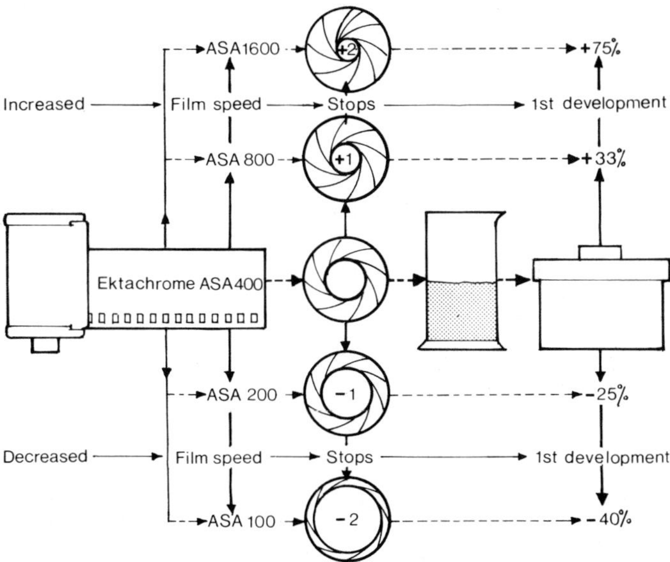

Altering the first developer time offers a range of film speeds for colour reversal films

films can be uprated by up to two stops (four times the ASA rating) or downrated by the same amount. For example Ektachrome 400 can be rated at 100, 200, 400, 800, or 1600 ASA and processed to produce reasonable transparencies.

Generally, processing is modified by lengthening the first development time to produce a higher-speed film for use in low light conditions, which can be important for sports and other action work indoors. Naturally, with increased development the grain size is increased. Simultaneously, the colour may deviate from the optimum. At worst, the film may suffer from the 'crossed curves' that can make transparencies look off colour and negatives impossible to process, the shadows and highlights showing different colour casts. Some films take better to 'push' processing than do others, so it is worth experimenting before pushing any special shots more than two stops. Naturally, it is normal to rate the whole film at the same speed, and not to try and process different sections for different times.

Downrating films is usually a cure for faulty exposure settings, not a practice to be recommended as normal procedure. It does little to improve the grain, and can spoil the colour. To reduce the effective film speed, allowing overexposure, reduce the first development time. Again, the effect varies slightly from film to film, and needs careful testing before it can become a reliable regular practice.

Exact film speeds and processing

The best exposure level for any film is determined by the emulsion and the processing. Small variations in processing alter the optimum exposure, calling for a slightly different meter setting; that is, using a slightly different exposure index (film speed setting). In practice, this is only of real importance with transparency films. Photographers who use commercial processing learn the best exposure index to use with their equipment so that their chosen processor produces the transparencies that best suits them. The home processor has an alternative: alter the process times to produce the best slides at the normal rated film speed. Just as with making gross changes, increasing the first development time lightens the film, decreasing the time darkens it. To a limited extent, decreasing the colour development time can result in a muting of the colours. This, though, calls for considerable experiment with any combination of film and chemistry before one can be sure of the results.

Basic reversal processing

Reversal processing has more steps then negative processing. Time and temperature must be rigidly controlled. Use a water bath for chemicals and tank. These are the basic steps for Kodak E6 and E4, Agfachrome 41 and Unicolor, a typical substitute E6 kit.

All processes after the first wash can be done in the light.

	Kodak E6		Unicolor E6	
	Temp °C	*Time (min)*	*Temp °C*	*Time (min)*
1st developer	38±¼	6¼	27.7±0.2	6½
Rinse	33–39	2	33–	2
Reversal bath	33–39	2	33–39	2
Colour developer	38±½	6	37–8	6
Conditioner	33–39	2	–	–
Stop	–	–	33–39	1
Wash	–	–	33–39	2
Bleach	33–39	633–39	3	
Fixer	33–39	4	33–39	2
Stabiliser	Room	½	Room	½

	Kodak E4		Agfachrome 41	
			20°C±0.5	24°C±0.2
	Temp °C	*Time (min)*	*Time (min)*	*Time (min)*
Prehardener	29.5±¼	3	–	–
Neutraliser	29.5±1	1	–	–
Wash	29.5±1	1	–	–
1st developer	29.5±¼	6½	18–20	13–14
Rinse	–	–	¼	¼
Stopbath	29.5±1	2	4	3
Wash	27–32	4	10	7
Reversal exposure	–	–	½ min to 2 photofloods	
Colour developer	29.5±1	15	14	11
Intermediate bath	–	–	5	5
Stop	29.5±1	3	–	–
Wash	27–32	3	15	9
Bleach	29.5±1	5	5	4
Wash	–	–	5	4
Fixer	29.5±1	4	5	4
Wash	27–32	6	10	7
Stabiliser	29.5±1	1	1	1

To increase film speed by 1 stop, increase first development by 33%; to increase it by 2 stops, increase development time by 75%. To reduce film speed by 1 stop, decrease first development time by 25%, by 2 stops reduce it by 40%.

Reversal exposures

While most modern processes depend upon chemical reversal of the image, it is quite possible to use light instead. Some older processes always used reversal by light, and some substitute formulae still do. After first development the film is bleached to remove the negative image then exposed to bright light to convert the remaining (positive image) silver halides to metallic silver. The film is then given second development.

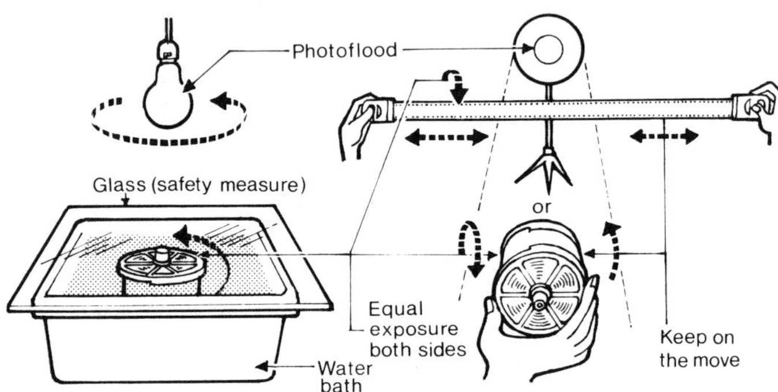

Three ways of exposing a reversal film to light after first development when chemistry does not contain a chemical reversing agent

The film needs much more exposure than would seem probable. Using a No. 2 Photoflood (500 W) expose the film for half a minute a side. It is possible to make the exposure with the film still coiled on a *clear* plastics spiral, but the film needs to be taken off a metal spiral or a more opaque plastics one. It is quite easy to reload a plastics spiral under water after the exposure.

Slide quality

Most slide films change colour and density as they dry, so do not try to evaluate wet transparencies. Once dry, the transparencies should have a neutral colour balance and show a good range of tones between clean whites and strong blacks. Push processing tends to increase the contrast, while reducing the film speed setting and development time reduces it. This can be a way of achieving rather different results.

Faults in processed slides can be grouped in any or all of three categories: exposure faults, developing faults, and post-development faults. Nothing can be done about exposure or first development faults. It is possible before the film is bleached to re-expose it and return it to the colour developer, but faults are seldom detected at that stage. However, bleaching and fixing faults can be corrected at a much later stage.

An analysis of faults in slides is shown on the next page.

Faults in processed slides

Fault		Cause
Film completely clear – no edge marks	*	Film fogged before processing
Film completely clear – with edge marks	*	Gross overexposure in camera
Transparencies pale	*	Overexposure
Transparencies pale and blue-green	*	Overdevelopment in first developer. First developer contaminated by fix
Transparencies pale and greenish	*	Insufficient colour development. Reversal time too short or exhausted reversal bath
Strange colour casts over pictures and edges	*	Fogged to coloured light, e.g. safelight
Film dark overall, sometimes reddish	*	Underdevelopment in first developer. Underbleached
Film dark in blotches	*	Underbleached, or underfixed. Patches touching and unprocessed.
Film black all over – no edge markings	*	First development omitted
Film black with normal edge markings	*	Unexposed film

See also the physical faults listed under black-and-white negative processing, page 74.

5

Black-and-white printing

Printing involves forming a latent image of a negative on light sensitive paper, then processing the paper so that the final (positive) picture appears. Early photographers exposed the paper by holding the negative in close contact with it (usually in a specially designed printing frame) and allowing light to fall on it for a suitable length of time. Nowadays however, virtually everyone uses small-format cameras and the image has to be enlarged, so it is projected on to the paper from an enlarger.

Papers

Monochrome paper is coated with a silver-halide emulsion, similar to that on black-and-white film. though it is much slower. Making a 25 × 20 cm (10 × 8 in) print from a 35 mm negative calls for perhaps 10 seconds exposure at *f*/8 or *f*/11 with a normal enlarger lamp.

Most paper used nowadays is 'resin coated' and has a thin layer of polyethylene or similar plastics coating on each side. This has two major effects: processing time, especially the washing time, is dramatically reduced, and the material lies virtually flat before and after processing.

During manufacture, the upper polyethylene coating can be embossed with a number of different designs. The top protective layer of emulsion itself can also be applied smoothly or with one of a number of surface textures. Each manufacturer offers his own range, but there are four commonly available surfaces: glossy, smooth matt, lustre and silk. Resin-coated papers dry to their own surface without any special techniques.

Glossy paper has a shiny surface, especially brilliant if it is hot-air dried. This gives the densest blacks and clearest whites possible, thus offering the greatest contrast range and impact. Pictures for reproduction in books and magazines should be printed on glossy paper.

Smooth matt is perhaps the least obtrusive surface. It is ideal for display and decorative prints, because it produces no distracting reflections. However, the maximum black possible with a matt surface would merely be a dark grey on glossy paper, so matt prints may have a rather dull or dead look. True matt finishes are rare: most resin-coated papers are available in a semi-matt finish.

Lustre or *pearl* surface paper offers a compromise between high gloss and matt. It has a stippled surface which reduces the chance of strong reflections, but retains much of the blackness of glossy paper. This type of surface is widely chosen for display and exhibition prints. As each manufacturer offers a slightly different version, it is well worth comparing them all.

Silk or *rayon* finish has a regular pattern. For some years it was the first choice of colour printing companies, but is also available in black and white. Its main advantage is that the texture tends to mask any slight unsharpness in the picture, but this should not deter experiments with it.

Traditional papers

Resin-coated papers meet considerable opposition from some quarters. The main arguments are that nobody knows how soon prints may deteriorate, the papers do not offer as

Some scenes need extremely accurate exposure to give delicate highlights (Robert Ashley)

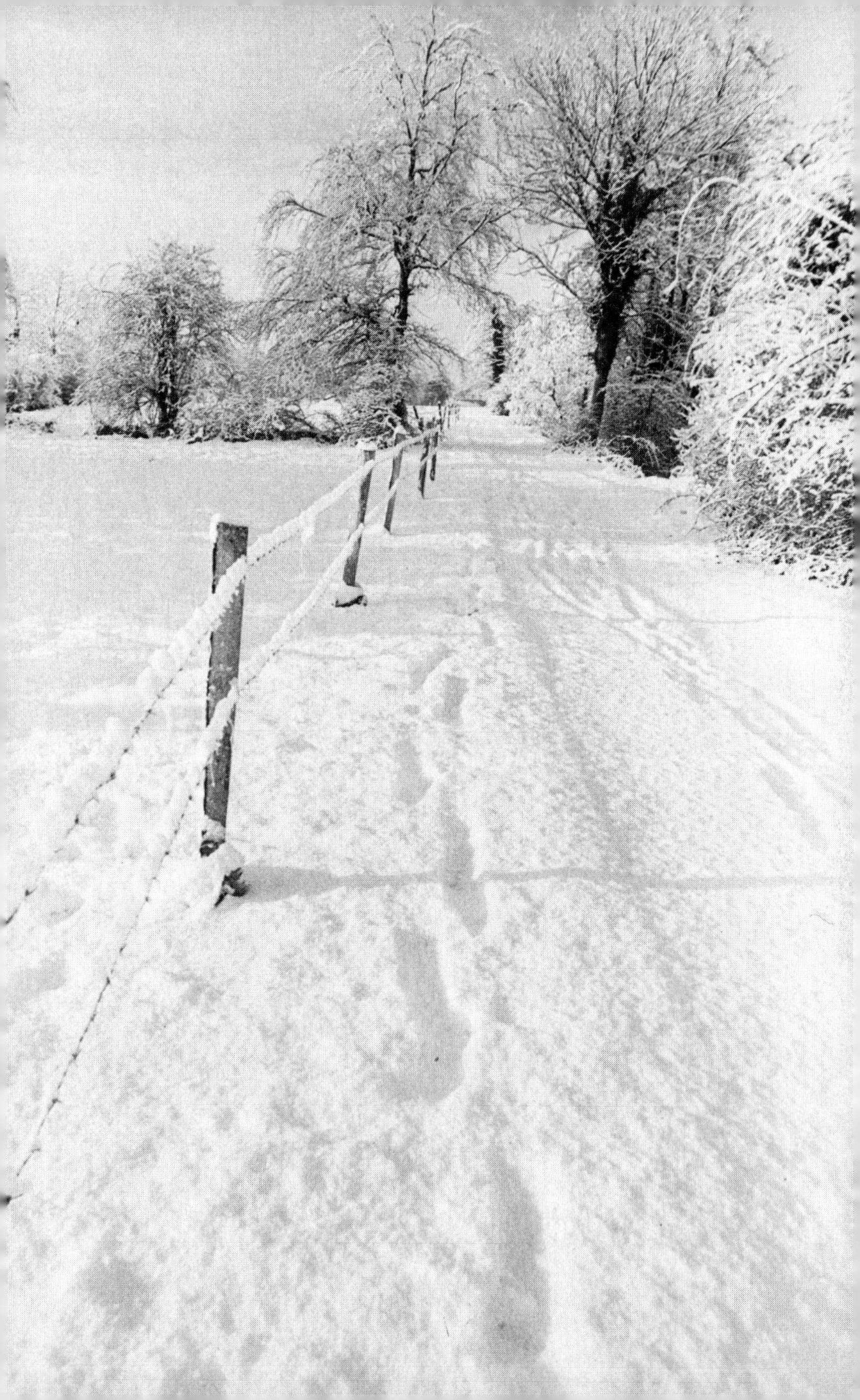

good a tonal range, and that the range of surfaces and emulsions is limited.

The first objection is probably of interest only to the archivist; treated with reasonable care, resin-coated prints should outlast most photographers. The quality of the emulsion is a much more important point. Undoubtedly, the first resin-coated materials produced less 'rich' looking prints, but they are continually improving. However, resin-coated materials tend to be much less tolerant of processing deviations. To achieve good results, they must be processed exactly according to the instructions, so it is not possible to compensate for more than minor exposure variation by varying the developing time.

The third objection is undoubtedly the most important. Traditional ('fiber-based') papers were available in a staggering number of surfaces and thicknesses. They also offered a choice of base colour, typically white, cream and ivory, and of emulsion type. Normal papers have an emulsion made largely from silver bromide in ordinary developers, giving a slightly cold bluish black image. Warmer (browner) tone images are produced on silver chloride papers, and the especially popular chlorobromide types. Both these papers respond strongly to warm-tone developers, which thus offer the choice of image colour to suit the subject.

So non-resin-coated papers are the choice of the fine print enthusiast. They still offer more choice of texture and image colour than do the resin-coated ranges. They tolerate quite wide changes in developing time, and can be manipulated during development to produce specific effects. They are also far more suitable for toning, and for hand colouring. These advantages have led manufacturers to concentrate their attention on providing extra quality papers. These have a higher silver halide content, and after particularly subtle reproduction of shadow detail. Naturally, such materials are expensive, about 50% more than normal resin-coated papers; but they do after the best available print quality.

Non-resin-coated papers are capable of extremely fine results, reproducing subtle variations in tone in both highlight and shadow areas (Clyde Reynolds)

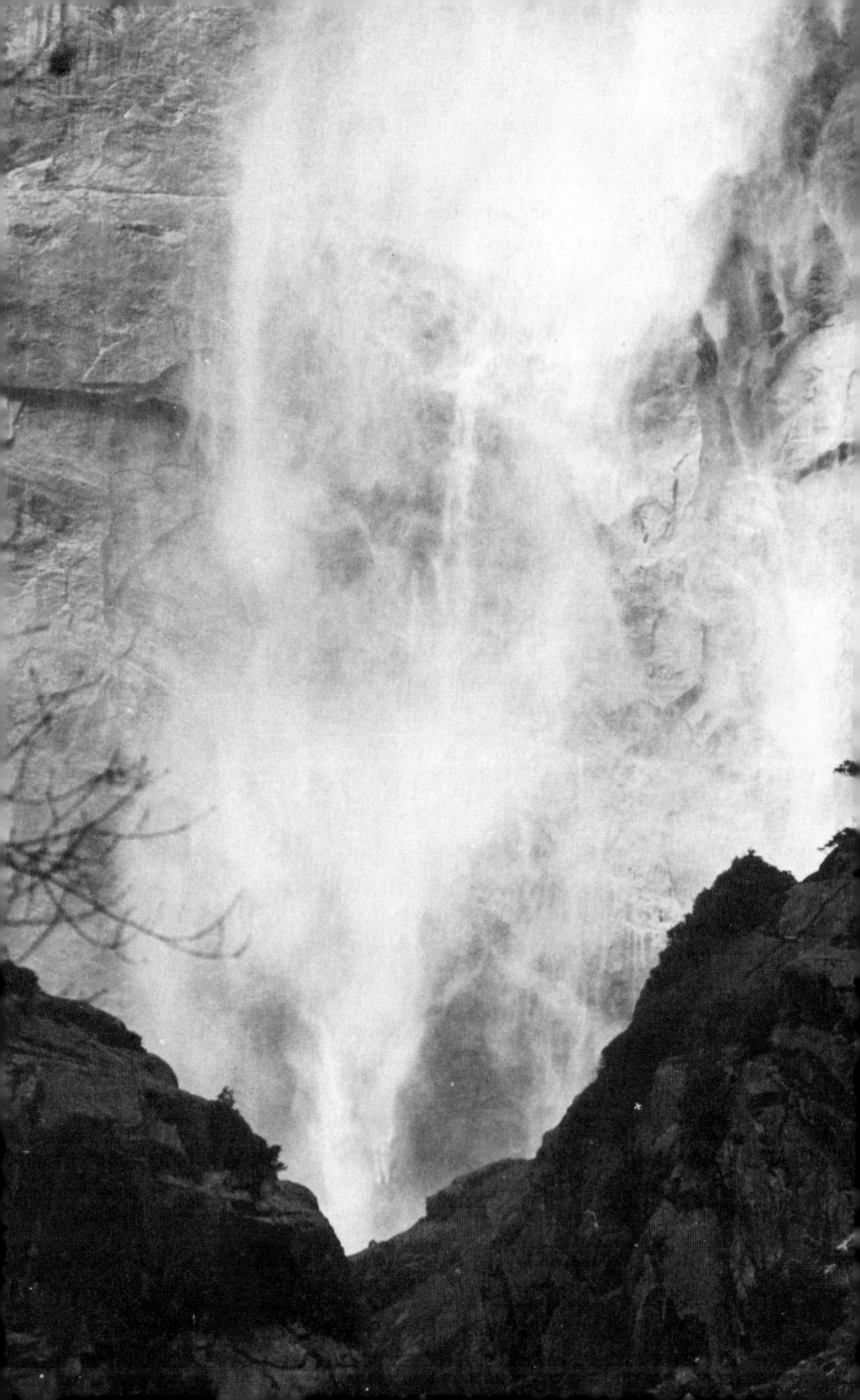

Because the paper base absorbs chemicals, non-resin-coated papers take longer to fix (while all the developer is neutralised) and need a much longer wash. They also tend to curl up, especially after processing, thus making a masking frame (for exposure) and a print dryer or glazer virtually necessities.

When air-dried, glossy surfaced papers finish matt. To give a high gloss, they must be glazed (see page 132). A well-glazed print, though, has a much finer gloss than does a glossy resin-coated print.

Document papers

Apart from true photographic papers, most manufacturers offer a range of document-copy papers. These are normally quite thin, and often in a restricted range of contrasts. Some, but not all, can be stabilisation processed (see page 110). The main advantage is that they are often considerably cheaper than normal materials, and are thus useful for experimental and proof printing.

Image colour

The colour of a metallic silver image varies with the silver particle size and distribution. It can be a neutral black but it can also be quite blue, or quite brown. This depends not only on the emulsion (chloride, bromide, chlorobromide, etc.) but also on the developer.

Coloured papers

Black-and-white emulsion is coated on a variety of brightly coloured bases and this offers an extra dimension in display prints. Some subjects can be lifted right out of the ordinary with a brightly coloured background. Metallic colours produce results that look almost like prints on sheet metal. As

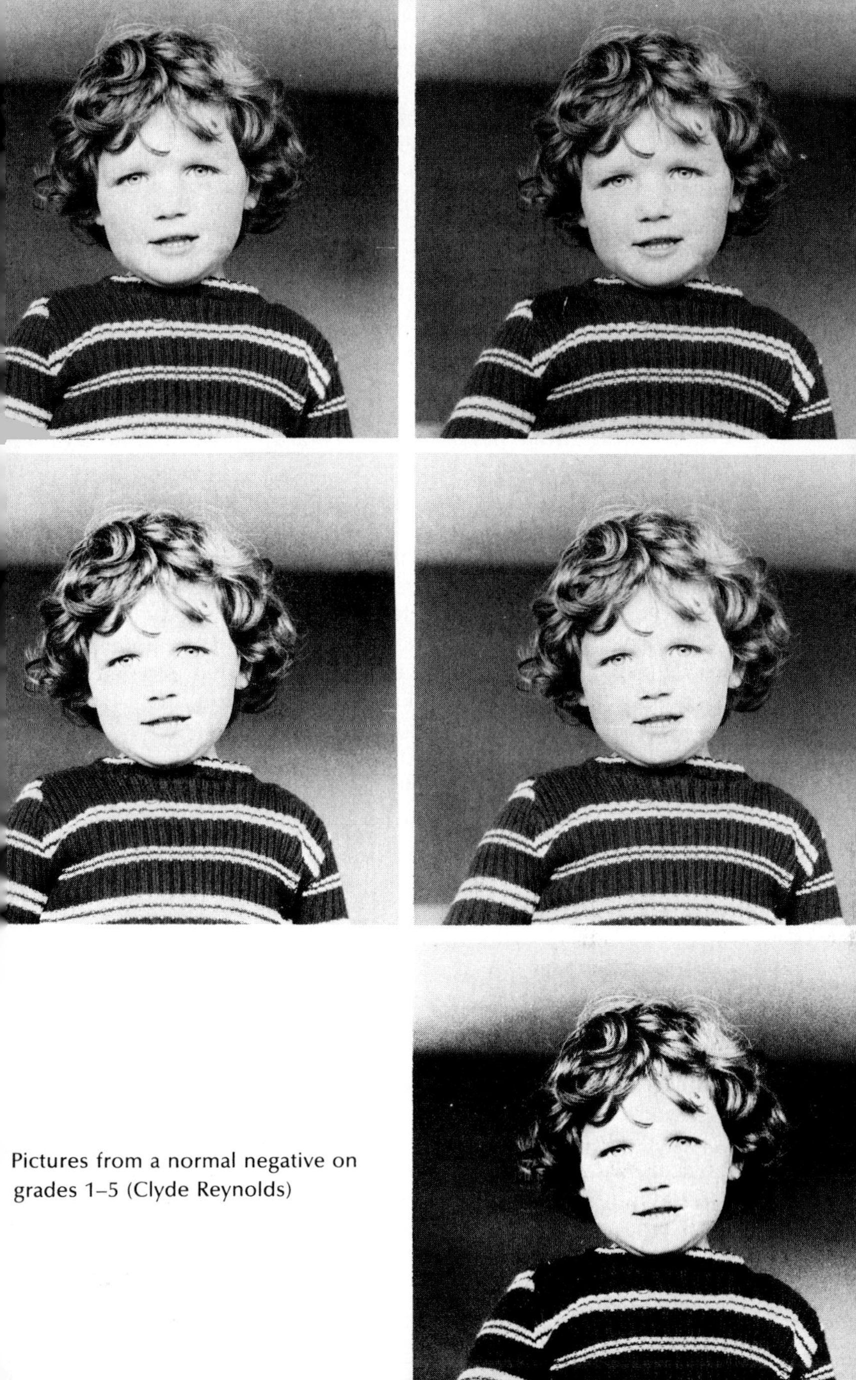

Pictures from a normal negative on grades 1–5 (Clyde Reynolds)

the colour takes the place of whites in a normal print the overall contrast is considerably reduced, so the most successful subjects for these materials are those with bold designs. Often it is better to print from high contrast or line negtives (see page 183).

Paper weight

The base used for photographic print material can vary from the thinnest India paper to thick card. Most traditional materials though are produced in either single weight or double weight. Single weight resembles good quality cartridge paper, and double weight is like thin card. The latter should be chosen for display prints where stiffness is important, otherwise, single weight is the normal choice for mounted or unmounted prints.

The other weights are sometimes used – lightweight, like writing paper, featherweight, and airmail, the thinnest. These are particularly useful for making montages. The thinner the paper, the less obvious the cut edges.

Resin-coated material is almost universally supplied as medium weight. This is actually single weight paper, but it is bulked and stiffened by the two layers of polyethylene used to waterproof the base.

Contrast and grades

One of the joys of black-and-white printing is in choosing exactly the contrast to produce the best picture. some subjects – hazy days and dreamy portraits, for example – cry out for soft paper, while others – perhaps heavy industrial scenes and aggressive modern architecture – demand the harsh tones of hard material. Normal monochrome paper is offered in a choice of grades. The actual numbers vary from make to make, but a typical list is:

0	Extra soft
1	Soft
2	Normal
3	Hard
4	Extra hard
5	Ultra hard

The terms 'soft' and 'hard' are used to describe increasing contrast. For most purposes, grade 2 gives good prints from well-exposed and correctly processed negatives. Some photographers prefer the extra contrast of grade 3. Thus, either grade 2 or grade 3 should be right for most pictures.

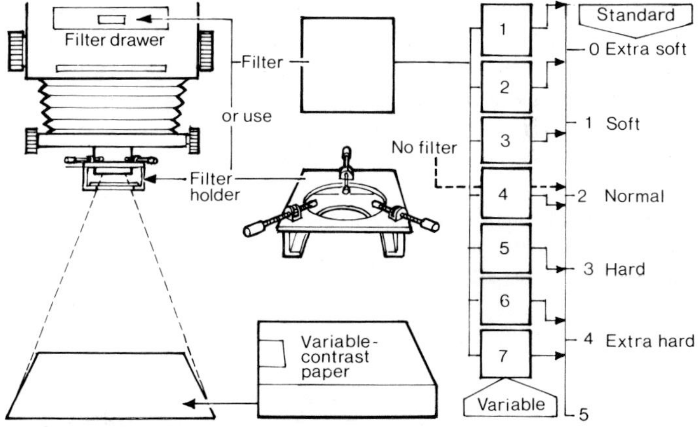

Variable-contrast paper offers a range of contrasts by altering the colour of the printing light with filters

The softer and harder ones are useful for special effects, and for the occasional aberrant negative. It is much better to adjust exposures and processing to give the correct contrast on normal paper than to print regularly on soft or hard material.

Variable-contrast paper

To be ready for any print, most photographers need a selection of paper contrasts and a variety of surfaces, so that they need perhaps 10 or 15 different papers, which can represent a considerable investment. There is also the problem that photographic materials have a relatively short life and after a few years, unused paper is likely to have lost some contrast, to give less brilliant whites and possibly poor blacks.

A neat solution to this difficulty is provided by variable-contrast papers. The emulsion is a mixture of high-contrast blue-sensitive and low-contrast green-sensitive material. When exposed to a mixture of blue and green light, as provided by a normal tungsten light enlarger, the paper gives normal contrast results (much the same as grade 2 paper). Changing the colour of the enlarger light alters the relative exposures given to the two components. Yellow filters absorb blue light, thus the green-sensitive low-contrast part prevails. Conversely, magenta filters restrict the exposure to the blue-sensitive emulsion, producing harder prints. Deep yellow and deep magenta have the strongest effects, while intermediate filters give intermediate contrasts.

The exact range of contrasts varies from make to make, and may vary with the exact colour of the light from the enlarger lamp. Each maker supplies suitable filters, and also suggests settings for use on enlargers with colour heads (see page 164).

Paper speeds

Short exposures are not an essential part of printing, so papers do not need to be as sensitive as films. They are given speed ratings according to ANSI standard PM2-2 1966. This cannot be directly related to ASA film speed ratings, but the paper scale uses figures about 50 times those on the film scale. With a normal enlarger, a 25 × 20 cm (10 × 8 in) print from a 35 mm negative usually needs about 10 seconds at *f*/8 on ANSI 250 paper.

Contrasty negative printed on variable contrast paper: a–1, b–2, c–3, d–no filter, e–4, f–5, g–6, h–7 (Clyde Reynolds)

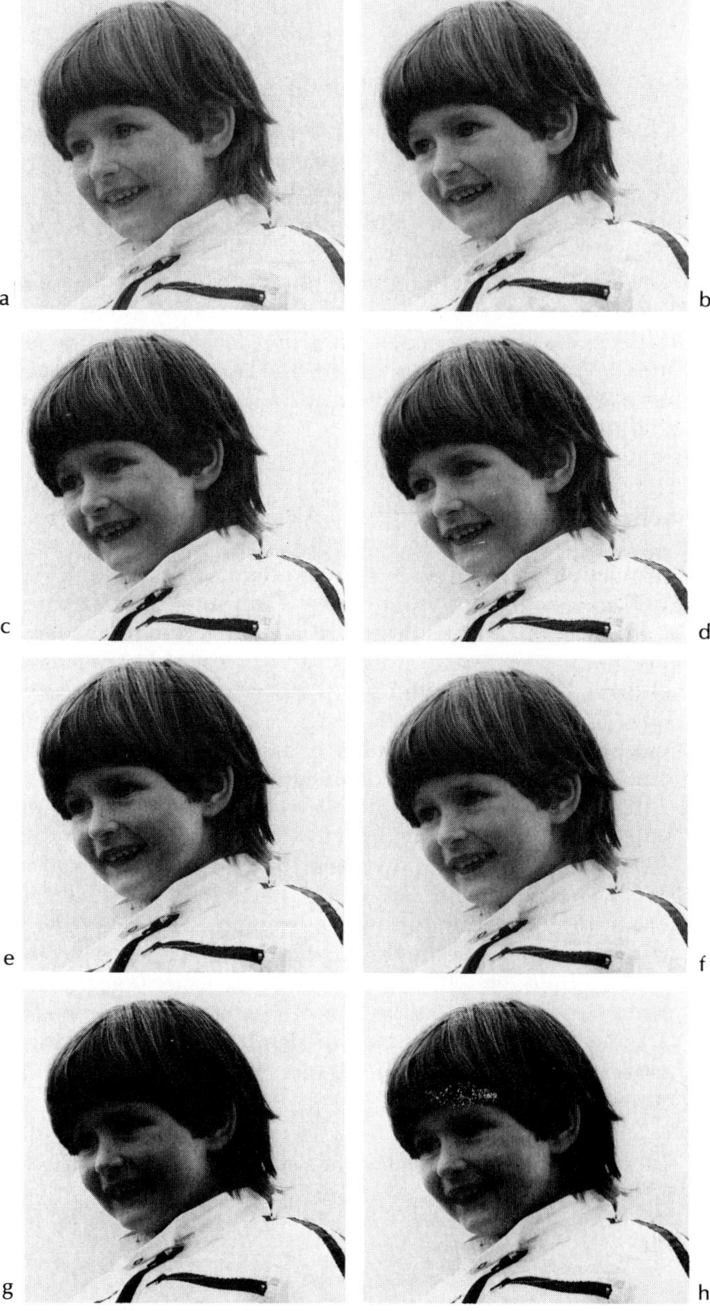
a
b
c
d
e
f
g
h

In general, higher contrast papers need more exposure, but some manufacturers have created ranges of equal-speed papers. This is a great convenience, because it allows exactly the same exposure times on all (or most) grades. Variable contrast papers usually have different speeds through different filters, but some allow the same exposure for the normal grades.

The ANSI speeds are on an arithmetic scale, so it is easy to calculate the change in exposure time. Simply multiply the correct time by the speed of paper in use, and then divide the answer by the new paper speed. For example, if a negative needs 8 seconds on paper rated at 250 it needs $8 \times 250 \div 160 =$ 12.5 seconds on 160 paper.

Contact papers

Virtually all papers now are intended for projection printing with an enlarger. However, there is still some contact paper around. As the name suggests, this is intended for exposure in direct contact with a negative. The paper is very slow, allowing bright safelighting – some even accept dim room lights. It needs a relatively long exposure, 30–60 seconds with an enlarger at its brightest, or a bright table lamp as light source; 10 seconds or so in sunlight.

Printing-out papers (POP) were special contact papers which were exposed in contact with the negative until they had darkened sufficiently, when they were simply fixed or toned, development not being required. Most printing frames have two clamps so that one end of the print could be inspected in subdued light to judge whether the exposure was long enough while maintaining it in exact register with the negative. The exposure was often made in full sunlight.

Today, such materials are purely a historical curiosity; all papers are developed to bring out the latent image formed during exposure.

Low contrast negative printed on the same range of variable-contrast grades (Clyde Reynolds)

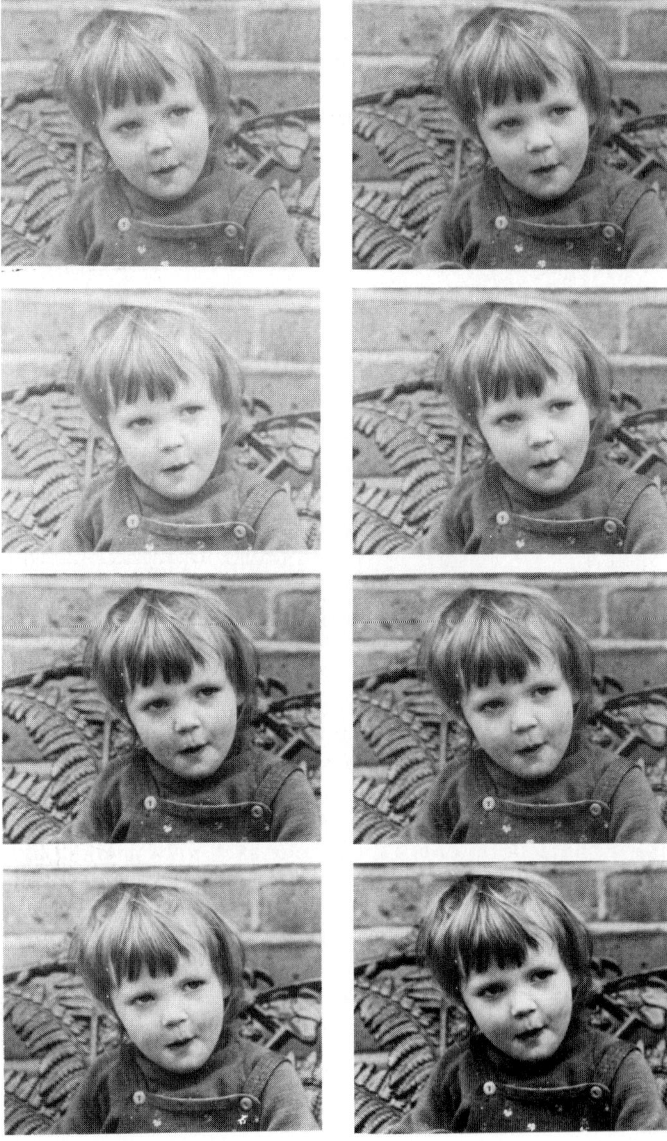

Contact printing

The main use of contact printing nowadays is in producing proofs. A single sheet of 25 × 20 cm (10 × 8 in) paper can show, for example, all 36 negatives on a roll of 35 mm film, or all 12 6 × 6 cm shots on a 120 roll film.

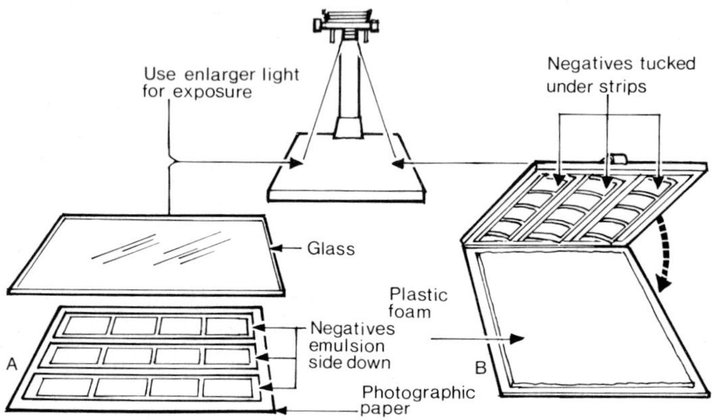

Contact prints in colour or monochrome provide a record of negatives. A. Using a simple glass sheet. B. Using a commercial contact printer

The emulsion (dull) side of the film has to be held firmly in contact with the paper, and the most basic way is to place the negatives on a sheet of paper (in safe lighting, of course) and hold them in place with a sheet of glass. For more regular use, a contact printer is a great help, as it holds a whole film (35 mm or 120 as chosen) and can be loaded in normal room lighting. The simpler versions merely hold the negatives in contact with a sheet of paper, as does a sheet of glass. The more sophisticated versions include a light source.

With a simple contact printer or a piece of glass the paper is exposed by switching on an external light. The easiest source is an enlarger with no negative in it. The exposure is around the same as needed when enlarging a negative to the whole paper size.

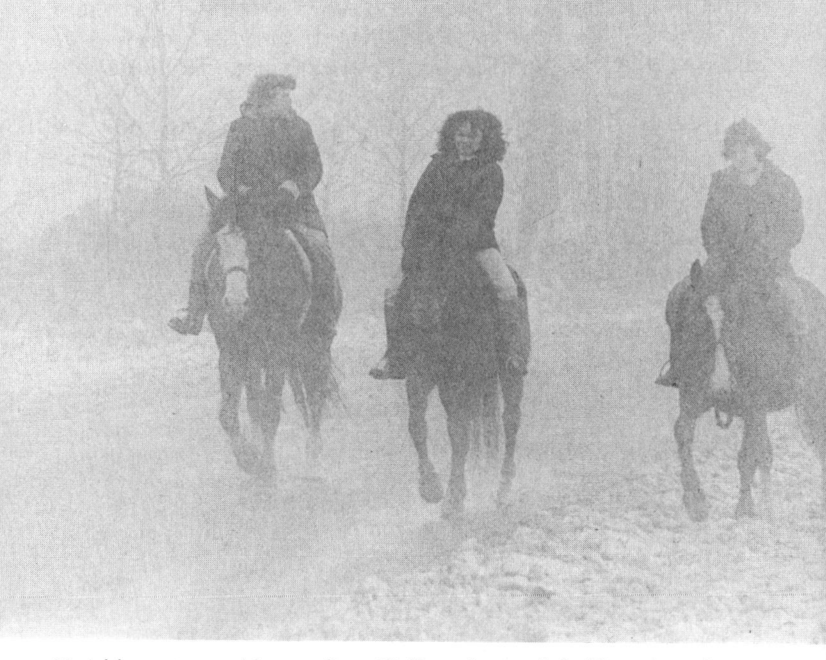

Variable contrast with a medium (4) filter gives a slight lift to the pale greys of foggy day (Paul Broadbent)

Processing paper

Paper is usually processed in open trays or dishes. These are rectangular, and the ideal size is about 5 cm (2 in) longer each side than the paper. As you can work in quite bright safelighting, the process is very straightforward. The chemicals can cause skin problems, so it is best to work with tongs or wear thin rubber gloves.

Holding the paper face upwards by one edge, place the opposite edge into the solution to one side of the dish and smoothly slide the paper under the surface of the solution so that the whole sheet is fully wetted as quickly as possible. Rock the dish gently so that a wave of developer flows back and forth across the print. Develop for the whole time indicated in the instructions. It is much better to develop for longer than necessary, especially if the developer temperature is a little low. For optimum quality, multiply the manufacturer's quoted time by 1.5. In the absence of instructions, develop resin-coated paper for 2 minutes and traditional paper for 3 minutes. Shortly before the time is up, lift out the paper by one edge and allow the liquid to drain back into the tray.

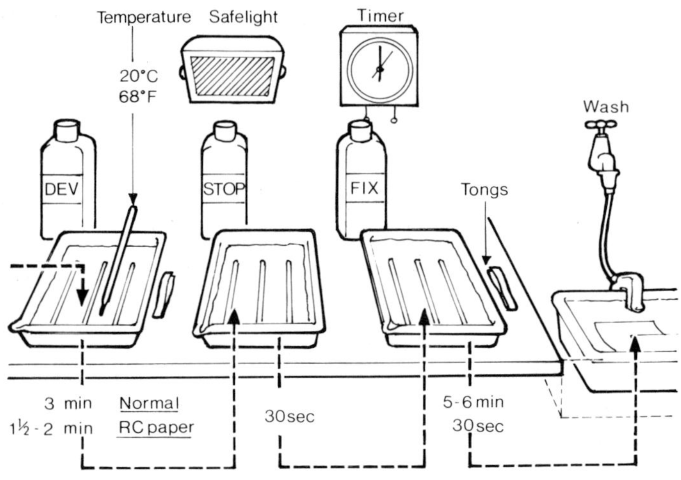

Basic black-and-white printing

Underdeveloping is the most common fault in printing. The result is a grey print because the paper has not had time to develop its full black. Even overall grey scenes need full development to achieve full rich tones. Working by safelight, you see the image appearing and a correctly exposed print looks dark and over-contrasty. It is very tempting to pull it out before its time and so lose its full potential. However, a worse fault is overexposure which can cause the image to develop so quickly that there is danger of the print becoming totally black. This type of print should go straight into the waste bin. Unfortunately, all too often it is lovingly fixed, washed and kept – another muddy grey and grey picture. If the paper goes too dark in the developer, there is only one solution: take a fresh sheet of paper and reduce the exposure.

Processing black-and-white papers

Paper should be processed in solutions kept at 20°C (68°F). Dilute all solutions exactly in accordance with instructions and agitate regularly. Several prints can be processed together if they are put face to face and back to back. Make sure that agitation ensures even processing, and that the face to face ones to do not stick together.

Papers are developed in universal or paper developer, resin-coated for 1½–2 minutes, normal type for 3 minutes. One litre of working strength developer will process about 60 25 × 20 cm (10 × 8 in) prints.

Development is stopped in a stop bath (2–4% acetic acid) or slowed in water for 30 seconds to reduce contamination of fixer with developer.

The image is then fixed in a suitable fixer. Traditional thiosulphate (hypo) fixers take 5–6 minutes to fix traditional papers. Modern high speed fixers can fix resin-coated materials in 30 seconds. Do not overfix resin-coated papers. One litre of working strength fixer will process about 100 25 × 20 cm (10 × 8 in) prints.

After fixing, prints must be washed. Conventional papers need at least 30 minutes in running water. Resin-coated prints need 2–4 minutes and should not be overwashed.

Dry traditional prints in a dryer or glazer. Air-dry resin-coated papers on a bench or in a rack.

After exactly the correct time, immerse the print in the stop bath (or water wash) and rock the dish gently for 30 seconds. Then remove the print to the fixer (once again allowing it to drain). Fix resin-coated papers for 2 minutes, and traditional ones for 5. Again, with stop bath and fixer, follow the paper or chemical instructions if they differ.

Now transfer the print to plain water, preferably running, and wash it thoroughly. Resin-coated materials need 4 or 5 minutes in running water. If you work away from a water source, keep the prints in a large dish of water for a while. However, resin-coated papers should not be soaked for too long – never more than 20 minutes. When several prints are ready, take them to a sink and wash them in running water.

Traditional papers require a *much* longer wash, and they are much less easily damaged by overwashing. The minimum is half an hour in running water, and some workers wash their prints for much longer than that.

Archival processing

Prints which have been processed and washed normally will outlast most photographers. Occasionally, though, there is call to produce a print which is as near everlasting as possible. Archival processing, combined with accurately air-conditioned storage, is aimed at this end.

The important part of archival processing is the wash. It is essential to remove virtually all traces of chemical from the paper, leaving only the pure silver image in the gelatin emulsion. This is done primarily by washing for a long time in running water. It is important that the water swirls past the prints; many special washing devices have been designed to achieve this, but the best is probably a simple cascade of three or four dishes.

One great help is a fixer eliminator, or hypo eliminator, to convert thiosulphate to sulphate, which is far more water soluble. A range of oxidising agents, including hypochlorites, permanganates, persulphates, iodine and ammoniacal hydrogen peroxide, have been used but probably the last is the most widely used. The basic formula is: 125 ml of 3% H_2O_2 and 100 ml of 3% NH_4OH mixed and made up to 1000 ml. Immerse the well-washed print in the eliminator for 5 minutes, and wash again for a further 10 minutes to remove all trace of eliminator.

Unfortunately, such treatment tends to fade the highlight detail, so for most long-life purposes a simple washing aid is better. The most commonly used and effective is a 2% solution of sodium sulphite. After a short rinse, immerse the print in the solution for 2 minutes, then the washing time can be reduced to one sixth of that normally needed.

However well processed the print, it can soon be bleached or stained by contact with most normal papers or adhesives (such as the gum on envelopes). Long-term storage is effective only in specially manufactured papers.

Developers

Just as with black-and-white films, developer reduces the exposed silver grains to metallic silver, thus revealing the latent image. The developers, however, tend to be far more vigorous, completing their action in 1–3 minutes. The grain on a paper print is never enlarged and is therefore unseen, so there is no need to compromise between graininess and time as there is with film developers.

Most paper developers are basically metol/hydroquinone or phenidone/hydroquinone formulae and most conveniently they are supplied as liquid concentrates (some in two parts which are mixed to form a concentrated solution). Add water, usually about nine parts to one of concentrate, and the developer is ready. Concentrated developers, even after mixing the two parts, have a long life – often several years – if the container is kept well stoppered.

Some papers have developers made specifically for them and they usually produce a fully developed image in the shortest possible time. They may also be formulated to give the most neutral image colour with that particular paper. These special developers are unlikely to produce the best possible prints with other papers (especially those from the same manufacturer if he recommends a different special developer). The papers, though, will usually develop quite acceptably in normal developers, but will take quite a lot longer.

Special high-contrast or soft-working developers allow you to vary the contrast somewhat on any particular paper, although they are not a complete answer to providing exactly the contrast you want. At their most effective, they increase or reduce the contrast about as much as changing paper by a single grade, while mostly the difference is nearer half a grade.

Stabilisation processing

A number of document copy papers incorporate developing agents in the emulsion. The image appears after a very short immersion in strong alkali and it is then stabilised (rather than truly fixed) in ammonium thiocyanate. The paper does not need washing and the process produces damp dry prints within a few seconds in a simple roller-transport processer. Developed originally for document copy work, and used widely in phototypesetting and other reproduction processes, stabilisation processing offers a quick way of producing proof prints.

Most resin-coated printing papers incorporate some developing agent in their emulsion so that they can react more quickly to conventional processing. Some types can be stabilisation processed, but this seldom produces a really worthwhile time saving. Stabilisation papers can be processed in normal developer and fixer, when they react much like resin-coated materials.

Stabilised prints are not permanent and within a month or so the image can start fading. To make the image permanent, fix and wash the print in the normal way. This can be done at any time after the original process.

Careful exposure and processing on a contrast paper turn this everyday negative into a picture (Ben Storm)

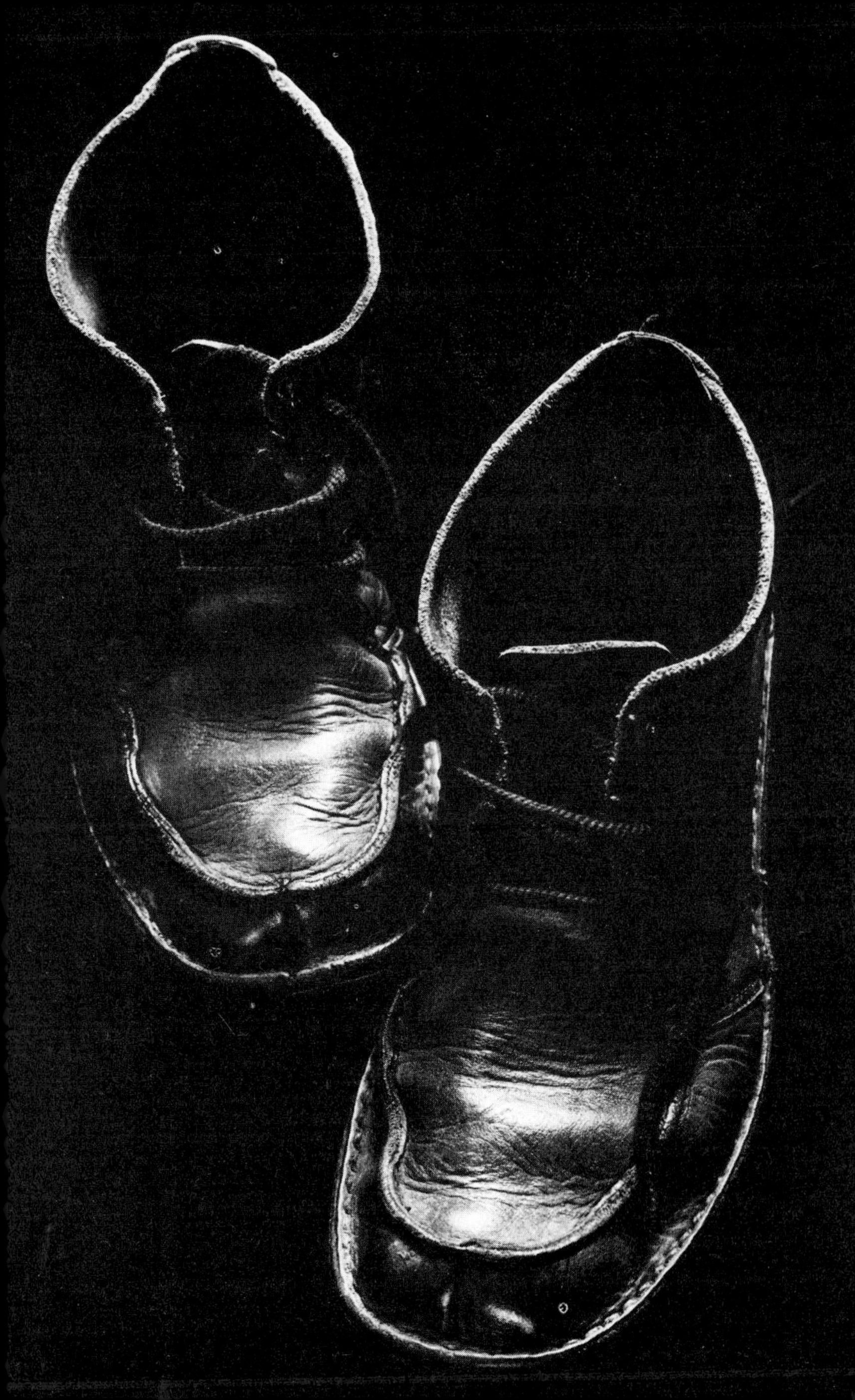

Projection printing

Today, most prints are exposed by projecting an image of the negative on to the light-sensitive paper. This has two major advantages in that it allows the size of the final image to be determined at the printing stage, irrespective of the original camera format, and it allows selection of exactly the required part of the frame. Therefore, one negative can form the basis of a range of different pictures, varied in size, shape and composition. Practically all projection prints are *enlargements*, so allowing convenient small-format cameras to be used. However, the principles are the same whether the final image is smaller or larger than the negative.

Enlarging

As noted earlier, an enlarger consists basically of a light source, negative carrier and lens all in a relatively light-tight

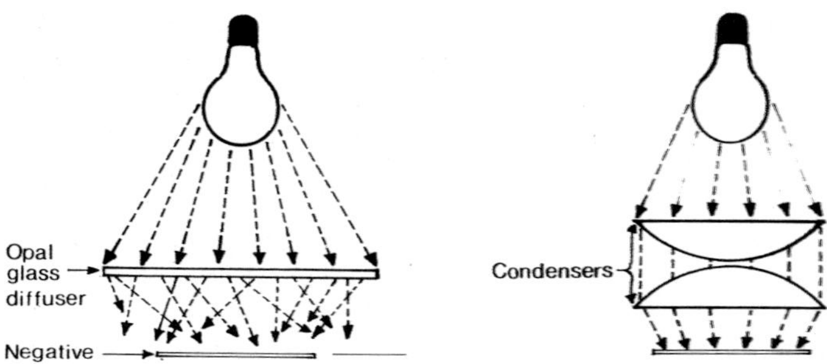

Diffusion and condenser light sources in enlargers

housing. The whole enlarger head can be raised or lowered to alter the image size, and the lens moved to ensure sharp focus. The most important features are that the negative is held flat and parallel with the base board, that the lens is mounted centrally under the negative with its axis at right angles to the negative and to the base board, and that the negative is illuminated evenly right out to the edges. The physical construction of most enlargers is adequate, allowing the image to be focused over the whole print area at the same time. The light source is more of a problem.

Basically, there are two illumination systems in common use: the light may be focused into a beam by one or more *condenser* lenses, or it may be spread evenly by a *diffuser* system. Because black-and-white negative images are granular, the dark areas can both absorb light and deflect it. With a focused beam of light the light loss by deflection significantly reduces the brightness of the denser parts of the negative, which increases the contrast of the image projected on to the baseboard. With diffuse lighting systems, the image on the baseboard is the same contrast as the negative (assuming no reduction by the lens). The effect of changing from a diffuser light source to a condenser system is about the same as changing to a paper one grade harder. This is why film and developer manufacturers give two different sets of developing times – to produce negatives to suit either condenser enlargers or diffuser enlargers.

Condenser enlargers produce prints which appear to be sharper, with better resolution of fine detail. However, they also tend to emphasise the grain structure of the image, and show up any faults or dirt on either surface of the negative. In practice, the normally accepted compromise solution, an opal bulb producing a diffuse light which is then focused on to the film, is as close to the ideal as possible. To use a sharply defined light source would overemphasise problems with the negative; and to use a totally diffuse system would lose some of the potential impact of a properly made black-and-white print.

Compose and focus the image on the white surface of an enlarging easel, the enlarger baseboard, or a sheet of plain paper. When the white area is larger than the printing paper, define the print borders with lines drawn with a suitable marker, or with pieces of tape. Do not worry about the thickness of the paper to be used. The depth of focus on an enlarger image is much greater than the paper thickness, so large that the paper can be tilted or buckled to distort the image without loss of focus (see page 129). If the image is sharp on the easel, it will be sharp on the paper.

Compose and focus at full lens aperture since this produces the brightest and most easily focused image. For small enlargements (up to about 10× the negative area) it is simple to focus visually. Beyond about 10× a focus finder is almost

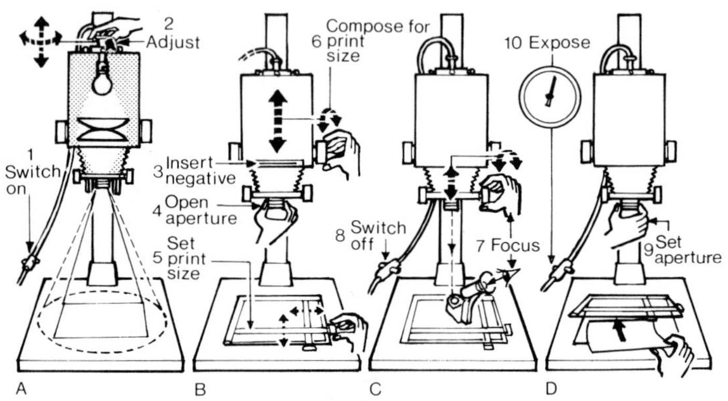

Setting up for black-and-white enlarging. A. Adjust enlarger for even lighting. B. Select print subject. C. Focus image sharpely. D. Insert paper and expose

essential (see page 37). Most focus finders magnify the image enough to focus on the grain structure, rather than the picture. After focusing, close the lens down by two stops to ensure optimum image quality. If the exposure times are inconvenient, you can rely on most *f*/2.8 lenses anywhere between *f*/4 and *f*/11. Good quality lenses of around *f*/4 produce excellent images down to about *f*/11, while low price lenses are often satisfactory only between *f*/8 and *f*/16.

Exposures

The density of a print depends on the image brightness and the exposure time. The brightness results from the enlarger

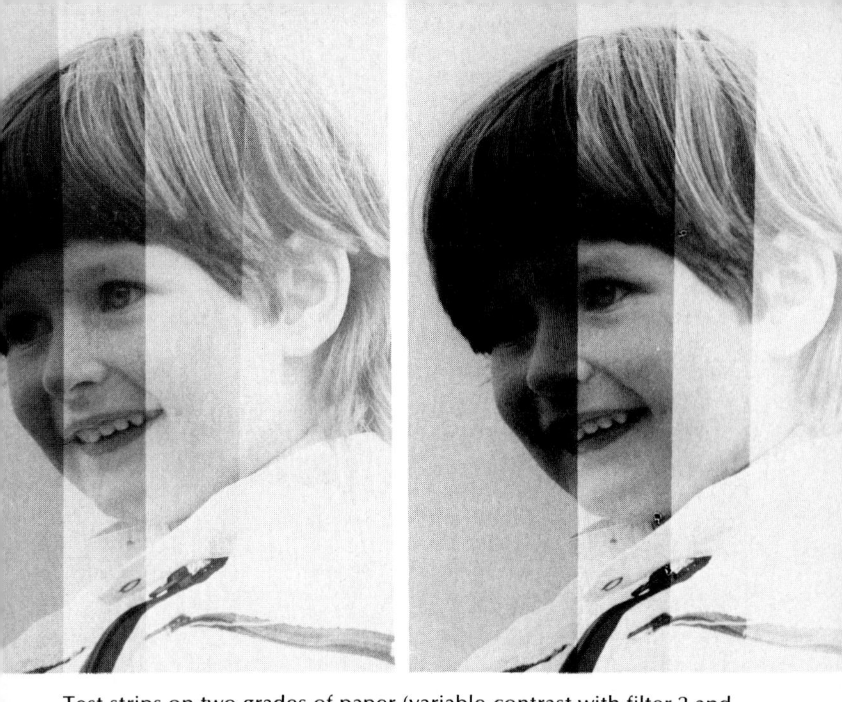

Test strips on two grades of paper (variable-contrast with filter 2 and 4) 5–10, 20 and 40 seconds (Clyde Reynolds)

light, the negative density, and the lens aperture. Simultaneously doubling the brightness and halving the time should maintain the same density, and it does over a restricted range of times and intensities. Outside that range, the paper needs more exposure to produce the same density. The range varies from paper to paper, but most are fairly even from 5 seconds to 1 minute or so. In most cases, the exposure time is the best factor to vary. Having selected the image and adjusted the lens aperture, make a test strip to decide on the right time. Leave the enlarger switched on, with its red safelight filter in position. Take a small piece of the paper you are using, about 10 × 8 cm (4 × 3 in), and put it on the easel or baseboard so that it will record the most important part of the picture. For example, for a portrait make the test strip from the model's face, not from the background.

Switch the enlarger off, and take the red filter out of its light path. The aim is now to make several different exposures (each double the last) on the test paper. The first time, you are working totally from scratch, but after a few prints, you learn where to start. With no other data, assume that you are most likely to need 10 seconds at *f*/8. So the ideal series is 2½, 5, 10, 20 and 40 seconds.

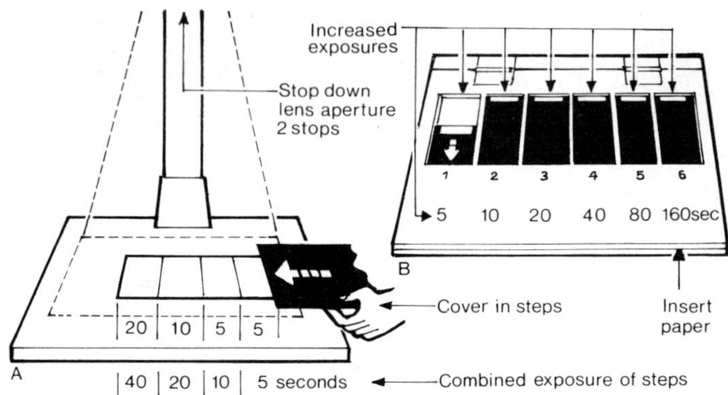

Making a test strip. A. Using a card allows the test to be confined to the important subject areas. B. A commercial test printer provides precise control with ease

Switch on the enlarger, noting the time carefully on a suitable seconds timer, or starting it. After 2½ seconds, interpose a piece of card to shade about one fifth of the test strip from the enlarger light; after a further 2½ seconds, shade off a little more; after a further 5, a little more, and so on. After the whole 40 seconds (which is given to only the last fifth of the strip) turn the enlarger off.

A timer wired into the enlarger switch actually complicates the production of test strips, but ensures much more accurate exposure control. You might, for example, set the timer for 5 seconds, switch on and cover part of the paper after 2½ seconds; shade off a little more, and let the timer provide another 5 seconds; shade a little more, open the lens by 1 stop, give another 5 seconds, open again and give another 5.

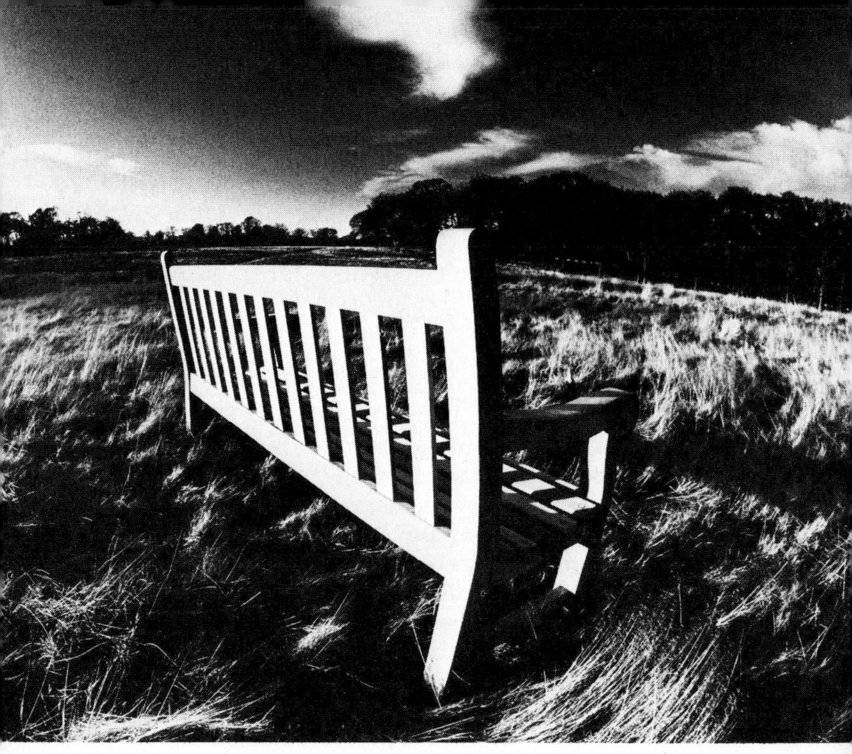

Extreme contrast printing is sometimes the best way to create a striking picture (Roy Pryer)

Assuming the lens diaphragm to be accurate, that gives an equivalent exposure series.

Once exposed, develop the test strip *fully*, rinse it, give it a short fix and another short rinse, after which it is ready for examination. Look at the test strip in full room lighting, or daylight if possible. With any luck the densities will range from too light, to too dark. Decide which is the nearest to your ideal, and work from that. In the unlikely event of one strip being exactly the density you want, then give the whole print that time. More often, the best exposure will fall between two steps. If the print needs to be exactly midway in tone, multiply the shorter time (which would be too light) by

1.4; if it needs to be nearer one or the other, bias the time for that effect.

Turn the lights off again and you are ready to make the first print. Put a sheet of paper on the enlarger easel. If you are in any doubt, put the safelight filter in the light path, turn on the enlarger, and verify the composition. Then give exactly the exposure worked out from the test strip, and develop the paper according to the instructions.

Choosing the paper grade

Sometimes, it is possible to tell from the test strip that the paper grade is unsuitable. Usually, though, you need the whole picture before it becomes obvious that the effect is too grey and flat or too contrasty. As with much in photography, it is largely a matter of personal taste conditioned by fads and fancies. Over recent years, the 'soot and whitewash' look of extra hard papers have been fashionable. To some extent this has been successful because photographers have favoured high-speed films and acutance developers, which produces obvious hard grain. So their prints have been almost akin to a half-tone picture, with greys represented by different dot patterns, rather than by apparently smooth midtones. I feel that this loses much of the attraction and precision of monochrome photography, and that fine grain with good midtone reproduction should be the norm. Modern cameras with multiple-coated lenses produce high contrast negatives which can be too contrasty for grade 2 paper. Still, grade 2 (or variable-contrast paper without a filter) is the best place to start. If the result (properly processed) is too grey, then move to a higher grade of paper; if it is too black-and-white, move to a lower grade.

Grades and exposures

Most manufacturers offer a series of papers with the same speed, in which case the same exposure is good for different grades. However, this does not apply universally; neither is it true of changing filters with variable contrast papers.

The subtler tones of a lower-contrast picture still need a good black produced by full processing to work well (Ben Storm)

If you use a number of different speed papers, the best course is to make test prints with each, and calculate the relationships between them. Call your normal paper (whichever grade it is) 1. Then other papers which need the same exposure can also be numbered 1. For papers which need more or less exposure, work out the factors by which you must alter the time (i.e. 0.7, 1.5 etc.) to match the print on the basic paper. Marked on the boxes, these factors give immediately calculable exposure time.

Filters for variable-contrast papers come with a calculator which allows simple conversion from the time needed with one filter to that needed with another.

Changing negatives

One of the great advantages of modern cameras is the consistency with which they can expose. This is essential for transparency photography, where the exposure must be right, and a great boon for printing. Carefully used, a camera will turn in roll after roll of negatives all the same density so they should all need the same print exposure, and this is largely the case. With a good set of negatives, you can give exactly the same exposure for each one. A variable set of negatives needs a test strip for each.

Of course, negatives of different sizes produce different intensities, even at the same enlarging ratio. So changing format calls for a new test strip.

Magnification

Moving the enlarger head up the column spreads the light further out and thus reduces its intensity. Doubling the height of the enlarger head reduces the intensity of illumination on the baseboard to one quarter of the previous level. This is true whether the whole area is printed, or just a section. To compensate, the paper now needs four times the exposure, or perhaps more if it is outside the range at which the paper obeys the reciprocity law; alternatively open the lens by two stops (say *f*/5.6 instead of *f*/11) and keep the time the same.

The most straightforward way to work out the change needed is from the linear dimensions on the enlarger baseboard. The light intensity (and thus the exposure time needed) varies with the square of the change in picture width or height. These changes are directly related to enlarger head movement. Thus, moving the head so that the lens is three times the distance from the paper magnifies the image three times (thus needing nine times the exposure time at the same

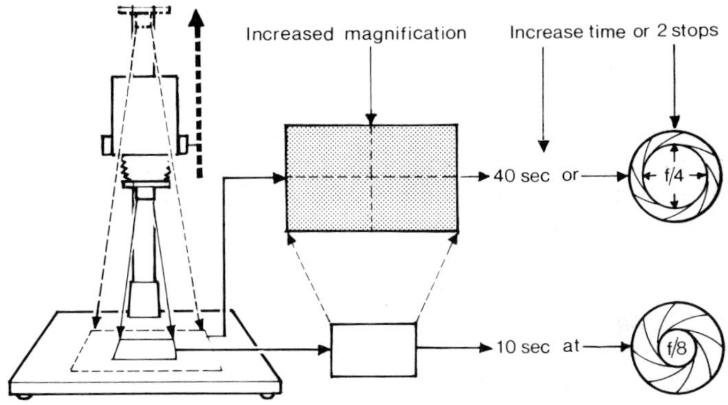

Changing print size calls for alteration in exposure

aperture). To help, many enlargers have calibrated columns, showing magnifications with various focal length lenses. It is simple to work out the change in exposure from the change in magnification by using the equation

$$\left(\frac{M_2}{M_1}\right)^2$$

For example when changing from 4½× image (a 160 mm wide print from a 35 mm negative) to an 11¼× image (a 400 mm wide print) the exposure time must be increased by $(11\frac{1}{4}/4\frac{1}{2})^2$ which is 6¼. So if the small print needed 4 seconds at *f*/8, the large one needs 25 seconds at *f*/8, 12½ seconds at *f*/5.6 or 6¼ seconds at *f*/4.

Exposure wedges

When it is impossible to calculate the exposure accurately, make another test strip based, of course, on the best calculation. For ever-changing negatives and magnifications, it is simpler to make the test strip in one go, through a step wedge. A step wedge is simply a piece of material with patches of several different tones. The *Kodak Enlarging Calculator* is a typical example. This is a disc divided into eight segments of differing densities. Each is marked with an exposure compensation factor. To use the calculator, lay it on the printing paper; open the lens by two stops, and give the calculated exposure time.

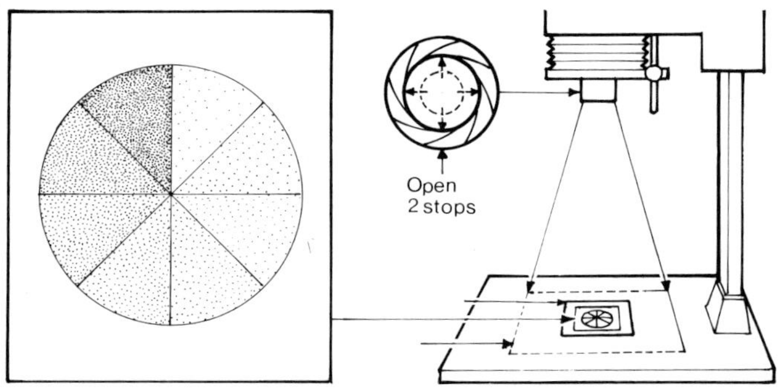

A density wedge allows a test strip to be made in a single exposure

After processing, the paper will show a series of different print densities. Select the correct one, and apply the marked exposure correction to the settings used to make the test.

It is quite simple to make a step wedge from a piece of film, by exposing it under the enlarger as if making a test strip on paper, then developing the film normally. The steps needed are about two stops apart, say, 1, 4 and 16 seconds at *f*/16. The best approach is to make a test strip on a piece of film with eight or ten gradations, then try this out on a print to decide which three or four steps are the best to use. After this make a second step wedge that can be easily calibrated.

Using an enlarging exposure meter

An enlarging exposure meter (see page 38) measures the light on the enlarger baseboard and displays the time needed to expose the paper fully. Some are combined with an enlarger timer to give the calculated exposure automatically. Once the meter is calibrated for the paper speed, it copes with negative density, magnification and lens aperture.

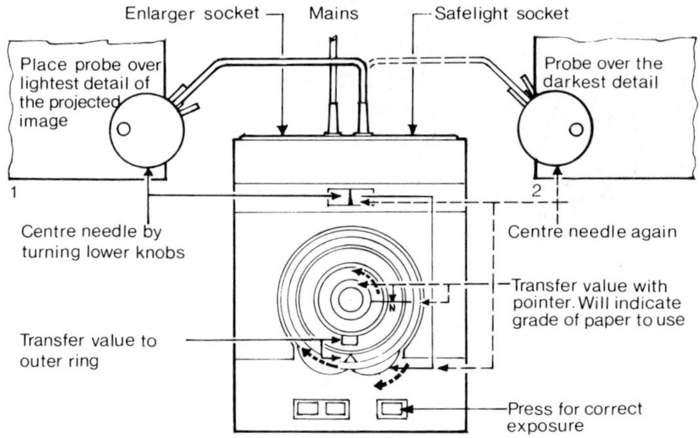

An enlarging mter can be used to estimate the paper grade and exposure time. Connected to the enlarger, some meters act as automatic timers as well

Most meters can measure either the whole negative on an integrated basis, or a selected area. The same meter setting can be used for an integrated reading or for a midtone reading. The latter is the best method if you can identify an area of the negative that you wish to become a midtone. Naturally, the meter needs to be calibrated differently to work out the exposure from highlight (dark) or shadow (light) readings. Comparing the times for the lightest and darkest negative areas (without recalibrating the meter) gives a measure of the projected negative density range, and thus the best paper contrast grade. Meter manufacturers supply tables to assist in the calcualtions, but once again the final choice is a matter of personal preference.

Holding back and burning in

Quite often the balance between light and dark areas of the print is unsatisfactory. Perhaps the light was too one-sided, or part of the subject too close to the flash; perhaps the subject was difficult – the difference in light level between a black suit and the bride's white dress is a classic photographic problem – or perhaps you just want to change the emphasis by altering the tones.

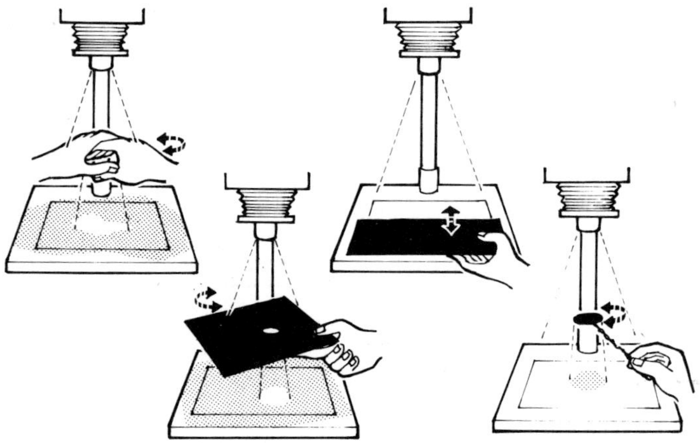

Some negatives call for extra or reduced exposure over part of the paper to reproduce the subject to its best advantage

Whatever the reason, the solution is the same: give the parts of the print that need to be darker more exposure than those that need to be lighter. Two terms are used: *holding back* (or *dodging*) and *burning in*. The only difference is in the proportion of the picture involved. 'Holding back' is shading a relatively small area so that it is finally lighter than the rest. 'Burning in' is shading a large area so that a relatively

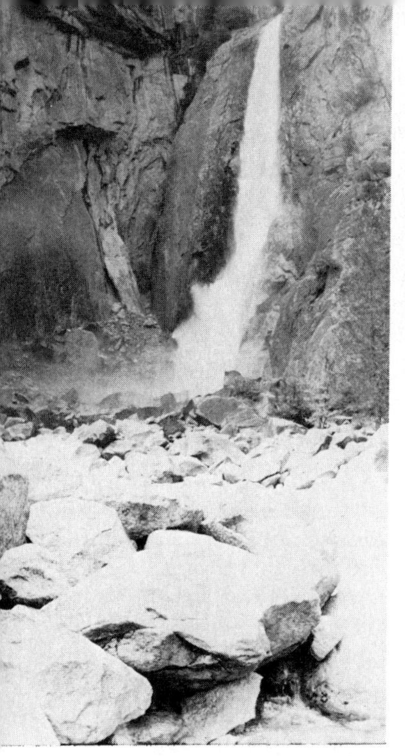
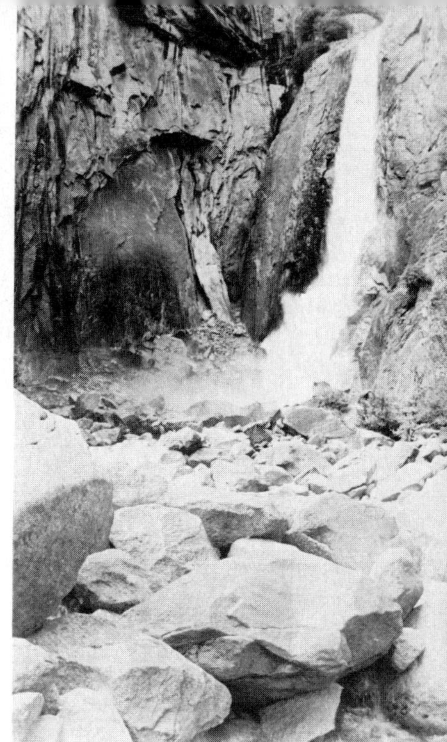

Contrast of foreground and background can be varied independently with variable contrast paper

small area comes out darker. Most holding back and practically all burning in can be done with the hands or a simple piece of card. Sometimes, when only a central area needs holding back, it is much easier to work with a suitably shaped dodger mounted on a piece of wire. Occasionally a card with a hole in it makes burning in simpler.

The difference in exposure needed obviously depends on the negative. However, reducing the exposure by about one third, or increasing it by a half is the least that makes a large difference in relative tones. The way to work is to calculate the best overall exposure and time that in the normal way. If part of the image needs holding back, then introduce suitable shading for one third or more of the time. If part needs burning in, after the full exposure, cover the enlarger lens with a hand or other opaque object, switch on the enlarger, and reveal the image where it needs more exposure.

For large areas, work quite close to the enlarger lens, and for more detailed work, move nearer to the paper. Keep the shader moving all the time, to make quite sure that the shaded area merges imperceptibly into the rest of the scene. There are few effects nastier than an obvious piece of holding back.

Varifiltering

One of the great advantages of variable-contrast papers is that they can accommodate otherwise unprintable negatives. For example, a picture taken indoors with a large window looking onto a sunlit scene. With normal material, no amount of holding back or burning in can get round the fact that the outdoor scene needs grade 1 to accommodate its high contrast, while the indoor part needs perhaps grade 4 to be anything other than a grey and grey border.

With variable-contrast material, you just make two separate prints, one framed by the other. Make two test strips (each through the appropriate filter) to determine the two exposures, then covering each part in turn make the print. In practice, it is often easier than this. One part usually needs much more exposure than the other. So expose the whole print through the filter appropriate to the thin parts of the negative (usually a high-contrast one), then cover those areas, and expose the remainder through its correct filter. The small first exposure will have virtually no effect on the contrast of the dense areas of the negative.

Multiple printing

There are many ways that two or more images can combine to form a better picture. The most obvious is the addition of clouds in an otherwise blank white sky. Here, unfortunately,

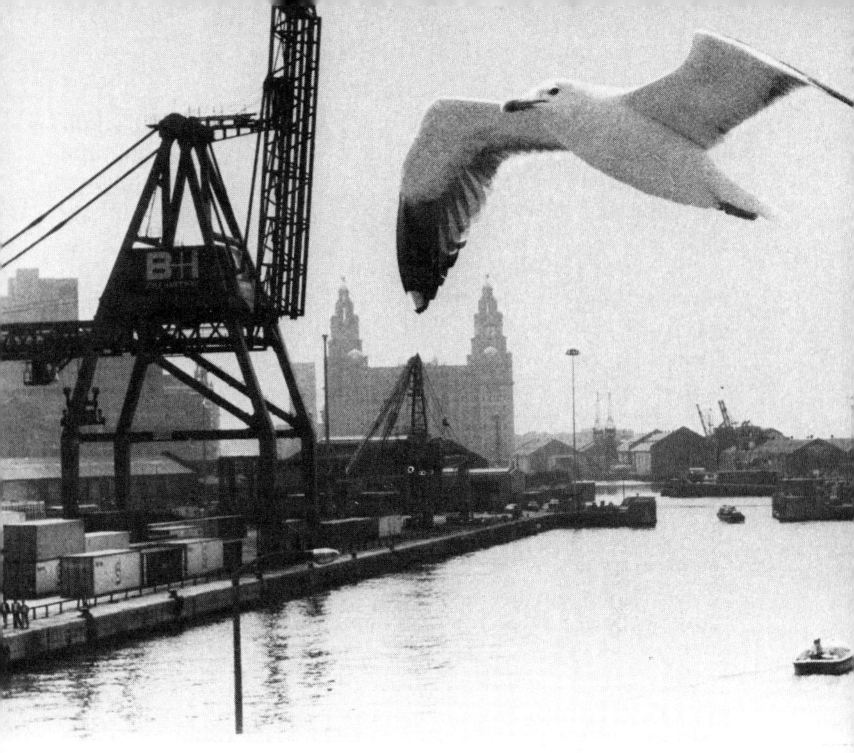

A second image can be simply printed into white areas

there is room to discuss only the basic principles. However, at least in monochrome, experiment is simple. Combination printing depends on one basic fact – once the paper is exposed, further exposure can only darken it. Thus, subsequent exposures can add dark detail to light areas, but not light detail to dark ones.

Assume that the landscape negative has a dark sky area which prints white. To add clouds, make a normal exposure, then change to a cloud negative. Restrict its image to the sky area (mark the paper with a soft pencil) and give a suitable exposure.

If the landscape has a mucky sky area (wires, for example), the the first exposure has to be confined to the land. It may be possible to use hands or a simple piece of card, but often the best way is to cut out a piece of thick card to match the skyline exactly and to place this on the paper before making the exposure (line it up using the enlarger's red safelight filter).

Given the right negatives, it is sometimes better to superimpose them in the enlarger carrier and make a single exposure, holding back or burning in as required.

With all combination techniques, there is a danger of producing hard edges. It is usually possible to soften these by handwork when the print has been processed (see page 188) but it is much more satisfactory to achieve the result during exposure.

Changing shapes

Most prints are made with the paper flat and level under the enlarger, so that each part of the negative is enlarged to the

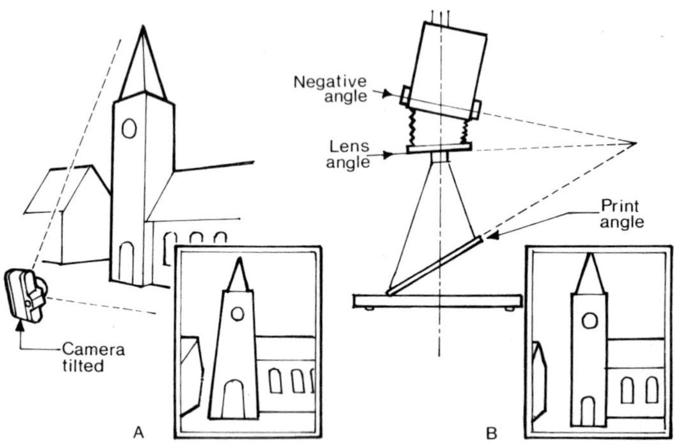

Converging verticals. A. Tilting the camera up to include the top of a subject produces an odd-looking picture. B. This can be compensated by tilting the paper. If the enlarger head can also be tilted, the whole is easily kept sharp, otherwise use the smallest lens aperture

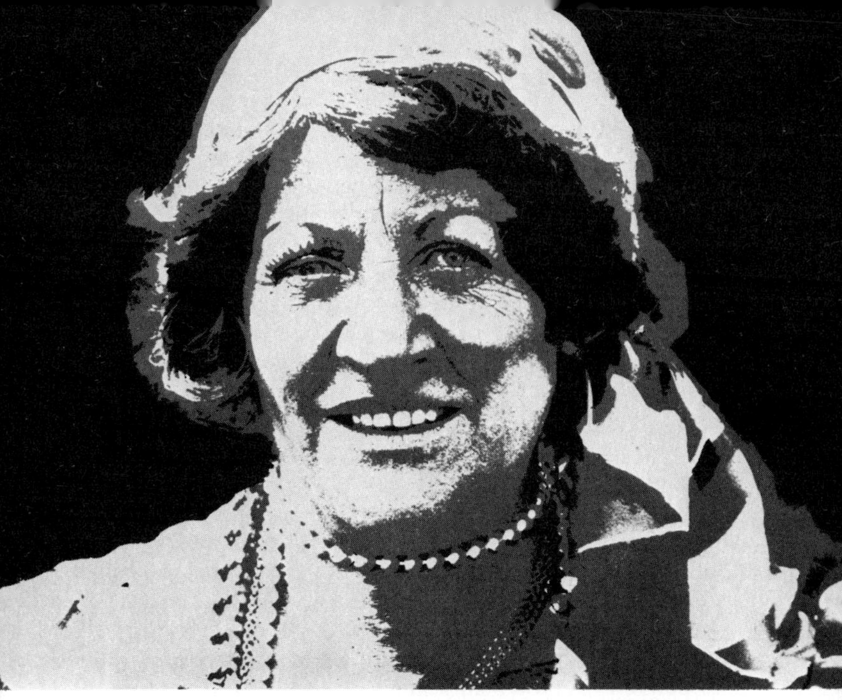

Multiple printing through lith negatives produces a posterised print with only a few tones (R. A. Hendra)

same degree. Sometimes, though, the negative calls for differential enlarging. Most frequently this affects pictures of buildings taken with the camera tilted, which uncorrected shows the building with converging sides (converging verticals). If the camera was tilted up, then the image tapers towards the top, making it look as if the building is falling backwards.

To alleviate or remove this effect, tilt the paper (on its easel) so that the bottom of the image is nearer the enlarger lens than the top. Support the easel in this position with books or pieces of wood, then focus the image in the midpoint and stop the lens down to give maximum depth of focus. It is surprising just how much tilt can be accommodated at *f*/11 or *f*/16. A sophisticated enlarger allows the negative to be tilted within the head, so that focus can be maintained even at full aperture with incredible degrees of tilt.

Tilting the paper can correct converging verticals, but not without distortion. Firstly, of course, the sides of the negative diverge 'in sympathy', but this can be overcome in trimming. Secondly, the image is elongated toward the top. This largely compensates for the compression introduced by the greater distance to the top of the scene. However, the result is to introduce some overall elongation. This is the same as the effect of using a rising front on the technical camera, or a shift lens on a 35 mm SLR.

Manipulating the process

For best image quality, the paper needs full development. In some circumstances, though, extra exposure and slightly curtailed development can produce adequate quality. This gives some freedom to play with the image during processing. It can be varied (slightly) in contrast, or darkened selectively, but the technique is no real substitute for correct exposure (including burning in) on the correct grade of material.

To darken specific areas, treat them with more concentrated developer by rubbing on undiluted concentrate. In practice, rubbing alone can work, for two reasons: it increases the temperature and it increases the agitation, both of which led to greater activity. One way to simplify the use of modified processing is to use water bath development. Once the image begins to appear in the developer, transfer the print to clean water and watch the image as it develops. Then apply developer to the areas which need extra darkening.

Toning

Monochrome prints are usually made on silver-halide paper, giving a nearly black and white image. The choice of paper and developer combinations allows a selection from cold blue-black to warm brown-black. To change the colour further, the image must be toned. In fact, toning was originally introduced as an effective method of fixing the image, so producing the sepia images of our great grandparents' time.

Toning changes the colour by replacing the silver image with another, the most common being silver sulphide or silver selenide. Sulphide toning can be a single stage operation using a thiosulphate-alum bath; or a double one, re developing the image in sodium sulphide after bleaching it with a ferricyanide-bromide solution. Two other toning processes produce subtle changes to the image colour – selenium and gold. Apart from the attractive results, these are used to give the prints even greater permanence when they are to be stored for posterity.

Replacing the silver with another metal produces more striking colour changes. Some used include: uranium, nearly orange; vanadium, yellowish; and iron, a bright Prussian blue. To give a virtually unrestricted range, colour chemistry can be used. After fixing, the image is bleached, then redeveloped in colour developer with a suitably coloured dye coupler or a mixture of dye couplers. All these processes are available in kit form, and come with detailed instructions.

Drying and glazing

Prints on resin-coated materials can be air dried. The simplest way is to lay them on absorbent paper and leave them. The best way is in a suitable designed rack with a gentle warm air circulation. The quickest way is with a hair dryer, which also gives the shiniest finish to glossy prints. It is important to keep the temperature below 95°C (200°F). Heat them up further, and the coating starts to melt and bubble, destroying the print.

Air drying traditional papers is less satisfactory. It takes a long time, and the prints usually curl up as they dry. Glossy-surfaced papers dry to a smooth matt finish, not to a gloss, so the best way to dry such papers is in close contact with a heated metal sheet. To produce a high gloss, the emulsion should be in contact with the scrupulously clean shiny metal. For unglazed prints (on any paper surface), the back of the print is placed in contact with the metal sheet.

Rotary or flatbed glazers must be spotlessly clean for glazing, but this is not quite so important if they are to be used as just dryers. To clean a new or used glazing sheet, wash it with an ammoniacal household cleaner (totally abrasive free, and without surfacing agents), followed by warm slightly soapy water. Then dust it with French chalk, and polish if off.

As an alternative to a heated glazer, prints can be glazed cold on a sheet of glass. Simply soak the print in glazing solution (or water and wetting agent), squeegee it on to a sheet of absolutely clean glass and leave to dry overnight. When it is dry, the print should drop off with a perfectly glazed surface. If it is stuck, it must be washed off and the process begun again.

Faults in black-and-white prints

Fault		Cause
Image too pale	*	Underexposed
Image too dark	*	Overexposed
Image all black or white	*	Contrast grade too high
Image grey – no real blacks	*	Overexposed and under-developed. Contrast grade too low
Small white spots or squiggles	*	Dust or hairs on negative or negative carrier glass
Fine dark lines or patches	*	Paper scratched or abraded
Wide white lines	*	Scratches on paper emulsion, special problem with resin-coated papers
Blisters	*	Process temperatures too varied. Resin-coated paper overheated in drying or mounting
Image has grey veil overall, usually uneven	*	Fogging by stray light. Unsafe safelight
Purple patches appear after a time	*	Incomplete fixing, especially of resin-coated papers

6

Making colour prints

Colour slides are great for projecting to a willing audience as nothing approaches their colour fidelity and impact. Unfortunately, however, they are not particularly handy for showing Grandma a few holiday shots, and virtually impossible to put on permanent display in the home.

The answer to these two uses, and a host of related ones, is to make paper prints from the transparencies. There are two basic ways of doing this: make negatives from the slides and prints from them; or make prints directly on reversal print materials. The best, and the most difficult, way is to make negatives and to print from them. It is possible to copy transparencies on to normal camera negative film just like copying transparencies. However, this calls for a series of trials to achieve the optimum lighting, exposure and processing. Using specially designed 'internegative' film is no less complicated, but produces better results.

Modern materials, including Cibachrome, have greatly improved direct prints from transparencies. So now the complications of internegative films can be left to the purist or at least to the custom lab. Reversal printing is relatively simple, but the processing more complicated than the latest colour-negative print processes. The results, unfortunately, are still not perfect. Making colour prints directly from slides can be disappointing, especially with really bright high-contrast pictures. The print materials have a much lower brightness range than the film, and tend to reduce highlight and shadow detail, producing a result with excessive contrast. Also, because a transparency cannot have the built-in orange mask of a colour negative, the colours may not be as true to life as in a print from a good negative.

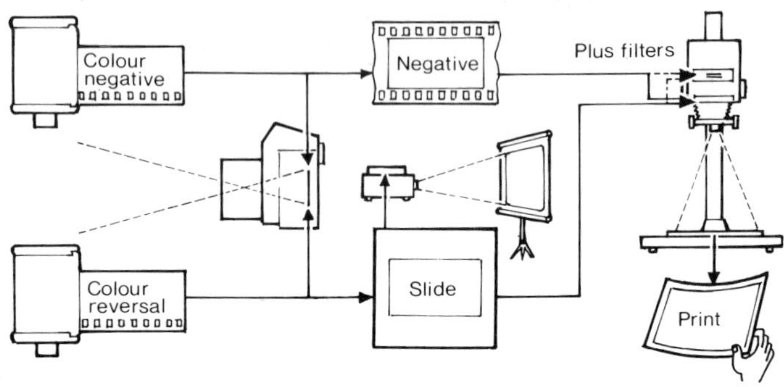

Colour prints can be made from negatives or slides

However, while most colour prints are made from negatives (the next chapter concentrates on that process) prints from slides should not be overlooked, especially as so many photographers concentrate on taking transparencies. Since reversal printing is simple to understand and most of the equipment applies equally to working from slides or from negatives, we will start with slides.

More equipment

Colour printing differs from black-and-white work in two ways. First, the enlarger light has to be altered to give exactly the correct colour, and secondly, the paper is sensitive to light of all colours.

The most economical way to change the colour is to put filters in the enlarger light path. Most recent enlargers have a drawer to hold filters, which are squares of pale tinted acetate (see page 33). It is usually possible to improvise with older enlargers and often one can lift off the lamp housing

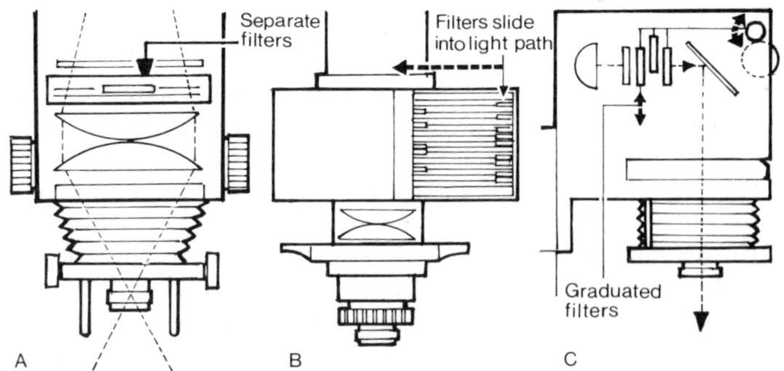

Colour printing needs coloured light. A. Filters can be placed in a drawer. B. Slide-in filters, introduced by Paterson, are an economical way of colour printing. C. Full colour heads have dial-in dichroic filters

and lay the filters on top of the condensers. Such enlargers may need to be equipped also with heat-absorbing glass to prevent heat (as infra-red radiation) reaching the film. If it is quite impossible to put filters inside the enlarger, then the answer is to use Colour Compensating (CC) gelatin filters in a simple holder below the lens. These filters are manufactured for use on camera lenses and a pack of up to three or four will not seriously degrade the print. If you intend to work this way, it is well to fit out the enlarger with a heat-absorbing glass and an ultra-violet absorbing filter (an old camera filter will do very well if it can be mounted conveniently).

The paper can be handled only in the dimmest safelighting, so it is better to learn to work entirely in the dark, and to process in a light-tight drum. The only actions that need darkness are taking the paper from the packet and putting in on the easel, switching on the enlarger, removing the paper to its processing drum and fitting the lid. The rest of the time the room lights can be on.

Chromogenic and dye destruction materials

There are two quite different transparency printing materials – chromogenic and dye destruction. Chromogenic materials use the same basic reversal principles that apply to slide films. They are processed first to a black-and-white negative, then fogged and redeveloped to form a colour image. At this stage they are totally black. To reveal the dye image, the silver is bleached and then fixed out. Until comparatively recently, this type of material tended to muddle dark blues and greens, but the most recent versions are a considerable improvement. The most widely available chromogenic reversal print materials are Kodak Ektachrome papers.

Dye destruction materials are currently available solely as Cibachrome. This material is made with the three dyes in three layers closely associated with colour sensitised silver halide layers. After exposure, it is processed to form a normal black-and-white negative. The next step is to bleach the negative back to soluble silver compounds; during this bleaching, the nearby dye particles are also bleached. Wherever there was a fully exposed and developed silver image, there is now no dye. The dye remaining in the emulsion forms a positive image corresponding in colour and tone to the original transparency and all it now needs is fixing and washing. Because the dyes are bleached, rather than formed in the emulsion, they can be more permanent compounds, so Cibachrome prints are less prone to fading.

Paper surfaces

The choice of materials for reversal printing is somewhat limited. Most types are available in glossy, lustre, and smooth matt. Glossy prints are especially effective in colour, but one of the other two surfaces may be more attractive for album prints. Most commercial colour prints are now made on lustre-surfaced papers, because that helps to mask slightly unsharp negatives and still provides good contrast.

Printing from slides

Most enlargers are designed to take negatives, which are unmounted. To reproduce from slides, the carrier must have the space to take a transparency frame, which rules out a number of carriers which locate the film with pins. However, it is possible to get a slide carrier to fit most enlargers. Clearly when working from mounted slides a glass carrier has no influence on film flatness. In fact for reversal printing a glass carrier is a nuisance. Any speck of dust shows on the print as a black mark which is very difficult to remove (unlike the white marks that dust produces on a print from a negative).

In the absence of a specially designed slide carrier, it is often possible to use half a normal glassless carrier. Tape the mount on to the carrier so that the film coincides with the cut out, then put the half carrier in the enlarger. It may be necessary to improvise some lightproofing as well.

Making contact sheets can be rather more tricky. It is difficult to arrange 20 slides on a sheet of print material working in total darkness. One solution is to tape the slides together before starting. With plastics-mounted slides, the tape is easily removed afterwards. With card mounts, how ever, the tape usually damages the mounts.

The ideal transparency

Printing from transparencies, just as from negatives, allows the density to be determined by the enlarging exposure. Thus it is possible to improve on incorrectly exposed pictures. However, it is seldom possible to get a good print from a pale overexposed transparency. In fact, as originals for prints, slightly underexposed slides are often better than correctly exposed ones. So if you intend to print from your pictures, it is worth using a bright projector so that you can standardise on quite dense slides.

Most transparency printing processes are rather high contrast, so that prints from pictures taken in bright sunlight are often disappointing. When starting transparency printing, choose a well-exposed picture without excessive contrast. Ideally, select one with people in the picture and a normal colour balance. Once you can make a good print from that, it is easy to progress to more difficult subjects.

Deciding the exposure and colour

The most direct way of deciding on the exposure is to make a test strip in the usual way. The only additional thing to remember is that increasing exposure lightens the image (unlike black-and-white printing).

To decide on the colour requirements means making a series of tests each with slightly different coloured light using a range of filter packs or colour head settings (see page 163). Transparency, enlarger light, paper batches, processing and personal preferences vary so much it is impossible to do more than suggest a starting point. For reversal papers such as Ektachrome 14 RC, a filter pack of around 40C + 20Y is a good start. Cibachrome dye destruction paper comes with a filter pack recommendation on each pack and that is the best start.

It is quite easy, but time and material consuming, to make a series of test strips or prints with different filter combinations. It is much easier to use a filter mosaic, of which there are several on the market consisting of a series of patches of filter material. Place one in contact with the printing paper, diffuse the enlarger image (with an opal screen held under the lens) and make an exposure. After processing, one of the patches should be a neutral grey and that patch corresponds with the change in filtration needed to produce a correctly coloured print. Most mosaics also include an exposure wedge, thus giving information on alterations to the time.

Perhaps the best way to start off is to make four separate exposures on a single sheet of paper. Set up the starting filter pack, and calculate the likely exposure time, which is probably a little less than that needed for a black-and-white print of the same size. Use a multiple-mask easel or an L-shaped card to restrict each of the four exposures to one quarter of the area. Make first a normal exposure of a part of the picture, then three different exposures through the mosaic, one at the same setting, one at two stops more and one at two stops less.

Process the paper and examine the result. With luck, the picture section will be near enough to be a guide to the right exposure. Thus, if it is a bit dark and a bit yellow, it needs more exposure, and less yellow filtering. Basically, with prints from transparencies, a 10 unit change (e.g. −10Y) is the smallest noticeable. If the print is definitely yellow, take out 20Y; if strongly so, remove 30Y, if it is really yellow all over, then the light is 50Y or 60Y too yellow. If there is too little yellow to remove it all, then add equivalent densities of cyan and magenta instead. For example, with a starting pack of 40C + 20Y, to 'remove' 40Y the new pack needs to be 60C + 20M.

The names of colours used in photography are a little different from the everyday meanings of the same words. At least, the way the colours appear on the prints can be confusing. 'Yellow' and 'green' are quite as expected; 'Cyan' looks sky blue; 'Blue' almost lavender or mauve, 'Magenta' pink or purple, and 'Red' orange or brown. Note, too that colours and densities vary slightly from system to system. Thus to achieve the same effect with different filters or with a colour head may need a numerically different filter pack. As long as you stick with one system, this causes little confusion.

The mosaic results can confirm the test print, or if the exposure and filtering were too far off to give reliable information can indicate the best exposure. Look first at the exposure series and choose the print in which about half the steps are easily seen. Then look at the coloured patches. One should be near enough neutral grey. Some mosaics come with a viewing card for comparing each spot with neutral grey. The mosaic instructions then explain how to alter the filters. Remember to follow the transparency instructions, not the negative ones. Most instructions have tables to make it easy to calculate the exposure as well.

Naturally, this method depends on the assumption that the transparency is one of a normal scene. That is, one with the usual range of tones, and equal representation of all colours. Such a scene integrates (averages) to a neutral mid-grey. If the subject is especially dark or light then the exposure wedge will be wrong. If there is a preponderence of one colour, then the wrong colour patch will be neutral grey. In both cases, following the mosaic exactly will alter the overall tone or colours to make the print match a normal scene. Thus, for example, a sunlit field of green corn will come out a little dark, and rather grey. A man in a white shirt standing in the field will take on a definitely pink tinge.

None but the most sophisticated methods (see page 168) can get round this problem directly. The simplest solution is to use the same exposure and filters as needed for often good slides on the same film. If the odd one is alone, the answer is to make a test print whenever the transparency is out of the ordinary. In practice, because transparencies are high contrast, transparency print materials are low contrast, so they have considerable colour and tone latitude. Thus exact exposure and filtration is less important than it is with negatives.

One accessory that helps greatly is an exposure meter and one which can be used for spot metering is especially useful. Once calibrated for, say, flesh tones the meter can be used to assess exposures on all transparencies which include people – however bizarre the lighting. Of course, the meter needs different calibrations for each box of paper, and for different skin tones. Meters that read light reflected from the paper can be a problem with Cibachrome, because its dark brown surface absorbs most of the light that reaches it.

Preparing to process prints

Before exposing the first print, the chemicals should be ready. Basically, there are two types of kit: those with several solutions or powders for each solution, and those with ready mixed chemicals. The more complicated kits usually have to be made up all at once. Each constituent is added in the specified order and the solution finally made up to the total volume. Naturally, this requires a set of suitable bottles to store all the solutions, which should be dark and airtight. Collapsible bottles are an attractive proposition since all the air can be squeezed out to help reduce oxidation. However, concertina bottles are rather a problem. Once dirty, they are almost impossible to clean.

Filter pack variations in printing from transparencies

To change the colour of the print the enlarger light is changed in colour. each of the three subractive primary colours – cyan, magenta and yellow – adds it own colour *and* reduces that of its complement, red, green and blue respectively. Mixtures of filters have intermediate effects.

To make a print less	*or more*	*add*	*or subtract*
Red	Cyan	Cyan	Magenta + Yellow
Green	Magenta	Magenta	Cyan + Yellow
Blue	Yellow	Yellow	Cyan + Magenta
Cyan	Red	Magenta + Yellow	Cyan
Magenta	Green	Cyan + Yellow	Magenta
Yellow	Blue	Cyan + Magenta	Yellow

If the unwanted colour is very strong, subtract 50 or 60; moderate, 30 or 40; slight, 20; and barely noticeable, 10. Remember, too, that the cast may not be exactly one colour.

Adding or subtracting filters changes the exposure time as well as the colour. Use a calculator disc or multiply the exposure time by the required factor for each filter added, or divide it for filters removed. All yellow filters have a factor of 1.1× and a CP8OR a factor of 3.4. For cyan and magenta filters, the factors are:

05C	1.1	05M	1.2
10C	1.2	10M	1.3
20C	1.3	20M	1.5
30C	1.4	30M	1.7
40C	1.5	40M	1.9
50C	1.6	50M	2.1

Filter combinations with all three colours are unecessary. They absorb extra light. For example, a filter pack of 20C, 60M, 80Y can be reduced to 40M, 60Y without changing the colour. The change more than halves the exposure time needed at the same aperture and magnification.

The dilute-and-use kits have a major advantage. You can prepare just the right volume of working strength solution for each session. The unused concentrates keep much longer than do working strength chemicals.

In addition to bulk containers for working strength solutions, it is well worth using a set of calibrated beakers or jars, one for each step in the process. Each holds exactly the right amount of solution for processing one print. Thus, the solutions can be measured out quickly and conveniently with no chance of cross contamination. They can be placed ready in the temperature control system before exposing each sheet of paper and loading it into the drum.

One of the most important steps in colour processing is washing and drying the print drum. The whole drum must be clean and dry to process prints reasonably. Even a trace of fixer can totally upset the developer balance. This is especially obvious with Cibachrome and when printing from negatives. Thus, the drum needs to be rinsed thoroughly with clean water after each print is taken out, drained and dried thoroughly with a clean cloth. Be especially thorough with the light-trapped lid. Water or chemicals trapped there can drip down on to the print and spoil it before processing starts.

Processing colour paper

The best way to process colour prints is in a light-tight drum. After exposure, the print is loaded into the drum. Then, working in the light, the chemicals are poured in and out in turn. Most kits call for total discard of used solutions, and the small volumes needed make this economical. Thus, each print is treated with fresh chemicals. A few systems have simple replenishment routines, which can extend to the life of the solutions, but cannot offer quite such consistent processing.

The volume of chemical needed is controlled by two factors. First, the amount needed to be sure of even develop-

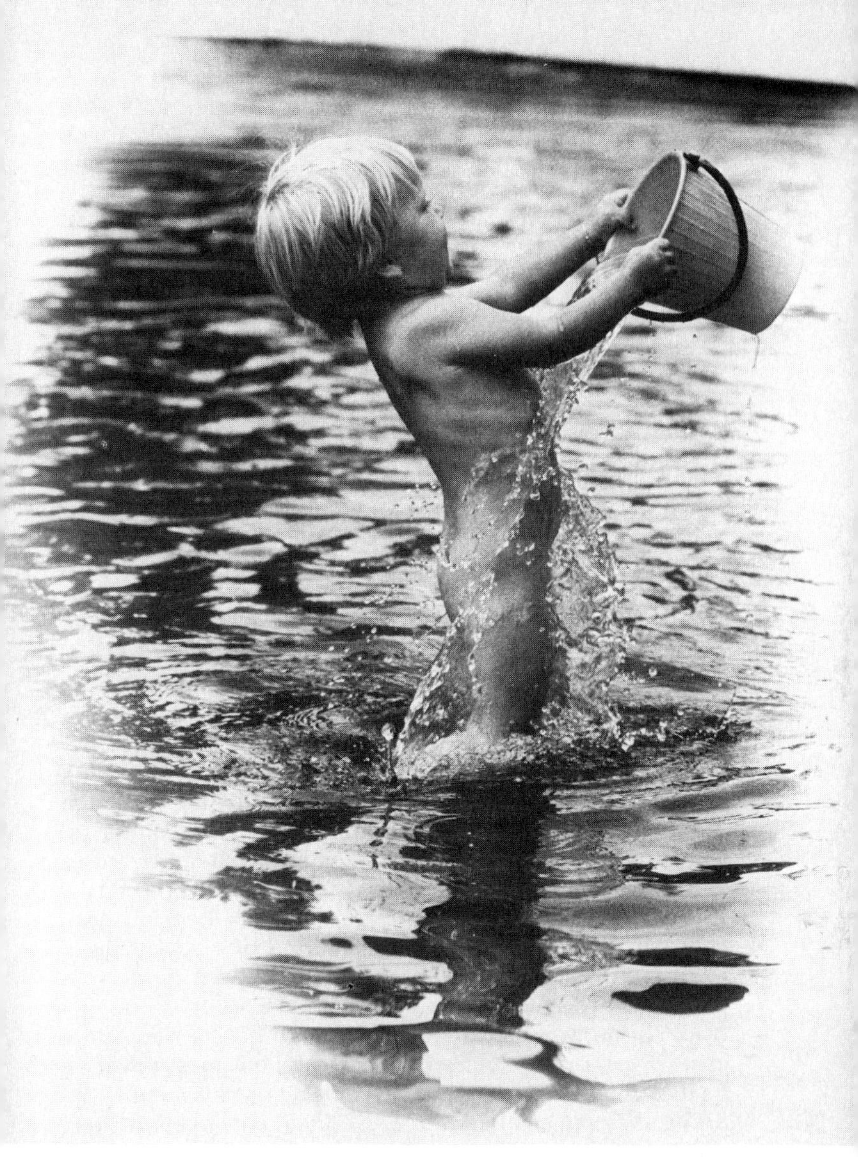

Shading the edges white while printing produces a vignette, concentrating attention on the subject (J. Easter)

ment in the drum. This is usually about 50–90 ml for 25 × 20 cm (10 × 8 in) size drum and 120–150 ml for one which processes 40 × 30 cm (16 × 12 in) prints. To use less than the stated volume is to court uneven development, even with a partly loaded drum. Secondly, the volume of solution must contain enough chemical activity to accomplish the processing in the time available.

Thus, there are instructions from both the drum and the chemical manufacturer. Always use the larger of the two quantities. It is always possible to re-use solutions if they have processed far less than their capacity. However, with or without replenishment, part-used solutions usually call for longer process times, so consult the marker's instructions.

Consistently maintaining temperature, concentration, agitation and time is essential for good colour processing – as important as it is for good transparency processing. Thus, it is well worth considering a thermostatically controlled motorised process drum.

About the least sensitive process of all is Cibachrome, which produces surprisingly good prints with quite careless processing. However, it produces even better prints when treated carefully.

One particular caution: colour chemicals are particularly sensitive to contamination. The smallest back contamination (bleach in the developer, for example) will completely ruin the process, resulting in low contrast, varying colour balance, and uneven density. Always use separate measures and containers for separate solutions. Many workers take fixed prints out of the process drum and wash them in a dish. However, washing in the drum has the major advantage of ensuring that the drum, with its lid and print holders, is thoroughly washed at the same time.

All currently available colour materials have a waterproof base. Thus, prints can be dried quickly, but must never be heated above 95°C (205°F). When making small numbers of prints, they can be dried with a hair dryer. For larger numbers a suitable dryer is better. It is essential to dry test prints before deciding on any filter or exposure changes that might be needed.

Colour-print drums

All print drums work on the same principle. The paper is curled round the inside, emulsion surface innermost. Larger drums can take two or more prints. The prints are separated by rods and clips. Sysems vary, but they all seem to work equally well. In some drums the print is held between two ridges to leave a trough at one side. When the solution is poured in, it runs into this area, not touching the paper. When the drum is rolled back and forward on a table, or better on a motorised base, the small volume of processing solution is washed constantly across the print surface. In some designs, the solution is retained in the end cap until the drum is rotated. Either way, the effect is the same. The timing starts from the instant the drum begins to roll. Before that, the print is out of the chemical. The timing ends when all the solution has been poured off. Thus, you should start pouring out about 15 seconds before the end of the required time.

Naturally, the way the drum is rolled determines the agitation, and thus the rate and evenness of processing. The drums which introduce some form of end-to-end flow are less likely to produce uneven development, but most work perfectly well. Rolling a drum up and down is rather a wearing occupation so a motor base is well worth considering. Each type of drum has its own motor while some drums work with other motors. Once again, there is little to choose between the many on offer.

Temperature control

The simplest way to achieve any exactly constant processing temperature is to work at a suitable room temperature, then the household heating (or cooling) systems can keep it constant. However, not all heating systems are capable of achieving or maintaining the temperatures exactly. In any case, many colour processes need to work at 24°C (75°F) and higher, which is uncomfortable.

If the room temperature differs from that required, then a water bath is the best way to get the process temperature correct. Some have heaters and thermostats which keep the water and anything standing in it at a constant temperature with little attention. Instead of one of the photographic types, it is quite easy to use an aquarium heater to maintain temperature in a suitably sized dish. In either case, calibrate the control against an accurate thermometer, and mark the processing temperatures clearly on the dial. The crudest system is to run a mixture of hot and cold water into a bowl, maintaining the necessary temperature by turning the taps on and off. This system is a nuisance, wastes water and tends to be messy, but it works perfectly well.

Most drum process routines are calculated on the basis that the drum will cool a little during the processing. It is normal to preheat the drum with water above the process temperature, thus making up for the heat loss. Use the recommended volume of preheat water. Too little can reduce the heating effect, too much can wash the print away from its perch, or wash multiple prints on top of one another. Some systems use the preheat to raise the temperature enough to obviate the need for a water bath. However, it is much better to keep the drum temperature constant throughout the process time. This is done by partly submerging it in (or floating it on) a water wath. The most convenient systems incorporate a motor to give optimum agitation. A processor of this sort is a worthwhile investment for anyone who wants to make more than a few prints.

However, the most important feature of any colour-processing routine is its consistency. It is not particularly important that the temperature drops exactly two degrees or any other amount. It is essential, though, that it drops by just the same amount every time. The process times, exposure and filtration can vary when changing from one drum to another (say a small one to a large one). Therefore avoid the temptation of using one piece of equipment for the test prints and another for the final enlargement.

Reducing chemical consumption

Small-scale processing depends for its uniformity on fresh solutions discarded after each print, which is fine when the drum needs just the right volume, and all the potential activity is used up. However, when using a large drum, or when making a few tests, the discarded chemicals may still be capable of processing more prints. One way round this problem is to use larger than recommended volumes, and re-use each solution three or four times. This, though, necessitates an increase in process time for each re-use. The material used in working out a completely consistent process may well exceed any potential savings in chemicals.

Some chemistry supliers suggest replenishment routines. The used solutions are saved, and returned to satisfactory state of activity by the addition of a small quantity of fresh chemical, often at a different dilution. This system has the advantage of offering good economy while using comparatively concentrated solutions and thus short process times. The disadvantage is that, however well planned the routine, the developer activity will change slightly from print to print. This is borne out by the suggestion that replenishment will work for about five prints. Beyond this, the dilution is too uncertain, and contaminants may have built up.

Thus, small scale replenishment is not equivalent to the systems used for commercial processing, where the processor can be run for months without a break. Each solution is kept exactly correct by the measured addition of replenisher.

One way of improving consistency with or without chemical economiser routines is to develop virtually to finality each time. In practice, all processes except the first development in reversal printing, or the colour development in negative/positive printing, go to completion. To take the first step to completion as well, increase the time by 50%. Of course, the enlarging exposure and filtration may need to be a little different. However, most papers respond well to this technique although some produce prints with excessive contrast.

Reversal paper processing

The widely available Kodak Ektachrome papers, such as Ektachrome 14RC, the compatible Agfachrome-R and similar materials, are processed in Ektachrome R14-3 chemistry. This is a 'three-bath' process, which actually has eight steps. There are a number of substitute processes for this type of paper.

Chromogenic print processing is in essence the same as transparency film processing. Just as with films, some processes call for reversal exposure; others accomplish the same result with chemical reversal. The results are equally acceptable. Once again, the first developer time is the most critical. In practice all other processes go to finality.

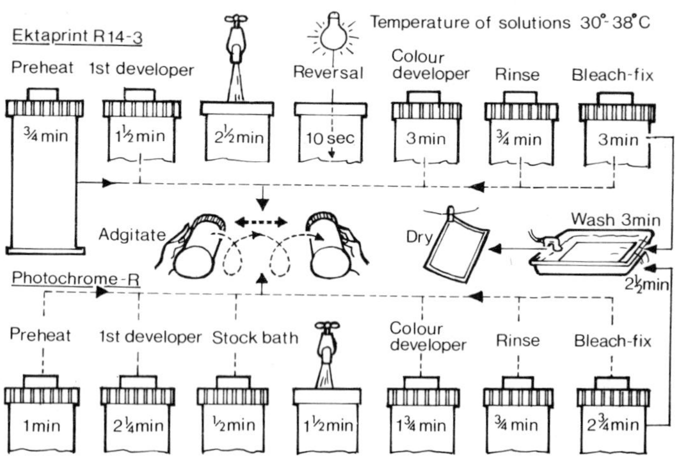

Processing a Chromogenic reversal print

After suitable first development time, the print is washed and removed from the drum and exposed fully to light. A 100 watt lamp about 35 cm away for 10 seconds or so is ideal and this is best done with the print in a dish of wash water.

During this wash, wipe out the print drum, ready to put the print back in it. Preheat the drum again, and pour in the colour developer; then rinse, bleach-fix and wash.

The major irritation in this process is the reversal exposure, which adds quite considerably to the time – that is why kits offering chemical reversal are a big advantage. The process time is around 12–13 minutes; usually with just three 'active' solutions and a number of washes. Commercial scale processes are altogether more complicated, needing more solutions and extra accuracy in control.

Reversal paper routines

Most Ektachrome print kits operate at 30–38°C (100°F). In practice, most can accept some variation in temperature and time. The main variation in small-scale processing is the requirement for a reversal exposure with some processes, but not with others. These are the times for Ektaprint R14-3 and Photochrome–R as typical examples:

	Ektaprint R14-3 *38°C*	*Photochrome-R* *35°C*
Preheat drum	¾ min	1 min
First developer	1½ min	2¼ min
Stock bath	–	½ min
Wash	2½ min	1½ min
reversal exposure	10 sec	–
Colour developer	3 min	1¾ min
Rinse	¾ min	¾ min
Bleach-fix	3 min	2¾ min
Wash	3 min	2½ min

Dry in the usual way.

As with all photographic processes, instructions can change from week to week. Thus, always check the instructions packed with *each* kit and make the recommended changes. This is one good reason for following the instructions as closely as possible. If you devise a very non-standard routine, unexpected changes in the process chemistry can cause considerable problems.

Cibachrome processing

Cibachrome material is coated with light-sensitive emulsion including three dye layers. So unlike normal chromogenic materials it is a dark colour – in fact brown, and it goes blacker when it is processed. The emulsion is coated either onto a white acetate base or onto resin-coated paper. The acetate base material which introduced simple slide printing to the home processor was especially noted for its very high gloss – achieved without any special processing techniques. The choice of surface is still limited, but adequate for most purposes.

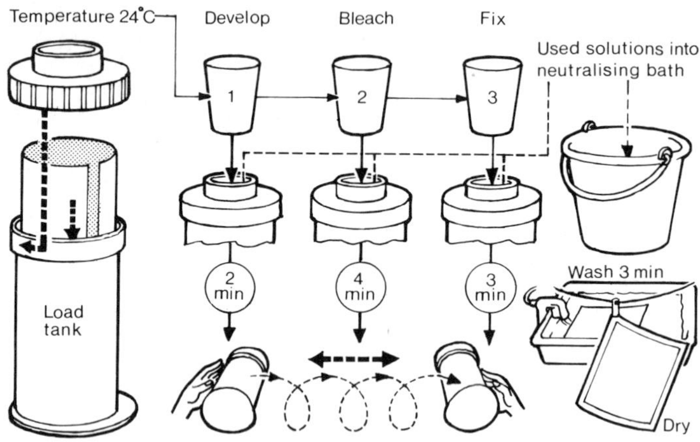

Processing a Cibachrome print

Cibachrome is best processed in a print drum with the usual continuous agitation by rolling or on a motor base. The first solution is basically a black-and-white developer. As with reversal paper processing the degree of development determines the print density – the more development, the lighter the print. Ilford supply a specially formulated developer, which is certainly the best choice for starting Cibachrome printing, and for occasional work. However, many photographers use ordinary monochrome developers to great success. Of course, changing the developer usually requires a change in development time, and probably in exposure and filters as well.

The bleach is the secret of Cibachrome. It is highly acidic solution, which must react exactly equally with each of the three dye layers in direct proportion to the silver image generated by the first developer. It is not an easy solution to replace, but a few chemical suppliers offer substitutes. The bleach must be used exactly according to the instructions. In particular, the whole powder must be mixed at once. This is quite simply because the chemicals are not mixed together in their package, and using part of the powder produces a liquid with the wrong proportions of each constituent. Further, the bleach includes a strong concentration of sulphamic acid (producing a pH of 0.3) and must be handled with extreme caution. The bleach should be neutralised before it is discarded. Neutralising powder (or tablets) is supplied with Cibachrome kits. Mixing discarded solutions without neutralising leads to a hearty chemical reaction – much foaming and the release of a pungent gas. If this happens inadvertently, dilute the mixture with water, and add neutraliser.

Fixing and washing Cibachrome is quite straightforward. The prints do not need stabilising, as their azo dyes are relatively stable – much more so than the chromogenic dyes in normal colour prints – from slides or negatives.

The Cibachrome routine

The recommended process temperature is 24°C (75°F), but any temperature between 20°C and 28°C can be used with suitable alteration to the times. In practice, temperature control is less important with Cibachrome than with other processes. Most workers achieve excellent prints time after time, as long as they are consistent in maintaining temperature.

Cibachrome process times (minutes)

	20°C	*24°C*	*28°C*
Developer	1½	2	2½
Bleach	3½	4	4½
Fix	2½	3	3½
Wash	3	3	3

Drying colour prints

Virtually all colour prints are now on resin-coated paper and they can be air-dried in a few minutes. The best way is in a specially made dryer. However, any suitable rack with a supply of warm air works well. Without a rack, a hair dryer is quite efficient. Be careful, though, to avoid overheating any part of the print. Temperatures above about 95°C can make the surface start to bubble.

High-speed drying is usually essential when colour printing. The materials tend to change colour quite markedly when wet. For example, Cibachrome takes on a chocolate-brown colour in the shadows, and generally looks far too red. Ektachrome papers, on the other hand, look rather cold and blue when wet. Thus, it is quite impossible to determine the colour balance until the paper is absolutely dry.

Changing paper batch

Once the optimum exposure and filtration are decided, then all good transparencies on the same film type should print with the same settings. Changes are needed only when the print needs to differ from the slide but that is usually obvious. In practice, different film types or film processed in different laboratories usually need slight changes to the filtration to produce the best prints. This, at first, calls for experiment. Soon, though, experience builds up a series of 'automatic' corrections. To keep these to a minimum, it is well worth standardising a few films, and sticking to the same processing routine, or the same laboratory.

Papers, though, vary from batch to batch. They can change in speed, and in colour balance. To help you get round this problem, each packet is labelled with exposure information. Cibachrome comes with a filter pack suggestion, the others with a recommendation for change from a hypothetical starting point.

A Cibachrome pack may, for example, suggest that for Kodachrome it needs 40Y, 05M and 00C. For the first test print, that is the place to start. However, you may find that your enlarger needs 50Y, 00M and 05C to produce the best print. If so, then use that combination. The next packet may call for 55Y, 10M, 00C as a basic filter pack. Modify that in the light of experience. 'Subtract' the original paper recommendation for your actual filtration.

50Y	00M	05C
40Y	05M	00C
+10Y	−05M	+05C

Now add this to the new basic recommendation

55Y	10M	00C
+10Y	−05M	+05C
65Y	05M	05C

As the new pack has all three colours, it is worth while to rationalise it by removing 05 from each to leave 60Y as the total filtration needed.

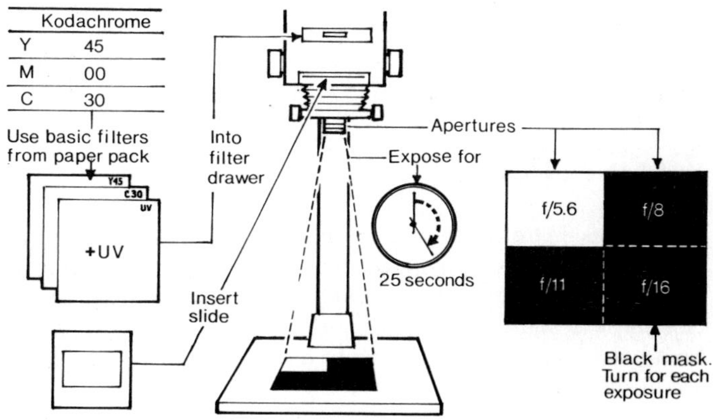

Making an exposure test for Cibachrome printing

The other materials suggest changes, but the effect is the same. For example: a packet marked 00C, 10M, 20Y may print well with 00C, 20M, 40Y. The next packet may be labelled 10C, 00M, 10Y. So make the change as in the Cibachrome example. Work out the basic filter pack by subtracting the correction from the filter pack you use

00C	20M	40Y
−00C	10M	20Y
00C	10M	20Y

Keep a note of that, then simply add the new corrections to it. Corrections can be negative or positive. The sum is usually straightforward, but it can result in a negative number. For example, a basic filter pack of −20C, 00M, 40Y is quite possible. Add that to 00C, 30M, 10Y, and the answer is −20C, 30M, 50Y. To achieve this, add 20 to each colour to achieve 00C, 50M, 70Y.

If the paper gives an exposure factor, the change in exposure time takes account of the filter changes. Divide the original time by the factor for the previous batch and multiply it by the new factor to give the optimum time for the first test print on the new paper.

One point, manufacturers vary in the order in which they present filter data. Kodak present the figures Cyan, Magenta, Yellow; while most European based companies reverse the order: Yellow, Magenta, Cyan. This is a trap for the unwary.

Kodak Ektaflex prints

The Kodak Ektraflex PCT Colour printmaking system, introduced in 1981, uses the image-transfer technology from their instant-picture system to simplify colour processing dramatically. The system uses a light-sensitive film, from which the image is transferred onto a white backing paper 'PCT' stands for Photo Colour Transfer.

Two film types are announced: PCT reversal film, and PCT negative film, for negatives and transparencies repectively.

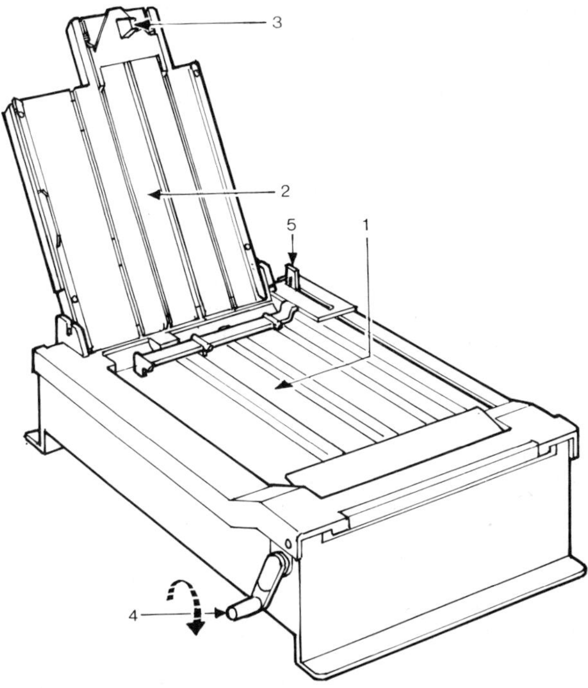

The Kodak 'Ektaflex' printmaker, Model 8 is a convenient, table top processor that makes possible one-solution printmaking from either negatives or transparencies. The printmaker produces a film/paper 'sandwich' that yields a colour print in 6–15 minutes, depending on room temperature.

The reversal material is exposed (in total darkness) just as is any other material as outlined in this chapter. Ektaflex PCT negative film is exposed to a correctly filtered colour negative just as a chromogenic colour paper – as described in the next chapter. In either case, exposure and filtration have the expected effects on the final picture. There is one major difference, though: the transparency or negative must go upside-down in the enlarger carrier, because the final image is reversed in the transfer process.

The film is processed for 20 seconds in activator solution, then rolled into intimate contact with a sheet of Ektaflex PCT paper. The sandwich is opaque, so that room lights can then be turned on. After 6–15 minutes (depending on the room temperature, the two are peeled apart to reveal the colour image transferred to the paper. The print does not need wasing; it dries in two or three minutes.

While it is possible to work in a dish of activator (wearing rubber gloves), to squeegee the film, and then roll it into contact with a sheet of paper, the process is considerably simplified with a Kodak Ektaflex printmaker. Model 8 works for 13 × 17 cm (5 × 7 in) and 20 × 25 cm (8 × 10 in) prints to make a print, first put a piece of Ektaflex paper on top fo the unit. Slide it under the lip to touch the roller. Then, in the dark, expose a piece of film in the normal way. Place the film, image side uppermost on the ramp, and slide it into the activator with the handle. After 20 seconds, push the film into the roller with the handle at the back, and turn the handle to roll the paper and film together; 'laminate' them in Kodak terminology. After a suitable time, peel the print from the film.

The Kodak Ektaflex Printmaker model 8 takes 3 US quarts (about 3 litres) of activator, which is sufficient for at least 75 20 × 25 cm (8 × 10 in) prints. After each printing session, empty the activator back into its container and seal it. This way, it lasts for more than 12 months. Left in the printmaker, it begins to loose activity within three days.

The negative and reversal film is sold in 8 × 10 and 5 × 7 sizes. The equivalent paper is a little larger to allow a margin of error in lamination. The receiving paper comes in two surfaces: F, smooth glossy; and N, smooth semi mat. Either can be used with reversal or negative film.

This entirely new process has yet to be thoroughly investigated, but the manufacturers claim print quality equivalent to normal chromogenic print making systems. Undoubtedly, Kodak Ektaflex PCT prints are easier to process than any other. They offer an economical system for the occasional user; who normally achieves less than optimum chemical usage. Because no processing variations can mar consistency

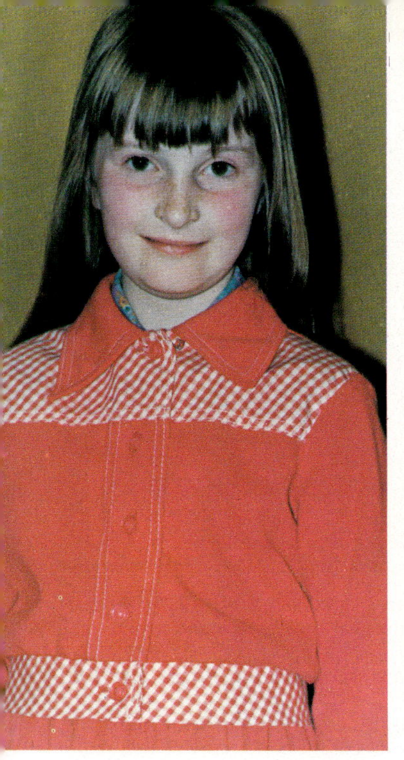

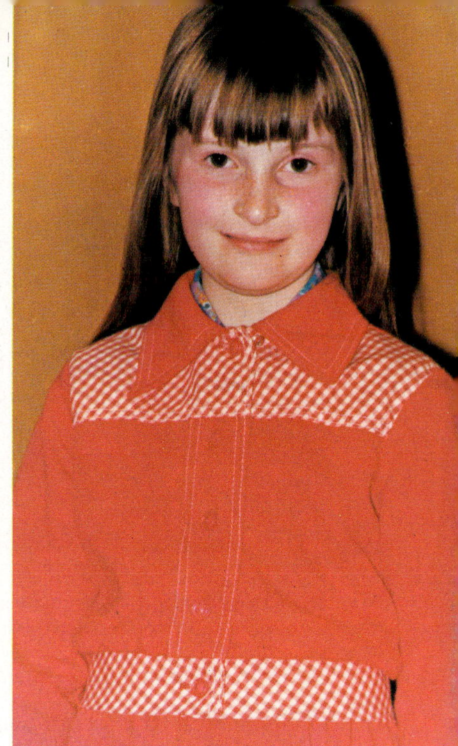

Following an integrated negative-colour reading, whether automatically or manually, produces an off-colour print (left) when the subject is strongly coloured. In this case the light had to be made 30CC less red to produce an acceptable colour balance (right)

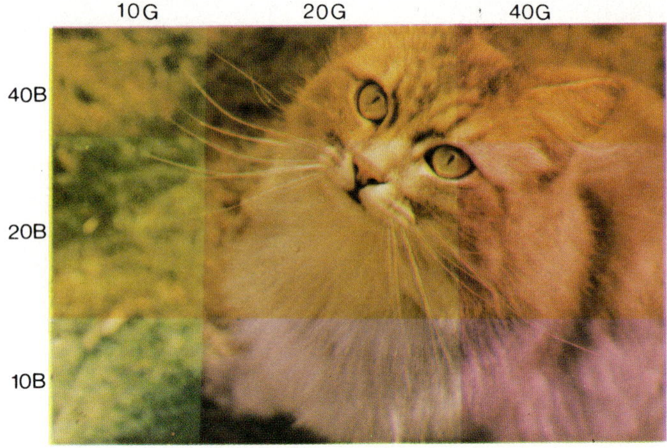

Top: Tricolour test made with an overall exposure of 10 seconds through a red filter and various times through blue and green

Below: A typical mosaic filter test with neutral block circled

Opposite: Contact print of a number of different colour negatives. All these can be printed with correct colour balance by changing the colour of the enlarger light, or the times through tricolour filters

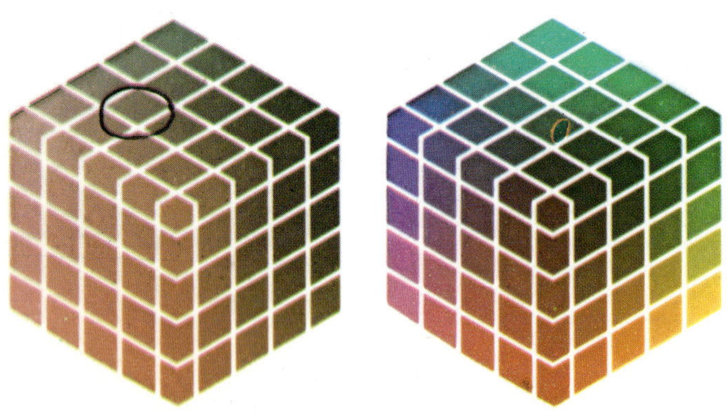

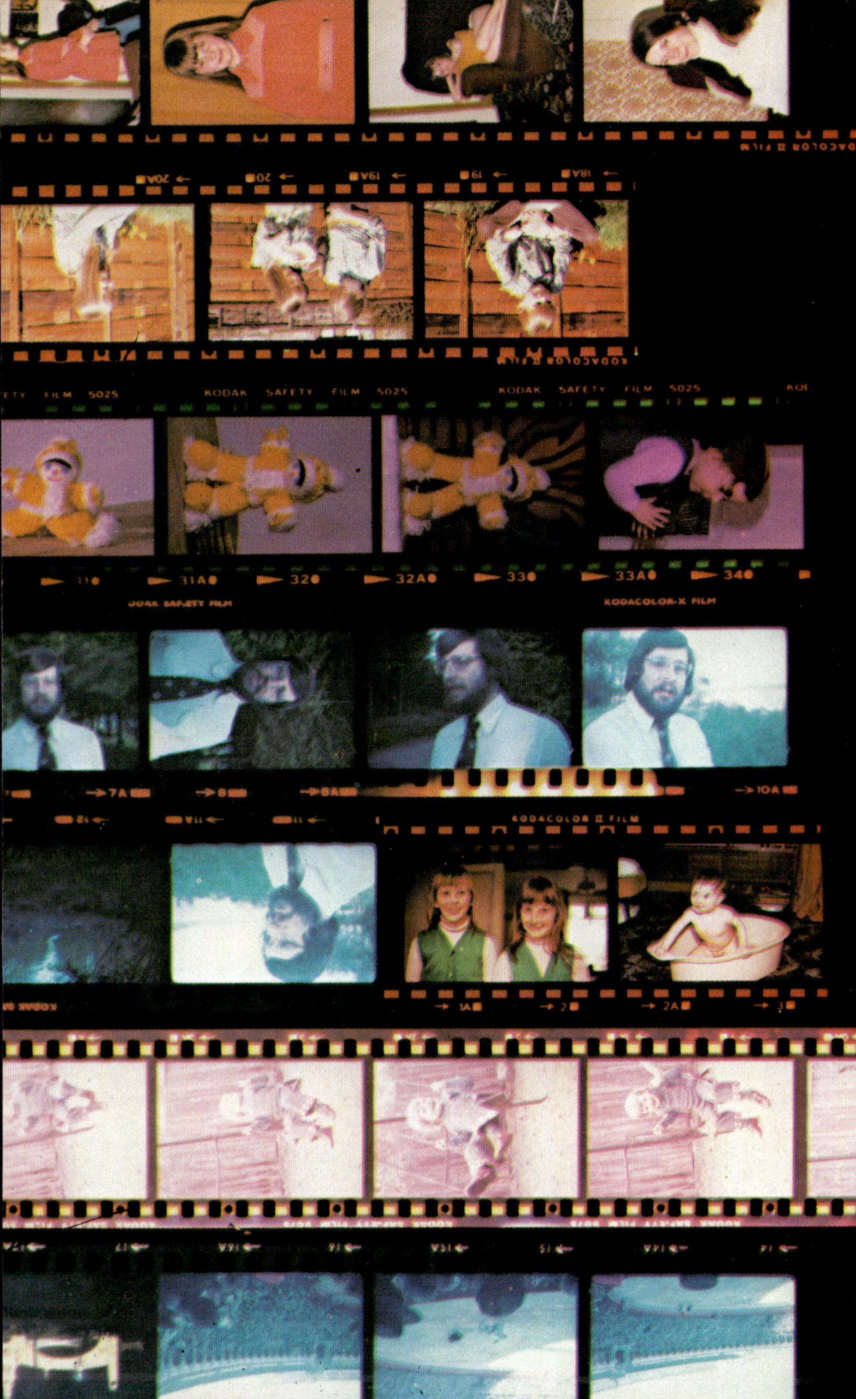

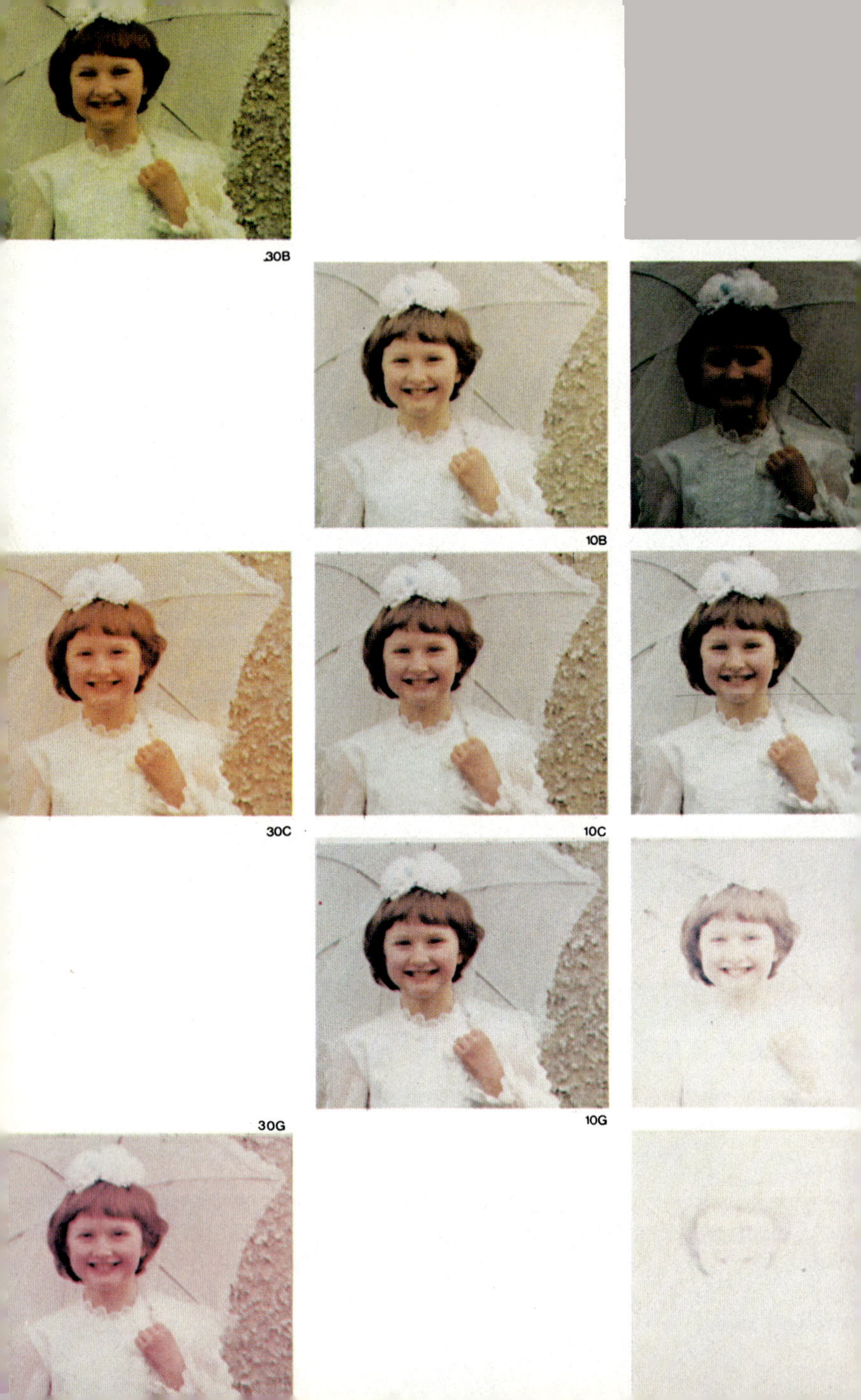
30B
10B
30C
10C
30G
10G

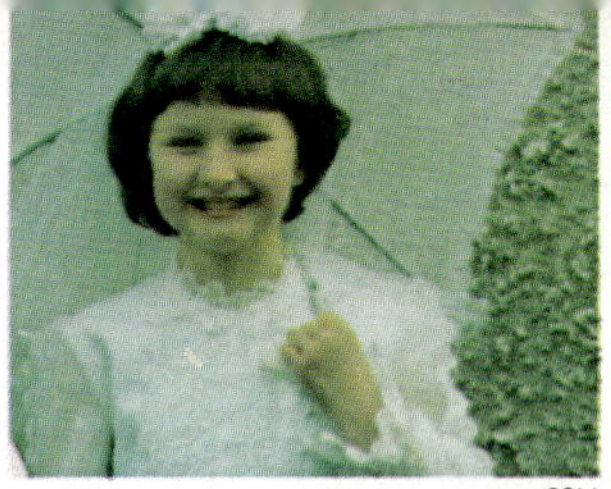

30M

Exposure and filter variation in negative printing. The pale tints need 10CC units to bring them to neutral colour balance though all are probably acceptable on their own. The stronger colours need 30CC units. The number on each print indicates the filter to be subtracted from the filter pack (or dial setting) to correct the colour balance.
When printing from transparencies the filters must be added to the printing light. As they have less effect, the stronger colours would call for a change of around 45CC units

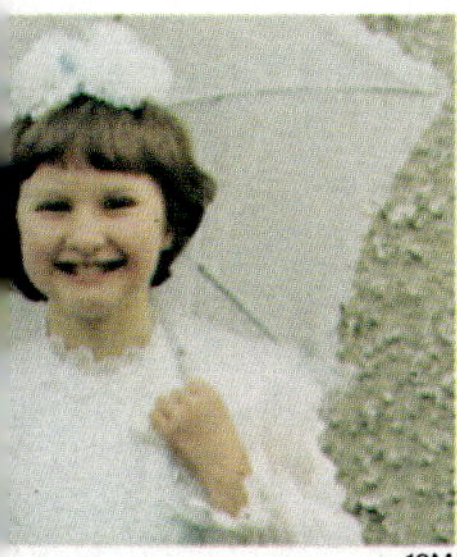

10M

10R

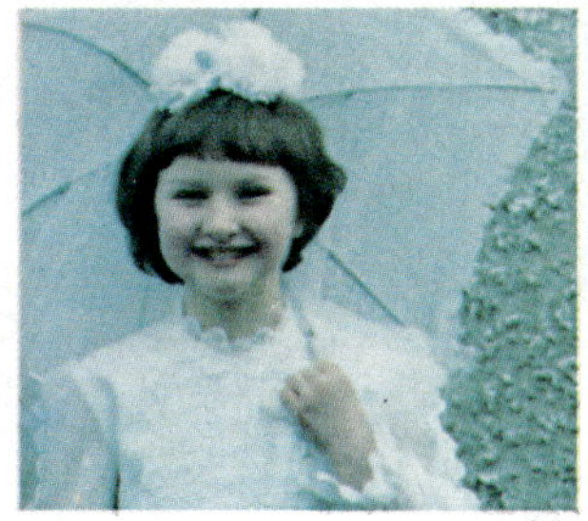

30R

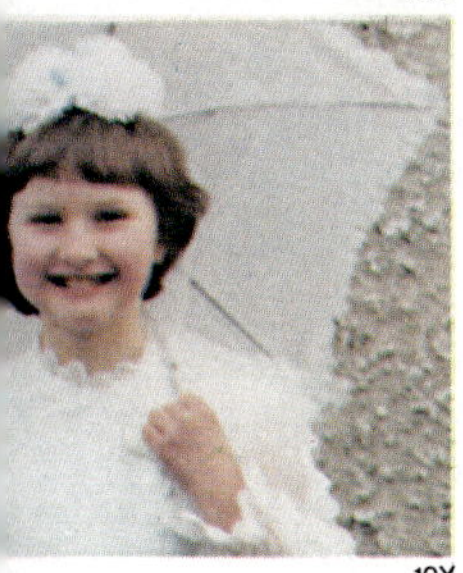

10Y

30Y

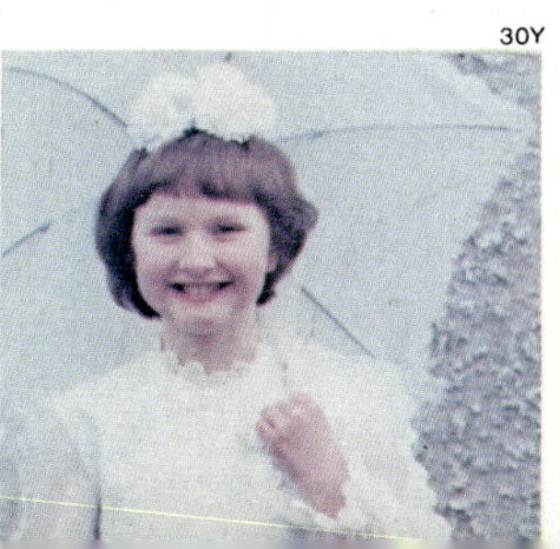

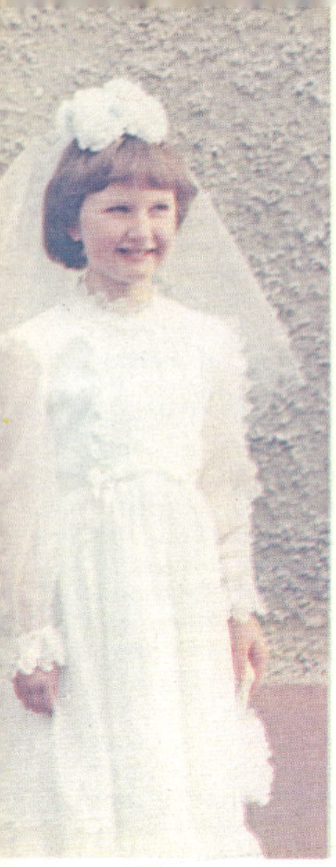

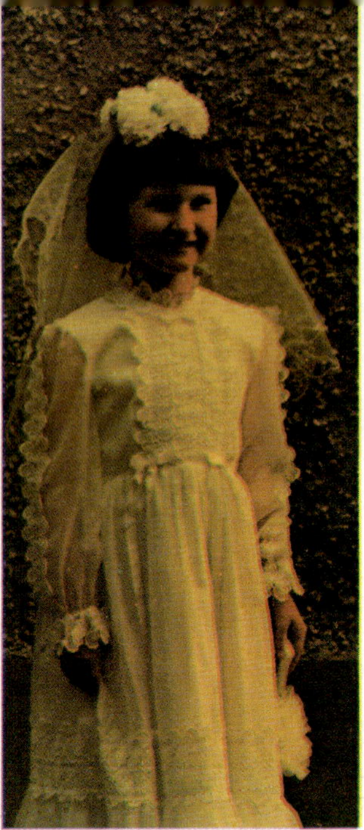

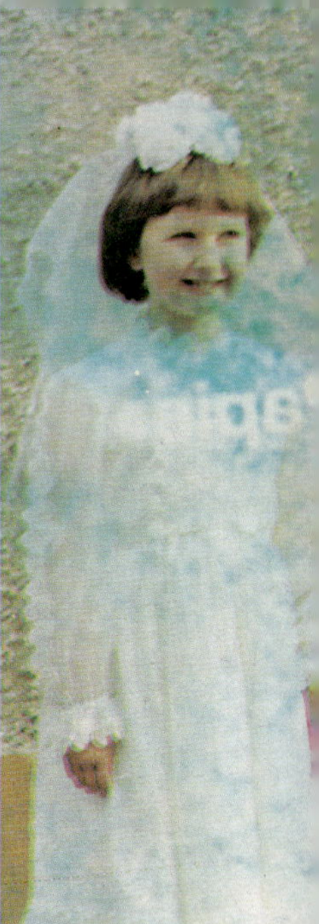

Underdeveloping (left) produces pictures with pale blue highlights. Fresh developer (centre) shows the amount of filter and exposure 'correction' that have been made to try to compensate for stale developer. Fogging through the yellow jacket is quite distinctive (right). Store paper in its black plastic envelope, not just the outer wrapper

Opposite: Some subjects allow colour changes to provide variations. CC30B added or subtracted from the correct filter pack provides three colour variatons here

Next page: Printing on colour paper allows brightening of monochrome pictures. Magenta subject detail obtained by exposing colour paper to the black-and-white negative through a Wratten 99 filter (green). The additional colour in the image comes from a second exposure, made without the negative, through a red Wratten 25 filter. This added cyan to the entire print (Alison Trapmore)

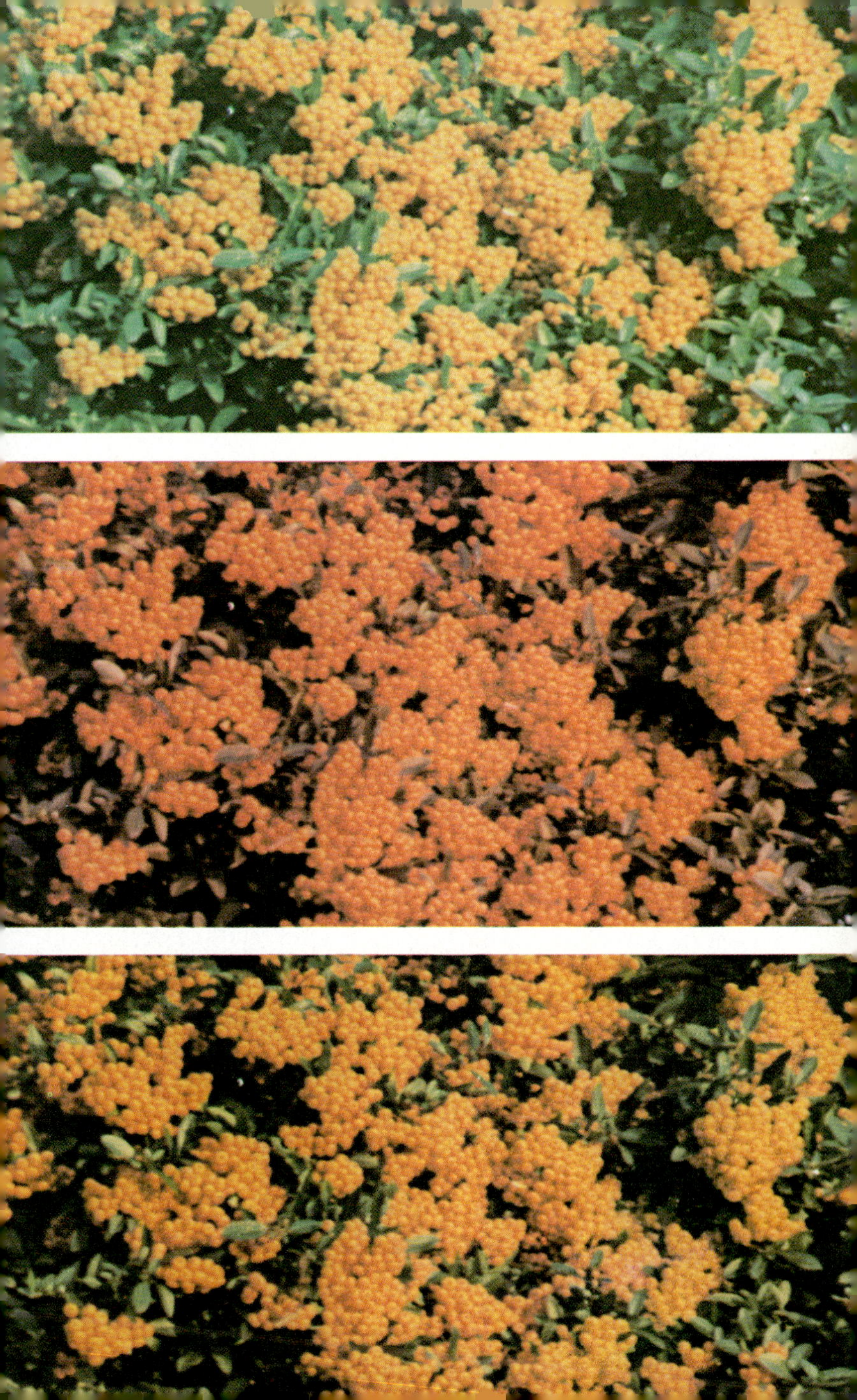

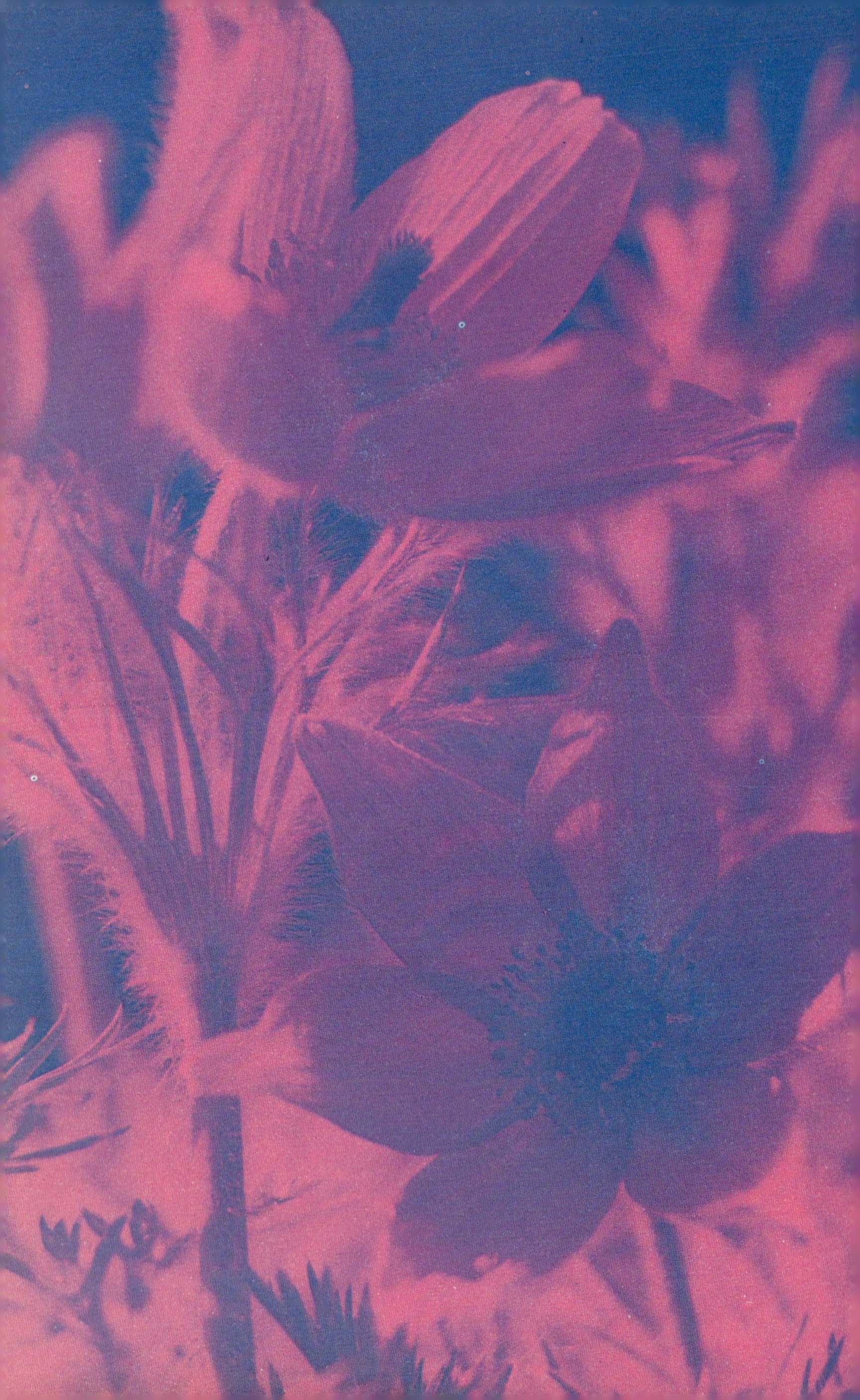

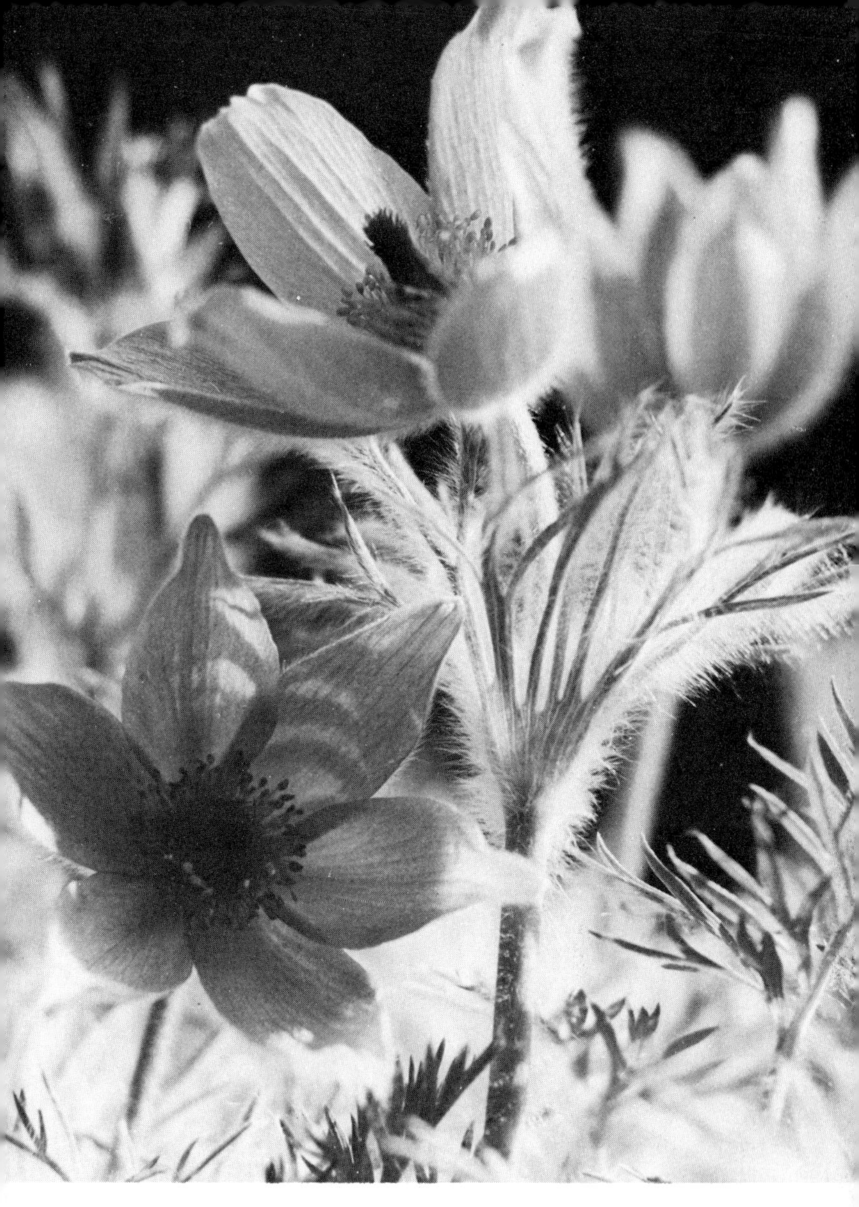

A black-and-white print from the same negative (Alison Trapmore)

of results, this is an ideal system for starting colour printing, expecially from negatives. The print maker has luminous numbers to make dark operation easy.

Once the correct exposure and filtration is found, the printmaker can be used to activate film about twice a minute. Offering a much faster throughput than most home processing systems.

7

Printing from colour negatives

While printing from slides may appear easier, printing from colour negatives has the advantage that the film is intended for print making. Thus, negatives are much lower contrast than are transparencies and incorporate colour-correcting dyes. That is why they are orange or brick red. The process, too, is simpler and quicker. So it is no problem to produce really good quality colour prints from negatives.

The basic equipment needed to print from colour negatives is the same as that needed for making prints from slides. The enlarger light has to be coloured with a filter pack or colour head, and the best way to process the prints is in a light-tight drum or a more sophisticated processor. A colour mosaic or analyser is a great help in achieving a good starting point for tests, but neither can really offer perfect prints first time every time.

There are two different ways to expose colour paper called 'white light' and 'tricolour'. With white-light printing, the paper is given a single exposure. The colour of the 'white' enlarger light is modified by the interposition of coloured material which *subtracts* the required amount of coloured light to give the correct colour in the print. Subtractive filters are coloured cyan, magenta, or yellow to remove red, green or blue light respectively. The colour balance is determined by the density of each colour in the light path, so the filters are needed as wedges (in a colour head) or in a set of varying densities.

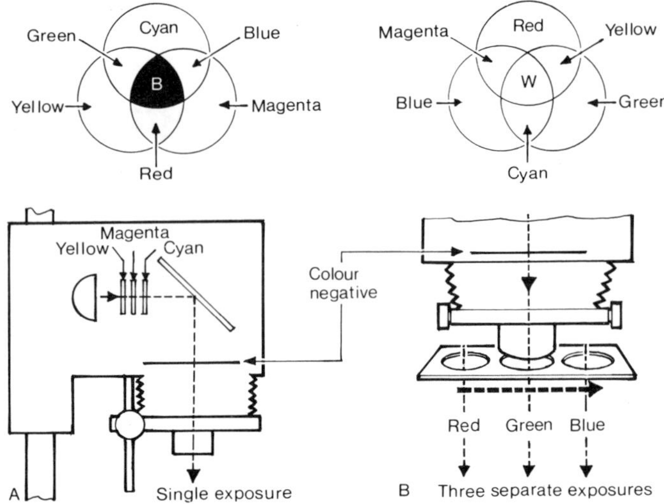

The two colour printing methods. A. White light printing uses a coloured light source to produce the correct colour balance in a simple exposure. B. Tricolour printing uses three separately timed exposures through three filters to produce a colour print

For tricolour printing, the paper is given three successive exposures through red, green, and blue filters in turn. The colour balance is determined by the ratio of the three exposures. The filter density is always the same and each filter restricts the light to its own colour. The normal way to control colour balance is by varying the time given through each filter. Since the three exposures are made sequentially and add up to the total colour, this process is sometimes called 'additive' printing.

Printing papers

Colour print papers all work chromogenically, producing coloured dyes at the same time as a silver image. The silver is then bleached and fixed out. Unlike monochrome papers, there is little choice of contrast grade. Some materials were in two grades – normal and soft. The range can be increased by using special soft-working developer instead of the normal solution, different brands of paper do offer different contrast, so it is worth trying several if the first is unsatisfactory. Avoid cheap offers of colour paper – outdated or unknown materials are more trouble than they are worth. It is disheartening to produce one off-colour print after another, which often happens on poor paper. Some chemistries allow a little contrast control by varying the process time – the longer the time, the higher the contrast.

Two different processes are now in widespread use. Kodak Ektaprint 2 (for Ektacolor 78RC and equivalents) and Agfa process 85 (for MCN 310 type 4). The chemicals are not totally compatible. However, most independent kits, while formulated for Kodak Ektacolor type papers, can be used for Agfacolor materials by omitting an additive. Agfacolor MCN type 5 papers, which are designed for professional and photofinishing use, employ process 90, which is compatible with Kodak Ektaprint.

As with all colour processing, the big film and paper manufacturer's chemistry is primarily designed for large-scale processing. Thus, while the paper manufacturers offer small kits, some independently made kits are easier to use and provide equally good results.

The choice of surface is somewhat restricted. Glossy, rayon, lustre and matt are available. Because of its greater naturalness, a colour print does not depend so strikingly on its surface as does a black-and-white one, so few workers find the limitation particularly irksome. It is always possible to have the surface textured after processing.

Negative quality

One of the problems with negative/positive colour printing is that it is difficult for even an expert to judge a colour negative visually. All that is normally possible is to select a negative with a good range of tones – one that looks crisp. The major problem of a poorly processed negative is what is called 'crossed curves'. That simply means that the contrast of one of the colours is out of balance with the others. Thus, the print may, for example, have green shadows and pink highlights. If that happens there is, unfortunately, no simple cure. Altering the filters to correct the shadows simply makes the highlights worse, and vice versa. Sometimes the effect occurs in the paper. Clearly this shows up by its presence in prints from different fims. If the negative is at fault, though, it has to be discarded.

Basic filter pack

Colour papers are not manufactured to print without filters. Most systems call for a strong red or orange filter pack. The unbalance was particularly drastic when type II colour films (starting with Kodacolor II) were introduced. These, by using a different system of internal masking, could be made much less orange than their immediate predecessors. Printing on Kodak Ektacolor 37 RC paper called for perhaps 100 or 120 units of red filter. Newer papers are more closely matched; but in the absence of any prior information, a starting filter pack of 50R (50M + 50Y) is advisable. Naturally, the enlarger should have heat-absorbing glass to prevent infra-red radiation reaching the film, and the filter pack should include an ultra-violet absorbing filter. Colour heads all provide absorption of both IR and UV as well as dialled-in colour control. However, some can reach their limit without providing enough red filtration. To avoid this problem with older papers, use a 50R acetate filter in the filter drawer, and use the colour controls to provide the rest of the filtration. Enlargers with colour heads may have their filter wedges calibrated on a different scale, so the exact needs may be differently described. For some with halogen lamps, a starting filter setting of 75M is recommended. Once the first good print has been made, the starting filter pack for any particular system is obvious.

Determining exposure and filtration

The most basic way of achieving correct density and colour is to make a series of test prints (or a test strip) through the starter filter pack. For a 25 × 20 cm (10 × 8 in) enlargement, 5, 10, 20 and 40 seconds at *f*/11 is a good start. It is very unlikely to be exactly the right colour. First decide which is the closest to the correct density, then examine this sector to decide how to change it to the correct colour.

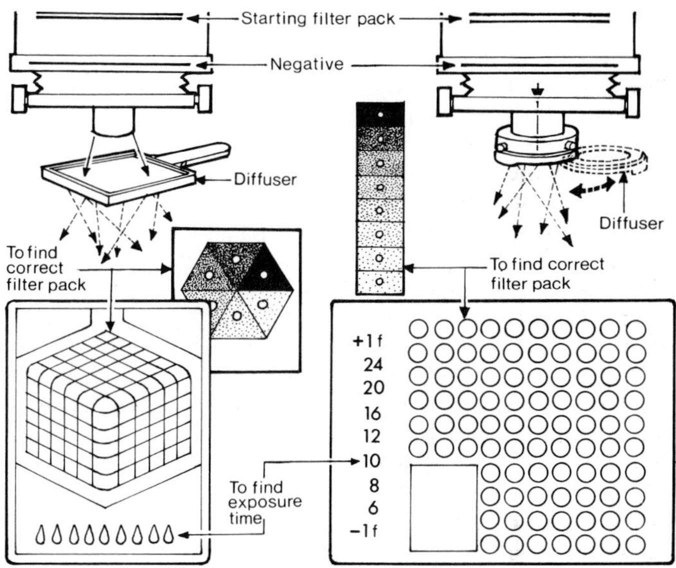

The correct colour balance and exposure can be found by identifying the neutral grey patch in a contact print of a filter mosaic made by the diffused light from an enlarger with negative. Most mosaics also have a density scale for exposure determination

Filter changes have a much greater effect in negative/positive printing than they do when printing from slides. Thus, a change of 05 makes quite a visible alteration; a change of 10 eliminates (or produces) a noticeable colour cast, 20 is equivalent to a strong colour cast, and 40 produces an image dominated by one colour. Rather than follow such a rule of thumb, many photographers prefer to use viewing filters. The normal acetate CP (colour printing) filters are fine for this purpose but colour-head users will not have any, so they need a separate viewing filter set. This is a little more complicated to use.

With a set of CP filters, select the one (or pack) through which the print looks the correct colour. Hold the filter(s) well away from the print, so that the light seen passes through the filter but once. A set of viewing filters offers just six filters of density 10. Viewing and interpretation extends the range of results. View normally, and if the filter overcorrects then the filter really needed is an 05; if it undercorrects,

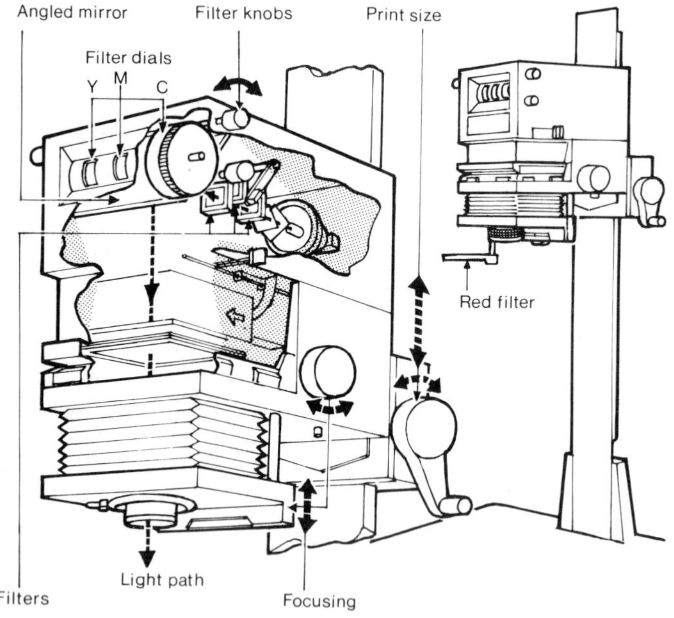

Components of a typical colour enlarger

Filter pack variations in printing from negatives

To change the colour of the print, the enlarger light is changed in colour. Each of the three subtractive primary colours – cyan, magenta and yellow subtracts its own colour and adds that of its complement, red, green or blue, respectively. Mixtures of filters have intermediate effects:

To make a print less	*or more*	*add*	*or subtract*
Red	Cyan	Magenta + Yellow	Cyan
Green	Magenta	Cyan + Yellow	Magenta
Blue	Yellow	Cyan + Magenta	Yellow
Cyan	Red	Cyan	Magenta + Yellow
Magenta	Green	Magenta	Cyan + Yellow
Yellow	Blue	Yellow	Cyan + Magenta

Approximate exposure factors for Kodak colour printing filters

Filter	*Factor*	*Filter*	*Factor*
05Y	1·0	05B	1·1
10Y	1·1	10B	1·3
20Y	1·1	20B	1·6
30Y	1·1	30B	2·0
40Y	1·1	40B	2·4
50Y	1·1	50B	2·9
05M	1·2	05G	1·1
10M	1·3	10G	1·2
20M	1·4	20G	1·3
30M	1·7	30G	1·4
40M	1·8	40G	1·5
50M	2·0	50G	1·7
05C	1·1	05R	1·2
10C	1·2	10R	1·3
20C	1·3	20R	1·5
30C	1·5	30R	1·7
40C	1·6	40R	1·9
50C	1·9	50R	2·2

then it is a 15. For stronger colour casts, place the filter on the print, which effectively doubles its colour. If that is right then the correction is equivalent to a density 20 filter. If it still undercorrects, the print colour is 30 or more out.

Assume that the print looks right when viewed through a CP20C and a CP20M filter together; it also looks right when a Blue (CP10B) viewing filter is placed on it. Thus, it is too yellow by around 20 printing units (CP20Y). Because the print is made from a negative, it is made more blue (less yellow) by adding yellow to the filter pack. In practice, about half the amount needed to correct the print visually. So in this case the print should be made with an extra 10Y in the filter pack (or dialled into the head). Thus, if working from the basic 50M + 50Y, the pack becomes 50M + 60Y.

The fact that adding a colour to the filter pack reduces that colour on the print is a little difficult to grasp at first, but it follows quite naturally from the negative/positive process. To darken a print (in monochrome or colour), increase the amount of light that falls on it. In the same way, to make it more blue, increase the amount of yellow light that reaches the paper. Increasing blue is the same as reducing yellow.

The exposure time can be estimated from the test prints. As usual, it is likely to fall between two of the original test steps. The time, though, is altered with each change in filtration. The exposure must be increased with the addition of filters and decreased with their removal. The most direct way to calculate the change is to divide the exposure time by each figure in turn for the filters removed, then multiply it by each for the filters added.

Suppose the best test was made at 20 seconds with 50R filtration, made up of 40M + 10M + 40Y + 10Y, and the print looks right through a 10C + 30M filter. So, the filter pack needs 05C + 15M subtracted from it.

As the filter pack is all M and Y, the 05C cannot be subtracted, so the equivalent colour change is made by adding 05M + 05Y. Subtract the extra 15M from that and the alteration is to add −10M + 05Y. Thus, the filter pack is changed by taking away 10M and adding 05Y. The exposure is 10 × 1.1 ÷ 1.3 or 8½ seconds.

Colour and density aids

Even with the use of viewing filters, it is hard to be sure of the right filters. Instead of test printing several times, a filter mosaic can provide the answers in one go – provided the negative represents a normal subject. Using these mosaics is the same with negatives as it is with transparencies (see page 139). Of course, the negative instructions now apply.

Instead of printing through a series of filter patches, it is quite possible to measure the colour of the light. Colour analysers do just that. They vary in their exact operation and efficiency but all do basically the same job. The probe is placed in the enlarger light beam, all other lights switched off, and the light-sensitive cell or photomultiplier tube measures the enlarger output. To produce filter recommendations, the analyser has to be programmed with the exact colour requirements of the paper being used. Analysers start from a perfect print from a good negative – decided by whatever tests are needed. Once produced, the 'perfect' exposure is analysed for red, green and blue content. In most cases, that is done by centering a meter needle, but other displays are available.

Once the analyser has been calibrated for a perfect print, the new negative goes in the enlarger carrier. Then the filter pack is adjusted until the needle is again zeroed for all three colours (usually in turn). Most analysers measure total exposure time as well.

This all sounds good, but there are snags. First, using an integrated reading always carries the risk of a 'subject failure' negative (as the photofinishers call it), that is one in which the subject does not integrate to grey. For these, an integrated reading is useless. The alternative is to calibrate the analyser for a specific subject, flesh tones, grass, concrete, or whatever is convenient, and measure the same subject in the negatives to be printed. Such a 'spot' reading is the best choice, but does depend on the chosen subject being the same colour in both negatives. There are some workers who measure from the film rebate. This is quite useless, taking no account of the subject lighting, camera exposure or processing. It is equivalent to (and no more informative than) the much less troublesome 'I use 70Y+50M for Agfacolor 400 processed in Photocolor II'.

The lower-priced analysers have to be recalibrated each time they are used, which makes them so troublesome as to be of little practical value to the small-scale worker. The time taken in recalibrating approaches the time saved by reduced test printing. More sophisticated models have numbered dials, and can be reset each time to the same figures.

Once calibrated, the figures can be written on the paper packet, and re-used whenever needed. This can offer considerable time saving when printing from several different film types, especially if spot readings are used. However, when working from a single film type it should not be necessary to analyse every negative. With accurate exposure (in the camera) and high quality processing, all the negatives on one film should print with the same filter pack.

Thus while analysers are clearly a boon to some photographers, they are by no means essential for colour printing. In practice, a low priced analyser may waste more time than it saves. With a more sophisticated model that can be recalibrated it is wise to build up a set of calibrations for different types of subject – including even a grey card if you carry one. Photograph it at the beginning or end of a session and then analyse the grey card negative to select optimum exposure

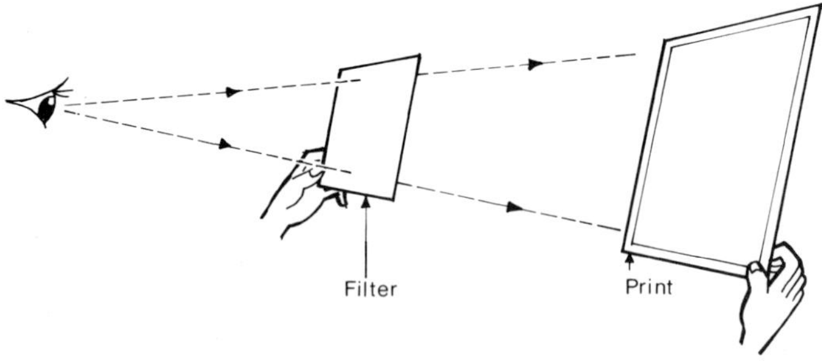

Deciding colour balance through a viewing filter

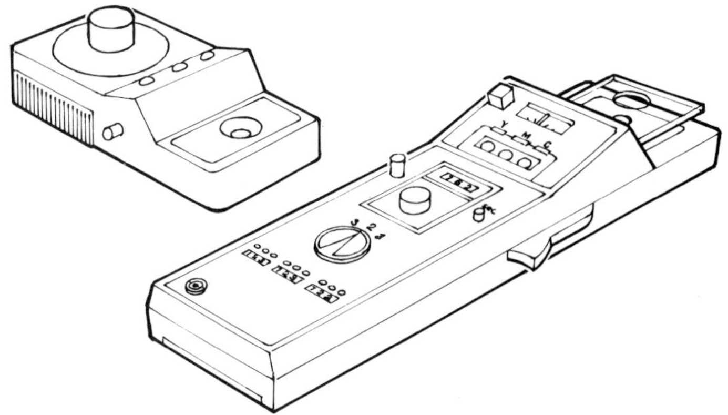

Colour analysers measure the red, green and blue content of the enlarger light (with negative and filters) allowing it to be matched to previous requirements of the paper in use

and filtration to suit the lighting and processing the film received.

Clearly to use a colour analyser easily requires an enlarger with a colour head. That way you can dial in exactly the right colours to zero the readings.

Tricolour printing

Instead of colouring the enlarger light with comparatively pale filters to make it exactly the right colour, it is possible to determine the colour balance of a print by making three successive exposures through primary coloured filters. This calls for a system for changing the red, blue and green filters between exposures without disturbing the enlarger.

The simple way is to hold the filters below the enlarger lens. This can be done by hand, but a card or plastics holder makes life much easier. As the filters go between the lens and the print, they need to be of the highest optical quality, scrupulously clean, flat, and free from scratches or blemishes.

To start from scratch, make four separate test prints on one sheet of paper. Make a single exposure (of different time for each print) through a blue filter, then a stepped exposure through red and green filters. Make the two step sequences at right angles to each other. Thus, each print now has an overall blue exposure, and a selection of red/green combinations.

Compose and focus the negative. Select the best area for making the tests; stop down to, say, *f*/8 for a 25 × 20 cm (10 × 8 in) print. Switch off the lights, and arrange a piece of paper on the baseboard masked so that the light will fall on to little under a quarter of it. Use either an L-shaped card or a sectional print frame. Give the paper a 5-second exposure

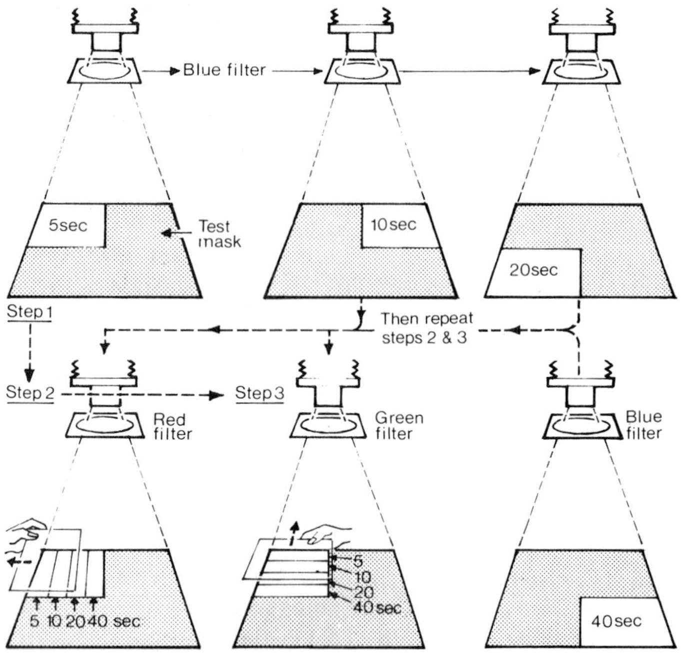

Tricolour printing exposures can be calculated form a series of test wedges. Making four on a simple sheet of paper is most convenient

through the blue filter. Then change to the green filter and make a test strip (just as in black-and-white printing) of 5, 10, 20 and 40 seconds across the paper. Change to the red filter and make a similar set of test exposures from top to bottom of the paper.

Then change to the next quarter and give a 10-second blue exposure and the same series of green and red exposures. Give blue exposures of 20 and 40 seconds to the other two quarters, followed by red and green steps. Then process the whole sheet.

The result is four prints, varying overall from pale blue to darker yellow. Each print has 16 differently coloured sections. The green exposures make each section increasingly more magenta; the red exposures increasingly more cyan. Choose the section most nearly correct in colour and tone. Decide the times used for this section, and use them to make a print.

The print may need a slightly different combination. The effect of changing exposure times is quite straightforward. To alter the density change all the times by the same proportion. To change the colour, alter them independently. Increase the exposure time to increase the complementary colour, thus decreasing the same colour as the filter.

To make the picture more	*Increase exposure through*	or	*Reduce exposure through*
Cyan	Red		Green and blue
Magenta	Green		Red and blue
Yellow	Blue		Red and green
Red	Green and blue		Red
Green	Red and blue		Green
Blue	Red and green		Blue

The test print density determines whether the proportion is best changed by increasing exposure through the suitable filter(s) or by decreasing it through the other(s).

This process sounds rather complicated, but it is quite practical. Unlike white-light printing, the enlarger needs no filter drawer or colour head, and some workers suggest that tricolour printing produces more saturated colours in their prints. The main use, though, is in automated printing equipment. Virtually all photofinisher printers use additive filtering. With a high intensity light source, the exposure times are so short as to appear virtually a single white-light flash. Also, it is possible to buy a colour enlarger which gives three sequential tricolour exposures in accordance with its built-in colour analyser. There are also colour enlargers which use three primary coloured light sources to adjust the colour of the printing light. These are not, though, tricolour enlargers in the normal sense.

The main disadvantage of tricolour printing – manual or automatic, is that it makes dodging or burning in a problem. Clearly, to maintain the colour balance, any section held back or printed in must have its three exposures in exactly the same proportions as those for the whole print. This calls for very accurate handwork. Any slight difference in the movement between the three exposures can produce strange coloured areas on the borders of the area held back. Thus tricolour printing is really only suitable for negatives which can be printed straight.

The other objection to the process is that the exposure times are much longer (in total) than those needed for white-light printing. This can, though, be reduced by giving an unfiltered white light exposure followed by suitable times through the two filters which need the longest exposure. For this, the enlarger must be fitted with a UV-absorbing filter. The test procedure, though, is virtually the same. Just replace the 'blue' exposure with a white one, and make wedge sequences with the other two filters in turn. Remember, though, that all three exposures will be much shorter or the enlarger needs a smaller lens aperture.

Contact printing

Making contact prints is especially useful from colour negatives. It saves making quite a large number of test prints. Even

Pieces of broken safety glass on a sheet of glass provide an unusual vignette (John Woodhouse)

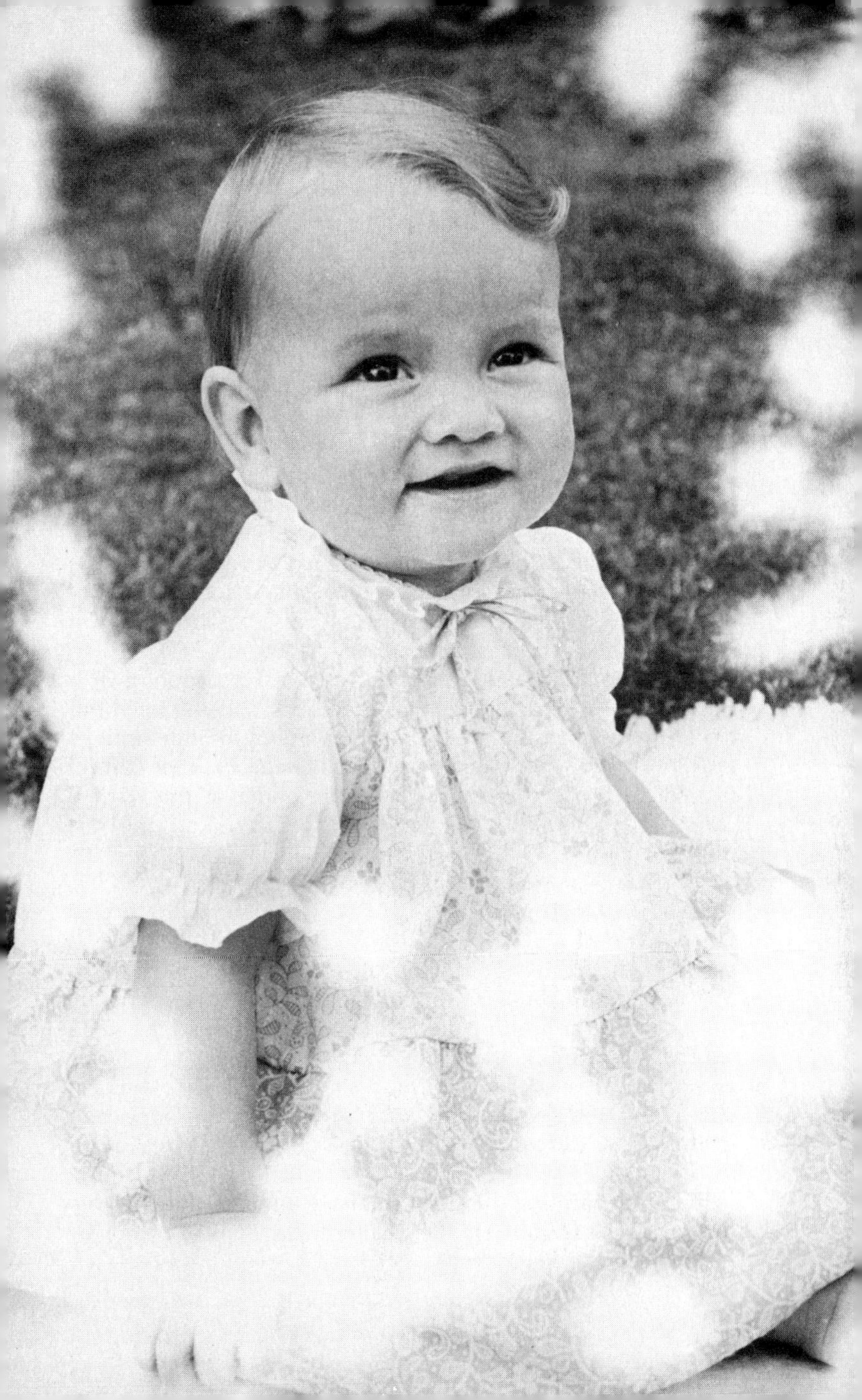

when working from 35 mm film, it is quite easy to see composition details in contact prints, and to select for such factors as facial expression. Also, a set of well-exposed negatives all taken under the same conditions should all print with the same filtration. However, this is not always the case, and colour balance changes show up in the contacts.

The main problem with contact printing colour is in arranging the negatives in contact with the paper. Working in the dark makes this difficult without suitable preparation. Undoubtedly, the best way is to use a contact printer. A good printer can be loaded with the negatives in the light, and hold them safely while the paper is inserted (in total darkness) prior to exposure. No printer which has a tendency to let negatives fall out is any real use for colour contacts

As an alternatives, tape the negatives to a sheet of glass using the smallest pieces of tape needed to secure them. Of course, the tape must not touch any image areas. Then, in the dark, lay the glass on the paper so that the film (emulsion side down) is in contact with it.

Once the negatives are lying against the paper, give a normal exposure with the enlarger set for a suitable height to cover the whole print area. Use the white-light filter settings that normally give good colour balance, or the correct tricolour exposure times. Process the paper in the normal way.

Holding back and burning in

When there are areas of the negative which print too dark or too light, they can be modified in white-light printing by holding back or burning in the area. This is done in the same way as it is in black-and-white printing (see page 124). Once again, hands, piece of card, and simple dodgers are worth using, and dodging times need to be a significant proportion of the whole exposure – a quick flick of the finger makes no difference.

In colour printing, though, you have an extra dimension – the colour. It is quite simple to alter local areas of colour by interposing a filter for all or part of the exposure time. As with altering the filter pack, the filter decreases its own colour. Thus, to increase blue, interpose a yellow filter, and so on. To make an intermediate change, use two or more filters together. Clearly, using any but the palest filter will reduce the density as well as changing the colour. So it is sometimes necessary to give the area held back some extra exposure to compensate for the change in density. For most purposes, interposing a 10CP filter for about half the exposure time will alter the colour balance a significant amount without needing a local exposure increase to compensate. With more filtering than that, use the filter to calculate the exposure increase needed, assuming that the area to be held back with the filter does not need lightening.

Composite printing

Adding clouds to an otherwise clear sky, or otherwise combining two negatives, is quite simple in colour. It is, though, important to bear in mind that a second or subsequent exposure can add density or colour, not take it away. Thus, it is not possible to add white clouds to a blue sky – only to print in the blue sky around the clouds on to white sky. The same principle applies in monochrome work, but there, blue skies often print white, allowing easy printing in of clouds.

To alter a blue sky in a colour print, the white cloud areas must receive no exposure. There are two solutions: bind a suitable (monochrome or colour) cloud negative together with the landscape so that its dense areas prevent the blue sky affecting the paper, or hold back the sky completely during the first exposure. Then change the negative and print in the sky while keeping the foreground covered. Clearly this needs some method of ensuring that the two images meet in the right place. The simplest is to draw a pencil line on the paper during the first exposure, and mask up to that during the second. Start by covering more area, the line is visible only with the enlarger switched on.

Colour print processing

Modern colour processing kits are simple to use; they can produce astonishingly good results in the simplest equipment. They each have precise time and temperature requirements. However, the exact times and temperatures are not as important as their absolute consistency. The print drums and processors already described (see pages 44, 146) were primarily devised for negative/positive printing.

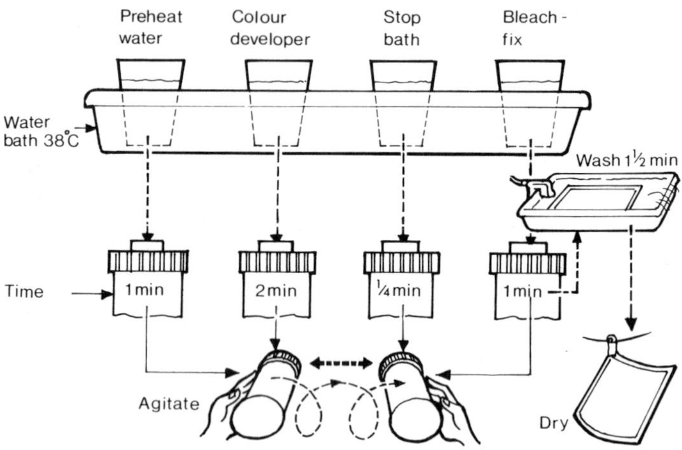

Processing a negative/positive colour print

The latest chemistry uses two active solutions: colour developer and bleach-fix, usually separated by a stop bath. Once again, the chemistry manufacturer's instructions are the ones to follow; they can change quite often, so an old instruction book may be out of date.

Many of the currently available Ektacolor type kits can process C41 films as well as papers. Virtually all come as two concentrates, with an additive for the developer for colour print processing. Most of these kits offer reasonably satisfactory results on Agfacolor MCN type 4 papers at relatively low temperatures if the print additive is omitted. Some kits include a final stabiliser; others do not. In general, stabiliser is going out of favour. However, there is some evidence that stabilisers do improve the life of prints, especially when they are displayed. For display prints, it pays to follow the paper manufacturer's instructions. Note that the stabilisation is done after washing. The formaldehyde, or salt, stabiliser should mostly remain in the emulsion.

Some chemistries allow a little manipulation of print contrast. Process about 30% longer to give the effect of one grade higher contrast. Naturally, this requires slightly shorter exposure times, and may result in colour changes.

Colour print routines

Most colour prints are processed at 38°C (100°F), but several systems allow a wide variation in process temperatures when compensated by different times. The simplest kits need diluting with water, and a small amount of additive adding to the colour developer. Here are the times at 38°C for two widely used processes, Kodak Ektaprint 2 and Photocolor II.

	Ektaprint 2	*Photocolor II*
Preheat	1 min	1 min
Colour development	3½ min	2 min
Stop bath	–	¼ min
Bleach fix	1½ min	1 min
Wash	3½ min	1½ min

8

Printing on special materials

Most darkroom work is straightforward printing or processing, producing the best normal print or transparency possible. Of course printing allows personal choice of colour, balance, contrast and composition; that is the main reason for doing it. However, there are also a whole range of materials designed to allow slightly different results. There are really two groups: materials for converting one type of image to another, colour to monochrome, and so on, and materials which allow derivations from the image – simplifications or elaborations.

Panchromatic paper

It is easy to print a colour negative on to ordinary monochrome paper. The exposure time is rather long, but processing is normal. Unfortunately, the results are often far from pleasing. Contrast tends to be too high, grain seems to appear from nowhere, and some colours print much darker than others. Red and yellow parts of the subject come out much too dark, blue parts much too light.

To make good prints, panchromatic paper is available. It is processed like any other monchrome paper, but like colour materials must be handled in the dark. In practice, the easiest way to process such paper is in a colour print drum. Thus working with panchromatic paper is akin to working with colour materials, without the need to filter the enlarger light.

Print films

To make transparencies from negatives calls for print film, colour or monochrome. Print films are designed to work like print papers. They are available in small sizes to make small-format projection slides (usually called slide film), and in larger sizes to make display transparencies. The easiest way to print on to small-format films is to use a camera fitted with suitable close-up equipment to make same size (or slightly different sized) copies. A bellows and slide copier is the usual choice. As many of the materials are intended for making movie release prints, they have to be loaded into suitable cassettes for 35 mm still cameras or roll-film cameras with 70 mm magazines.

Few print materials come with exact exposure information so exposure times have to be calculated from test strips. Colour materials have to be exposed to light of exactly the right colour, filtered as with any colour printing. Yet again, this has to be a process of test and develop before making any final judgements. To ensure results it is essential to buy a considerable quantity of film of one batch. The exposure and filter conditions remain constant if the film is kept in a refrigerator.

One of the main reasons for using a print film is to make enlarged transparencies. Clearly, this cannot be done in a small-format camera. It is quite possible to enlarge directly on to sheets of print film. This is just like printing on to paper, and film can be processed in trays or in a colour print drum. Cut film, though, is expensive, and making single exposures can be time consuming. The best way to handle the film is in dark slides, as used in cameras. These can be loaded quite easily (in the dark with colour or panchromatic materials) and allow the film to be exposed and stored until ready for processing.

For most 35 mm photographers, 6 × 9 cm transparencies are the largest needed. Black-and-white slides can be made on roll film quite simply using an old roll-film camera back as a film holder. Remove the bellows and lens panel and construct a simple light-tight cover. Then print on to the film using an enlarger in the normal way. Normal negative film developed for twice the recommended time produces quite good transparencies. Unfortunately, this cannot be done in colour.

Colour print and slide films use the normal colour negative film processing chemicals and routines.

Printing on to camera films

Starting with a transparency, it is simple to produce a colour or monochrome negative on normal camera material. Most transparencies are rather higher contrast than the scenes they represent, so it pays to use contrast-reducing techniques. For black-and-white negatives, expose generously and cut back on development. Do the same with colour negative film if the processing chemicals are designed to allow some variation in process times.

Once again, the simplest approach is to use the camera and a slide copier to make the negatives. However, there are attractions in having larger-format copy negatives, especially if they are to be used for derivative processes. Once again, an old 6 × 9 cm camera body makes an excellent film holder.

When making negatives, the exposure and processing are less critical because the final density and colour are decided at a later stage. However, it is usually best to make some tests before embarking on an important project. Try a range of exposures and in colour filters, choose the conditions which produce negatives most closely matched to normal camera negatives.

Reversal copies

To make a transparency from a transparency, or a negative from a negative, calls for a reversal film. Camera films can be used, but they often lead to excessive contrast and poor colour saturation. For serious work it is well worth choosing purpose-made materials. Reversal duplicating films are made

A texture screen adds its own feeling to a high-contrast print – this one was simplified by handwork as well (Paul Broadbent)

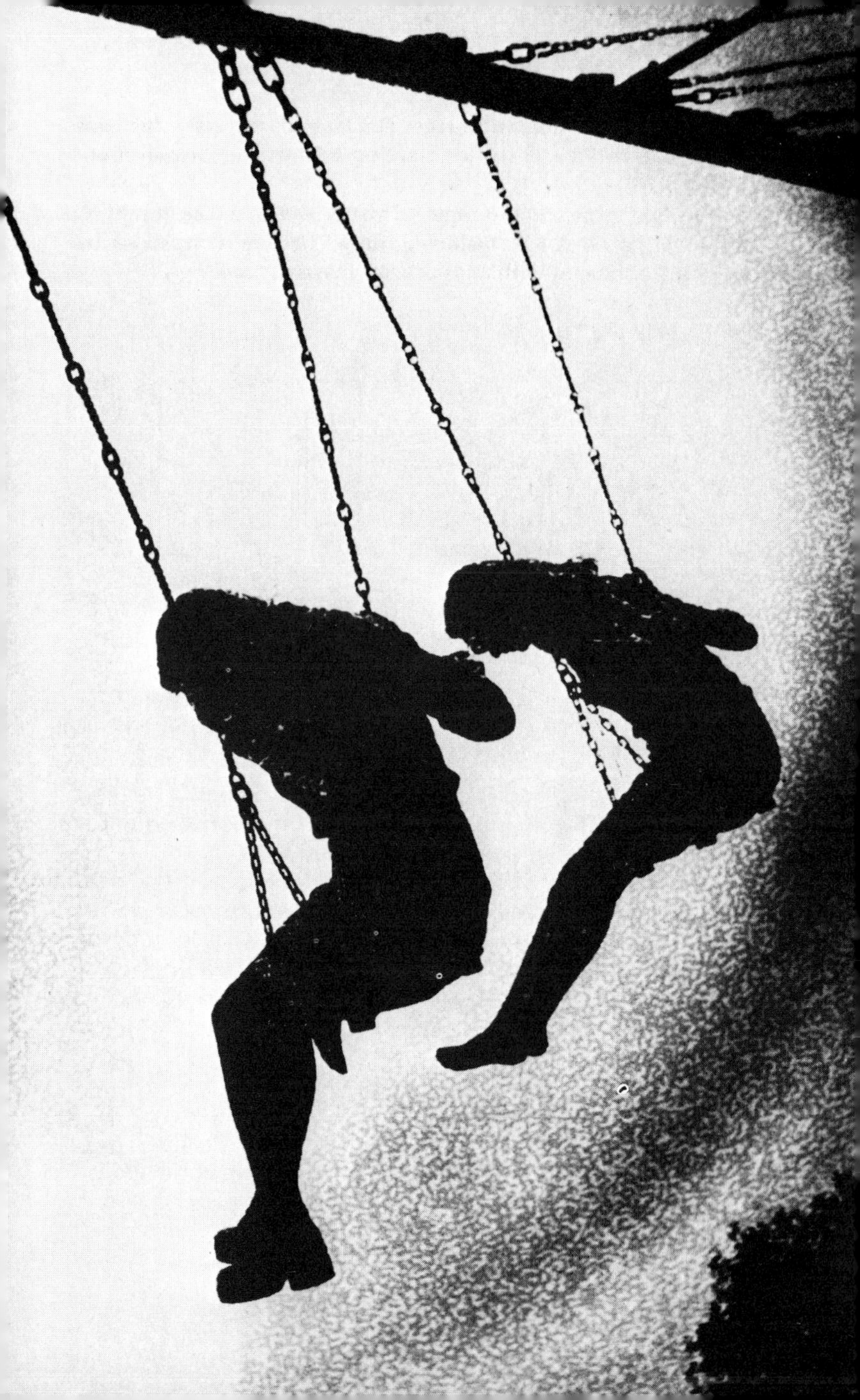

in 35 mm and sheet film sizes. The largest normally stocked is 50 × 40 cm (20 × 16 in) for making impressive display transparencies.

Unlike most camera films, virtually all the duplicating films are designed for tungsten lighting. The light must be balanced correctly with filters just as when making a reversal

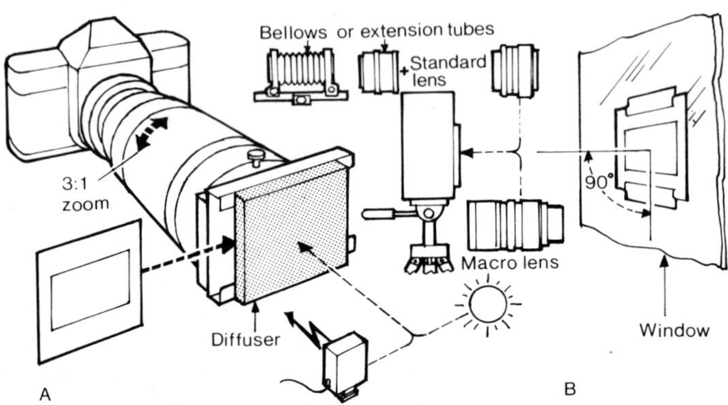

Making copy transparencies is easiest with a slide copy film in a camera. A. Using a zoom slied copier. B. With normal close-focusing equipment

print from a transparency. Direct reversal copies of negatives are often difficult to print, so the production of duplicate negatives calls for accurately recorded tests.

A typical slide duplicating film has an effective film speed of around 4 ASA and produces correct colour balance with a filter pack of around CP50C+CP85Y in 3200 K (tungsten) lighting and around CP30C+CP90Y by electronic flash. CP filters must, of course, gp between the light source and the transparency.

High-contrast materials

One of the most common ways of changing an image is to enhance its contrast. Using high-contrast paper has some effect, but materials intended for preparing material for photomechanical reproduction introduce much higher contrast. These materials, called 'lith' or 'line' can reproduce a subject in totally black or totally white. They come usually in moderately large sheets.

The most commonly used materials are either blue-sensitive or orthochromatic. Blue-sensitive materials can be handled in normal paper-type safelighting. Orthchromatic materials in red light. Of course, panchromatic materials (which are also available) have to be handled in total darkness.

Printing from a negative on to lith type film produces a positive in pure blacks and pure whites. The length of the exposure determines which parts are black and which white. The longer the exposure, the more becomes black. To remove all greys, the material must be developed in special developer. However, lith film can be processed in normal paper developer. The result is a high contrast, but not totally black-and-white, positive. Making a negative by contact-printing this on to another sheet of lith film further reduces any intermediate tones. The negative can then be printed on to normal grade 4 or 5 paper to produce a 'line' print in pure blacks and whites.

The best negatives for high contrast treatment are simple ones. Complicated subjects often become over-elaborate. One strange effect is that grain can be enhanced. A print from a grainy negative can look from a distance almost like a normal print. The intermediate tones are represented by areas of black stipple, each grain reproduced as a tiny black spot.

Simple high-contrast prints – positive or negative – can be attractive, but high-contrast materials are only the starting point for a whole range of potential effects. Making two or three negatives with different exposures produces a simple method of creating a small number of different tones, called posterisation.

Suppose one piece of film is exposed to re-produce just the highlights, and another the highlights and midtones; both, of course, go completely black where affected at all. Place the highlight negative on a piece of paper, and flood it

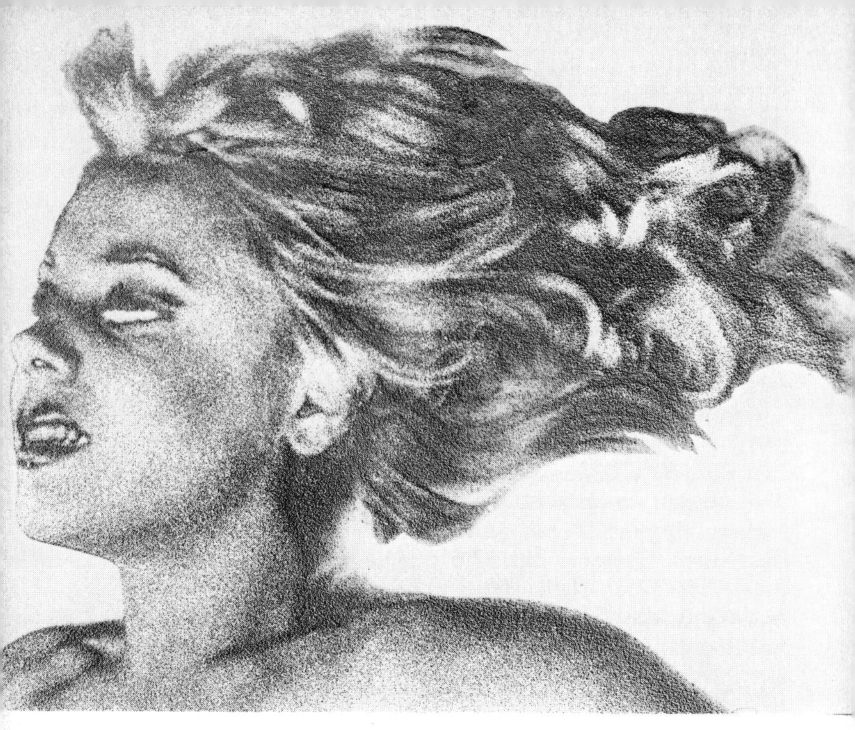

Exaggerating the grain and painting out of the background produces a strong image (Derek Lee)

with light for long enough to produce a grey image. Now place the midtone negative on the paper exactly above the highlight one. Fog the paper again to produce a good black, then process it. The result is white highlights, even grey midtones and black dark tones, nothing else.

Of course, to work, the negatives must be held exactly on top of each other and this can be done in a number of ways. The easiest (working with blue-sensitive materials) is to draw a cross outside the image area on each side, then line the crosses up. More complicated systems using adhesive tape or punched holes are also quite easy to prepare.

A high-contrast copy can simplify a stark scene to provide extra impact (Bill Bayley)

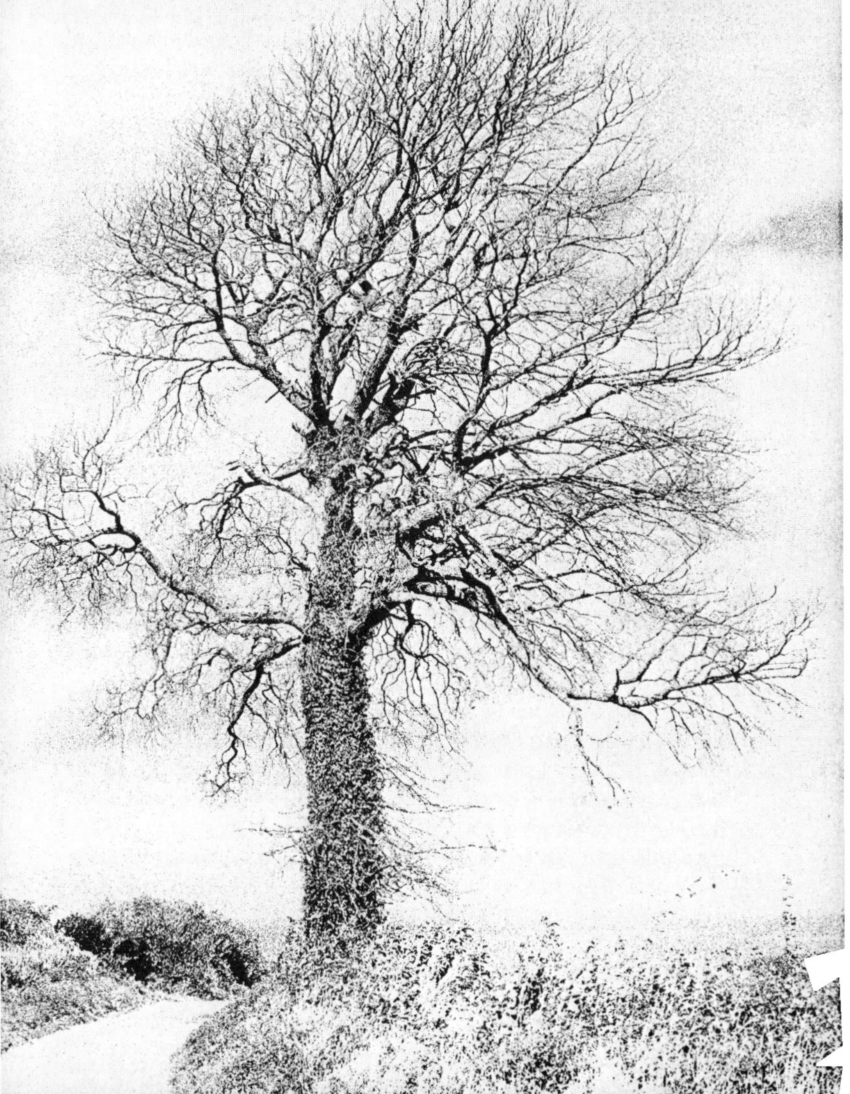

Working on colour paper, the tones can be substituted with plain coloured areas, each formed by fogging the paper through a strong coloured filter. Of course, where the paper is affected by two lights the colour is a mixture. Processing is perfectly normal colour development.

Line materials can be used in conjunction with texture screens to provide an enormous variety of effects which are widely displayed in graphic reproduction. They can also be used with sabattier effect to produce almost contour images, and by combining negative and positive produce just an edge line round the subject.

For many workers, this is the main purpose in their photography. The camera-formed image is purely a starting point for almost endless complicated manipulation. The end result may bear no resemblance to the subject, but may be an attractive and striking picture in its own right.

Mobile emulsion

While we normally expect emulsion to be coated on paper or film, they are not the only possible substrates. Photosensitive metal plates are available for making control panels etc. These can make attractive display prints and they are more durable than metallic-coated papers.

One stage further is to mix an emulsion and coat it onto any available base. In the past, photographers made their own emulsions from raw chemicals. Today it is possible, though sometimes difficult, to buy ready-made emulsions. These can be tipped or brushed on to paper, cloth, metal, eggshells and so forth to take your images. Smooth pale substrates look good with subtle-toned pictures; rougher and darker surfaces are much better suited to high-contrast pictures.

9

The final destination

Photographs are to be seen, otherwise they have no value, so they need to be presented in the best possible way. Transparencies, of course, are usually projected, perhaps with music or as part of a comprehensive audio-visual package. Prints, on the other hand, are made available for scrutiny – in the hand or on the wall. Often, the final presentation can make the difference between visual impact and total disregard, so the last stage in processing and printing needs as much care as the earlier stages.

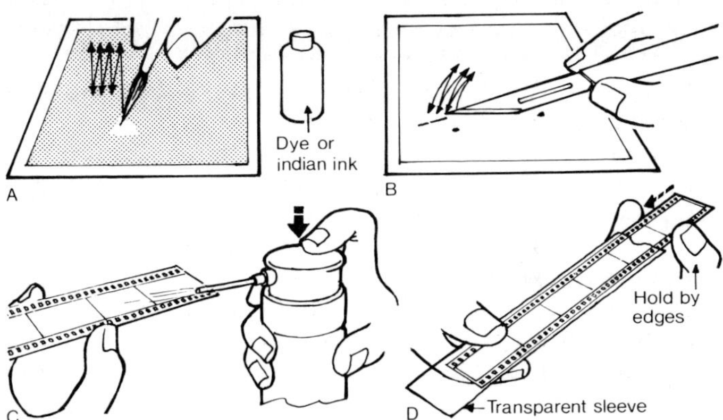

Most prints need some handwork to cover blemishes. A. Spot light areas with suitable colour on a fine brush. B. Scrape away unwanted dark spots with a very sharp scalpel. C. Take care to remove dust from negatives before printing. D. Store films in a suitable sleeve to keep them clean

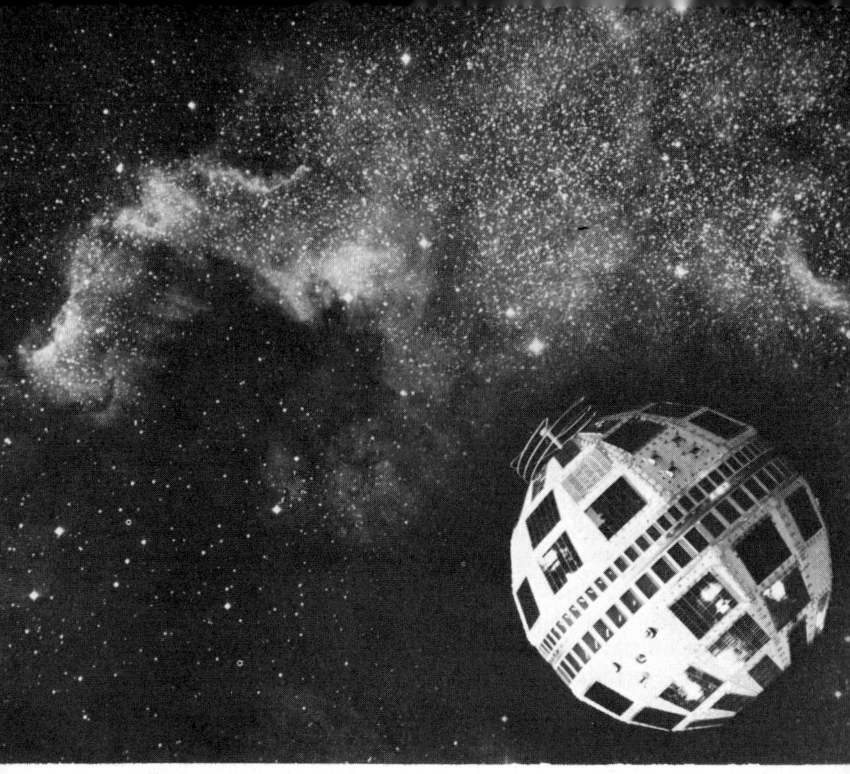

Montaging a studio shot onto an observatory sky scene can produce a realistic picture (NASA)

Spotting

Practically every print has some blemish. Most common are tiny white dots, caused by dust specks on the negative or on the glass negative carrier. Some prints may show fine lines from scratches on the negative, and even some larger white areas. All these can be removed, with care. Dark spots, which are common on prints from transparencies, are a greater problem which we will come to shortly.

White spots have to be filled carefully with suitably toned dye, ink or paint. The classic way to 'spot' a print is with a nearly dry fine-pointed artist's watercolour brush. There are many spotting colours on the market and they all work well. For monochrome work, choose one that most nearly matches the image tone of the paper. Alternatively, use Indian ink diluted with water or with a little white poster colour. For small areas on a colour print, use a correct tone of grey. For anything but a tiny spot, mix exactly the right colour.

Photographic images are made up of a myriad of tiny dots formed by the grain in the film. The aim of spotting should be to mimic these dots. Take up a little colour on the pointed brush and gently apply a stipple to the white areas. Small pinpricks can be filled with a single touch, but larger areas need patience. Allow the medium to dry between stipples and build up the density slowly. One or two spotting sessions strengthen the resolve of any photographer to be sure everything is as clean as possible – spotless, in fact – next time he makes a print.

While a fine brush and the recommended photographic spotting colours are undoubtedly the best choice, they are by no means the only way to remove blemishes. Some papers can be spotted with a soft pencil. This does rub off easily and cannot give a rich black, but pencil is easy to use. Alternatively, many fibre-tip pens produce black or grey spots quite suitable to the work. It is well worth retaining a few spotty scrap prints to try out new ideas.

Black spots

Black dots are common on prints made from transparencies. They are caused by dust specks on the transparency. Similarly, they are common when printing on negatives made from transparencies. Naturally, they cannot be removed by normal spotting. They must either be bleached away or scraped off.

Scraping (often called 'knifing') is a good method, but requires considerable practice. So make a series of tests before trying out the technique on an important print. The best implement is a sharp scalpel, or a single-side razor blade. The aim is to cut or scrape off the emulsion little by little without ever damaging the paper base. It is easy to remove all the emulsion from some resin-coated materials, leaving white polyethylene-coated paper which is difficult to recolour, so it is better to let a little emulsion remain. If, after careful scraping, the patch becomes a shade light, colour it again as if it were any normal white spot.

Of course, scraping away at the emulsion blemishes the surface. If a fine high gloss is needed, the print cannot be knifed; dark spots must be bleached out. By far the most widely used bleach for black-and-white work is a mixture of potassium permanganate and sodium thiosulphate (Farmer's reducer). This works rather slowly, and a iodine bleach is a better choice for removing spots. Dissolve about 8 g potassium iodide and 2 g iodine in 500 ml of water. Use at this strength for removing blemishes. After bleaching, rinse the print and refix it in normal fixer solution.

Bleaches for colour materials are rather strong, and best not made from raw chemicals. To work on colour reversal prints, use commercially available bleaches. Some of these (intended mainly for transparencies) bleach different colours selectively, thus they may be used to change the colour of unwanted spots.

Retouching

Clearly, there is no distinguishing line between removing photographic blemishes from the print, and in removing the images of natural blemishes. Thus, the skills gained in removing the results of dust or careless negative handling can be put to good use removing spots, wrinkles or hairs that the camera recorded faithfully. A skilled retoucher can virtually create a picture from nothing, but that goes well beyond what is normally accepted as photography.

However, it is often possible to improve a composition by removing a telegraph pole or a few power cables. It makes little difference whether they are masked out during printing, or bleached out on the print, the effect is the same. Naturally, any white voids have to be filled. That is where retouching becomes creative artwork.

Dry dye retouching

One of the best methods of applying dye to large areas of a colour print is to rub it on dry. Moisten a cake of retouching colour by breathing on it to produce condenstion. Rub a pad of dry cotton wool on the dye and transfer it to the clean dry print. Buff the print gently with the pad to reduce the dye, add more dye to increase the colour. Solid retouching colours come with a cake of reducer, which is used in the same way to remove any excess dye. The dry dye can be permanently fixed on the print by playing steam on the area for about ten seconds. Be careful not to overheat the print and cause the emulsion to bubble.

This method of retouching has the advantage of leaving the print surface relatively unblemished. Normally, even glossy prints need no resurfacing.

Reducing and intensifying

Sometimes it is necessary to alter the density of large areas on the print. Usually the best solution is to hold back or print in the area during exposure, but occasionally that does not work. Then a monochrome print can be 'reduced' by overall or selective bleaching. For this, Farmer's reducer, formed by adding about 10 ml potassium ferricyanide solution (100 g/l) to 200 ml sodium thiosulphate solution (200 g/l). The working solution should be pale yellow. Paint on the reducer, working in full room lighting, and wait until the reduction (bleaching) is satisfactory. Wash the print thoroughly.

The main use for reducers is in improving overdeveloped negatives. Simply immerse the negative in reducer and watch until it is about the correct density, then wash it immediately. Even with with greatest care, it is possible to lose shadow detail when reducing a negative. So it is important to make the best print from the negative before starting so that there is at least some record if it is damaged.

Intensifiers are used almost entirely for negatives, rather than for prints. There are numerous formulae and preparations. Most require the negative to be bleached and redeveloped. One of the simplest is a solution of potassium bichromate (10 g/l) with hydrochloric acid. A little HCl (2 ml/l) gives more intensification than a more concentrated solution (12 ml/l). Bleach the negative in the bichromate/hydrochloric acid solution until no image shows at all. Then, working in full light, redevelop it in a normal film developer.

Reducing and intensifying colour materials is more complicated. However, bleaches for transparencies or prints do work reasonably well. The difficulty with colour negatives is that aftertreatment may introduce contrast changes that make the negatives unprintable.

Trimming and borders

With modern resin-coated materials, it is quite simple to make borderless prints. The paper lies quite flat without a normal enlarging easel. A borderless print often has a greater impact that has one with borders, and is much easier to trim to shape. You can allow compositional reasons to dominate the trim, even if the original print was from the full negative area.

For deciding on the crop, make two L-shaped card masks, black or white as you prefer. Make a rectangular frame from these and lay it on the print. The masks allow you to adjust the shape exactly as you wish. When you are satisfied, make the print and trim it to size. To cut prints straight use a print trimmer. An old-fashioned paper guillotine is perfectly acceptable, and easy to use while the blade is sharp. The modern rotary trimmers are even easier to use, and seem to have less problem with blunted blades.

White borders are easily created when printing from negatives. Compose the picture exactly within the enlarging easel.

'Solarisation' of a line negative produces an outline image, which can then be printed to striking effect (R. A. Hendra)

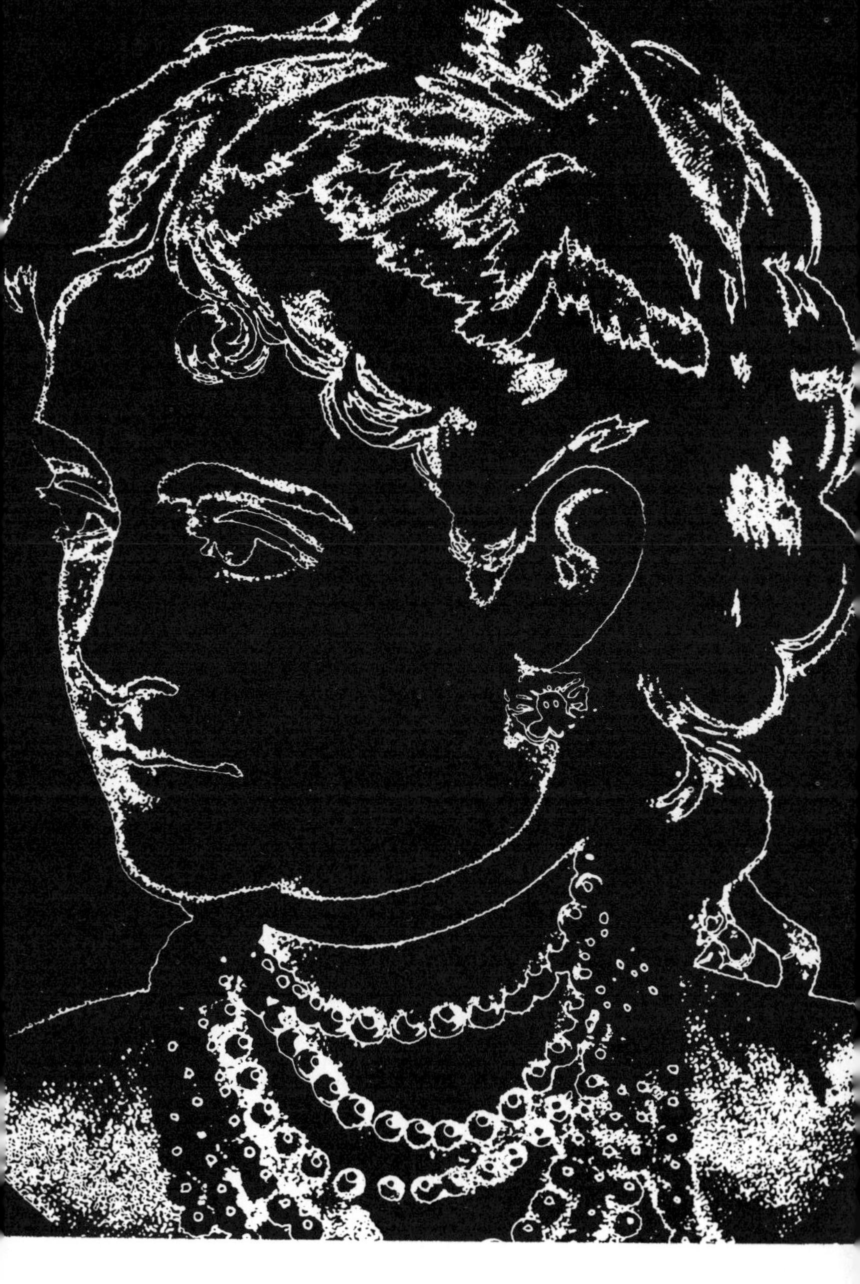

Then slide the paper under the easel blades, so that they mask off the edges. When the print is processed and dried, trim the edges to give the correct width white borders. Printing from colour transparencies, an enlarging easel leaves black borders. To make them white, they must be fogged. So make the print, then cover the picture area with a rectangular card placed exactly in the right place. After hingeing up the frame, turn on the light to fog the border. This technique can also produce black borders on prints from negatives.

Marking prints

Resin-coated materials do not absorb inks; normal inks will remain wet for a long time, thus potentially being transferred to other prints. Therefore, they must be marked with pencil, or with fast drying inks. A ball-point pen is often recommended, but this is extremely likely to damage the print surface by being pressed through from behind. Use either a soft pencil (2B or softer) or a spirit-based marker intended for writing on plastics surfaces. Special inks are made for rubber stamps to allow marking on resin-coated materials. For temporary markup, a wax pencil (such as a Chinagraph) is fine.

Print mounting

To display prints to their best advantage, they must be mounted on a stiff support. Card mounts are good for pictures up to about 50 × 40 cm (20 × 16 in). Larger sizes need firmer backing, for which hardboard is ideal. Before mounting a print, decide just how much border (if any) it needs. Look at a variety of coloured surrounds. The classical cream or white are by no means the only colours available. The

Sometimes the mounting is almost as important as the original scene (Manuel Torre Ursueguia)

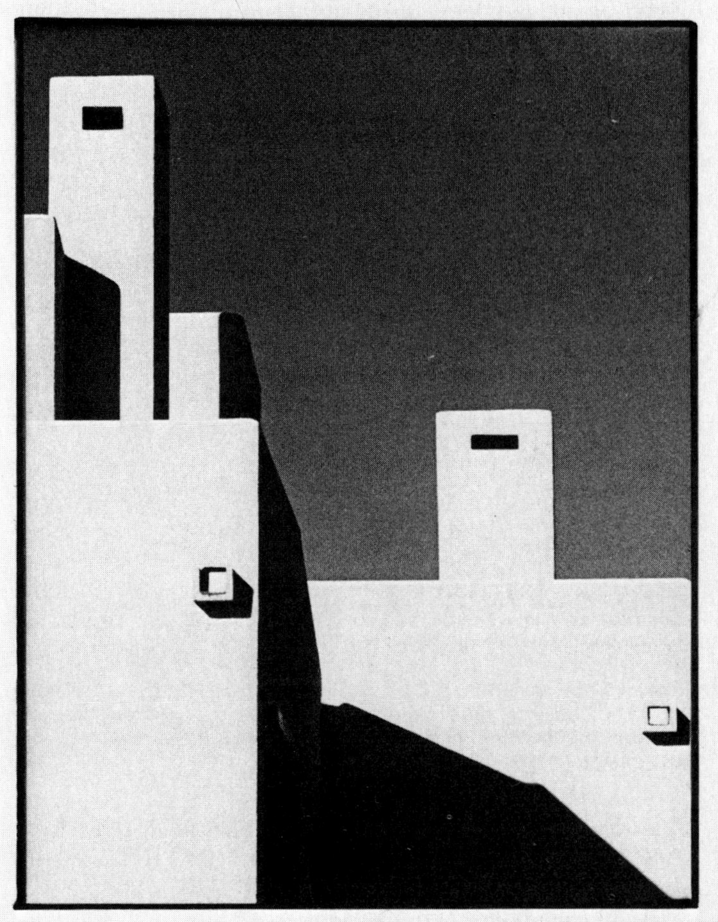

surround can go in front of framed pictures behind glass, so it can be changed at will. For unframed pictures the mount forms the border. One good borderless way is to mount prints on thick wood blocks to produce solid panels for wall hanging or standing.

There are three basic methods of mounting a print: adhesive, double-sided tape, and dry mounting tissue. Adhesives are specially prepared for photographic purposes; they are usually rubber gum based, and do not cause the image to

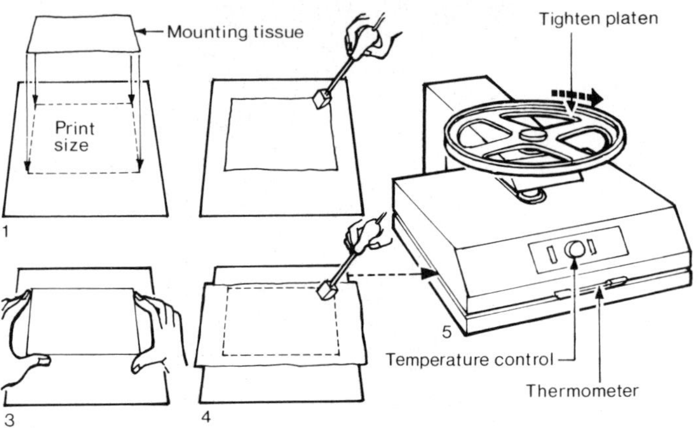

Prints can be glue-mounted, spray mounts are easy, but the classic way is to use heat-sensitive mounting tissure in a thermostatically controlled mounting press. Resin-coated materials must not be heated above 95°C (205°F)

deteriorate. The easiest to use are spray-on types in aerosol cans. Some stick rather quickly, so they need special care in aligning the print in its mount.

Double-sided tape is perhaps the easiest method. It is also often the least permanent. After a while prints may sag away from their mount unless they are firmly stuck all over.

A contribution of texture from a second reticulated negative, vignetting and careful framing produce a charming picture, showing the advantages of printing one's own pictures (Valerie Bissland)

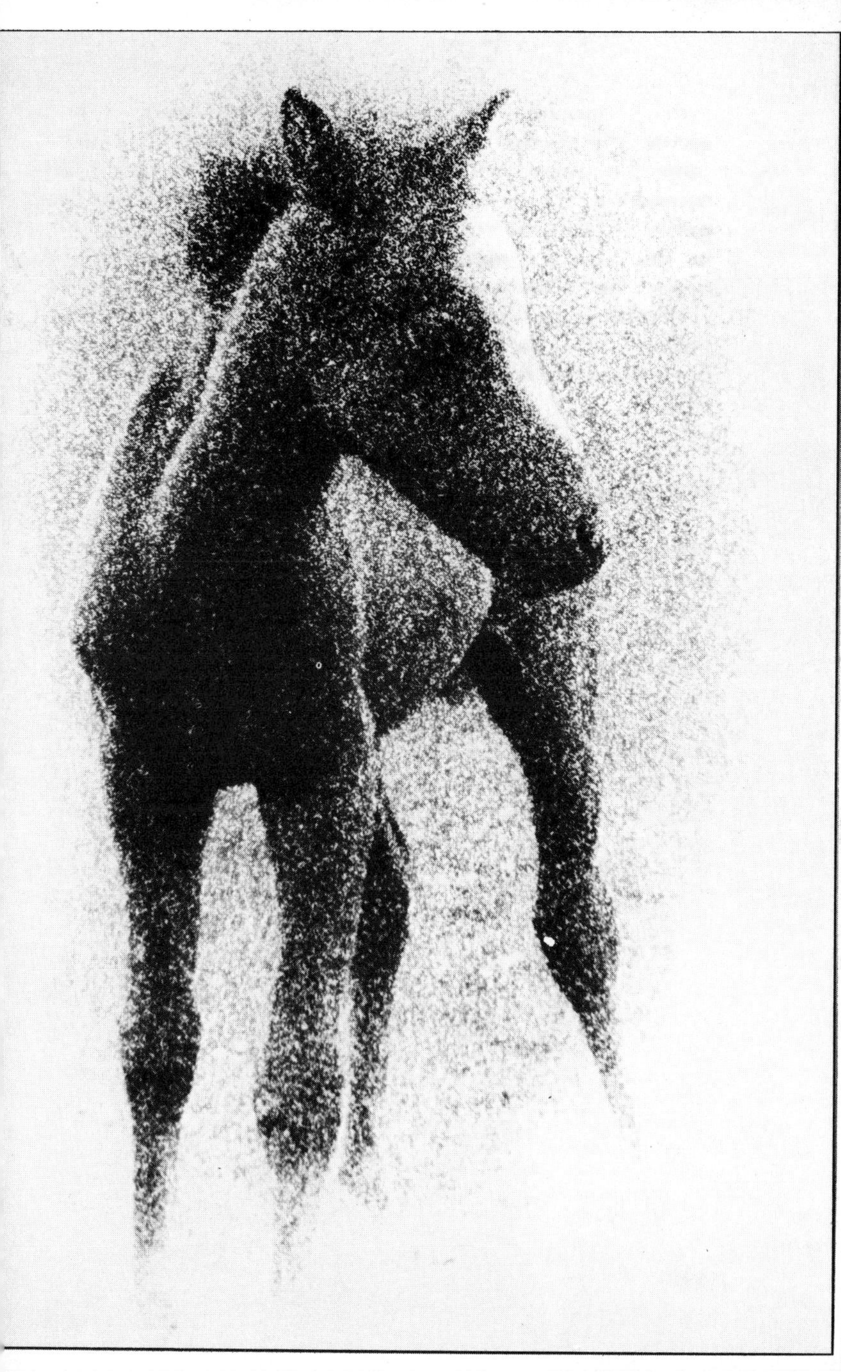

Dry mounting uses shellac impregnated tissue. Heated gently, the shellac melts and sticks. A sheet of tissue the same size as the print is tacked to its back using a small heated iron. The tissue is then tacked to the mount with the print in exactly the correct place. Once positioned accurately, the print and mount are placed in a heated mounting press. The temperature must be very accurately controlled with resin-coated paper, otherwise it may be overheated and bubble. It is quite simple to dry mount prints using a domestic iron, as long as its temperature can be kept below 95°C.

Print surfaces

Printing papers come with various surface textures. These can, to some extent, be modified afterwards. The simplest way is to spray on a matt lacquer. Such lacquers usually contain a UV absorbant, in order to increase the print life. Matt lacquer can be used on glossy, textured or matt prints. Conversely a glossy lacquer can add sheen to a matt image.

It is also possible to affix a textured surface to a print. A number of companies can laminate prints to resemble canvas, rough paper, silk and so on, as well as a series of more abstract surfaces. It is also possible to buy self-adhesive textured material.

Index